Over My Shoulder

11/18/2018

To Mary Ellen Kennedy –
Jade said you enjoyed my columns
in the Post-Star. I sincerely
hope you'll find them as
enjoyable this time
around.!
All the best!
Joe

Over My Shoulder

A Collection of
"Over My Shoulder" and "Passed Times" Columns
published in *The Post-Star* from 1994-2003
Volume 1: 1994-1997

by

Joseph Cutshall-King

matchless books

Over My Shoulder
A Collection of "Over My Shoulder" and "Passed Times" Columns published in
The Post-Star from 1994-2003; Volume 1: 1994-1997

Editor: Julia C. Cutshall-King

Cover design & all artwork © 2018 by Michael George King, Black Swan Image
Works, Frederick, MD

ISBN: 978-1-7200-5021-6

First Edition

Printed in the United States of America

A Matchless Books® production – https://pipingrock.wordpress.com/

DEDICATION

This book is dedicated with love to my wife, Sara, who for decades now has supported me in, and suffered through, my mania for history, and to my daughter, Julia, who has inherited that mania.

ACKNOWLEDGMENTS

My sincerest thanks go to my editor and daughter, Julia C. Cutshall-King, who helped me assemble these columns, reviewed them all, weeded out the boring and dated columns, and, finally, recommended those that are included here. She encouraged, prodded, and poked me to keep me on track. Without her, this book would not have materialized.

Thank you to my brother Michael George King of Black Swan Image Works, for his beautiful design for the cover. This is the second cover this very patient and very creative man has designed for me. His first was for my historical mystery novel *The Burning of The Piping Rock*.

I must acknowledge a debt of gratitude to the publishers of *The Post-Star*, to Editor Ken Tingley for the courtesy shown in allowing the reprint of these columns, and to my various editors over the nine years I wrote my columns, especially City Editor Bob Condon.

My thanks go also to educator, author, and historian Matthew A. Rozell, for his sincere encouragement and sound advice on publishing and related matters.

For their critiques of the formatting, I thank two Vermonters: my friend, coauthor, editor, and co-editor Charles R. Putney, a wonderful writer and editor; and my friend Cinda Morse, both of whom offered valued observations.

To author and friend Gail Terp, my thanks for her professional proofing.

Spouses always thank their spouses, but mine is a sincere one. Thank you, Sara, for your support and encouragement. As with my other books, this one could not have happened without you. I love you for your "nudges."

Finally, a huge "Thank you!" goes out to my readers, who have encouraged me to assemble a collection of my columns. During the nine years I wrote these columns, they faithfully read my work, helped me to create more of it with their ideas, corrected me when I was wrong in facts, sometimes railed at me when they disagreed with a position I took, but always kept coming back for more. What a pleasure for me to be back again!

Joseph Cutshall-King

OTHER WORKS BY CUTSHALL-KING

FICTION
2011: *The Burning of The Piping Rock*; a historical mystery novel; (Matchless Books).

HISTORIES
2017: *WATER & LIGHT: S. R. Stoddard's Lake George*. Chapman Historical Museum, publisher.
2008: *Cornerstone of the Future*; history of First Presbyterian Church of Glens Falls, NY. First Presbyterian Church of Glens Falls, NY, publisher.
2001: *Con Amore – The Italian History of Fort Edward*; with Italian Heritage Committee of Fort Edward Historical Association, Inc., publisher.
1987: *Hospital by the Falls*; History of the Glens Falls Hospital, publisher.

NEWSPAPER COLUMNS
1994-2003: *"Over My Shoulder"* – Weekly column of history and commentary in *The Post-Star*, Glens Falls, NY.
1994-1995: *"Passed Times"* – Seasonal column of history and commentary in "The Time of Our Lives" tabloid of *The Post-Star*, Glens Falls, NY.
1975-1985: *"Chapman Museum"* – Weekly column of history and commentary in *The Post-Star*, Glens Falls, NY.

AS CONTRIBUTING AUTHOR
2005: Section on "Washington County, NY" in *The Encyclopedia of New York State*, 1st ed. Syracuse, NY: Syracuse University Press.

AS CO-EDITOR
1996 - *Sherlock Holmes: Victorian Sleuth to Modern Hero*. Scarecrow Press/University Press. Co-editor with Charles R. Putney and Sally Sugarman; collation of presentations from conference "Sherlock Holmes: Victorian Sleuth to Modern Hero."

RADIO
1978-1988: Author/producer of *LEGACY*, weekly program of history and commentary broadcast on WWSC AM/WCKM FM, Glens Falls, NY.

Table of Contents

FOREWORD

The gift of a good storyteller is to take you outside of yourself and then subtly draw you back again, unfolding bits of the tale that remind you of yourself, and make the characters in the story relatable—no matter how long ago, nor fantastical the tale may seem.

I grew up having my father read to me at night. The Grimm Brothers and Mother Goose come to mind, but so do the tales he created from his memory and imagination. Once, out of desperation, he read to me from the biography of Elizabeth I; hundreds of pages long, it was dull reading bound to lull a child to sleep. I was hooked; I wanted to know what she did next, and why—as my father (I imagine) equally hoped to know the same about my sleep patterns, and when they would kick in.

That is the gift (and in that case, curse) of the true storyteller in action; I was in a time and place I'd never be able to conceive of, but I felt that I could. A story connects us, no matter who we are or what we've experienced. We understand because we're reminded that we are human, and that time and space separate little when it comes down to it.

My father's columns—whether you're familiar with them or not—foster that connection. I'm honored to have been able to edit them and know that you, dear reader, will enjoy them as much as I have.

Julia C. Cutshall-King, Editor

INTRODUCTION: WELCOME AND WELCOME BACK!

When City Editor Bob Condon first discussed my returning to write for *The Post-Star* in 1994, perhaps he was a little trepidatious. I certainly was! It had been nine years since my last column, written while I was Director of the Chapman Historical Museum. However, Bob said Editor Ken Tingley had approved my starting out with a column called "Passed Times" in a quarterly tabloid section, "The Time of Our Lives."

That tab tabloid was discontinued in 1995. However, that column had garnered enough interest from past and new readers by then for *The Post-Star* to offer me a bi-weekly column, "Over My Shoulder," combining local history and commentary. In 1996 it went weekly and stayed as such until March 2003. I ended it when I took a job out of the region.

In all, I wrote more than 400 columns, all but eight were "Over My Shoulder." This book is a selection from all columns from January 1994 to December 1997. As *The Post-Star* covers Warren, Washington, and Saratoga Counties, I wrote columns covering from Ticonderoga (Essex County) in the north to Saratoga in the south, east into Vermont and west into the Adirondacks. I wrote local history as well as commentary on events of day. Most of the latter were rants and, thanks to the editorial work of Julia C. Cutshall-King, you have been spared columns too dated, too topical, or just too dull. Spelling and punctuation have been corrected when necessary. An occasional endnote was added for clarity or to update information.

Speaking of editors, Bob Condon was not my only one. Others included Will Doolittle, Dave Blow, Fred Daley, and Mike Mender, to name a few. Bob comes to mind most often, as he was also my editor when I was a correspondent from 1995 to 1997, reporting on news of towns and villages in southern Washington County and eastern Saratoga County. I learned from all my editors and am grateful to them.

This is not a scholarly book. I have always written knowing history can be deadly but hoping I could make it enjoyable enough for all to read. However, I always used primary and secondary sources. Primary included newspapers, public records, booklets, pamphlets diaries, journals, correspondence, audio and video recordings, many of them mine. Secondary included every published history I could buy or borrow. Some have been cited; others not. Our house groans under the weight of paper collected. I wrote these before the internet had become the trove it is today. Since then, to my wife Sara's distress, I have added more paper to my own library, not to mention hundreds upon hundreds of gigabytes of scanned and downloaded documents, maps, photographs and the like. My mania.

So, I thank you for reading these columns. I really hope you will enjoy them!

Joseph Cutshall-King

SECTION 1: GLENS FALLS HISTORY

"PASSED TIMES" COLUMN; WINTER 1994 VOL. I, NO. 1.
A trip into the memory zone

NOTE: This was my first column to be published after my return to *The Post-Star* in 1994. This "Passed Times" column in *The Time of Our Lives* was exhilarating for me, as well as humbling. I implied in a rather superior tone that it snowed more in my youth. Right after publication, Glens Falls had a record snowstorm. I took a lot of good-natured ribbing—and learned to avoid weather as a topic.

There is one thing, above all others, which children, grandchildren – well, let's just say younger people – accuse us of as we age: exaggerating the conditions under which we grew up.

Weather is an example. As is the distance we spent walking to school. Put both together and you have the perfect example.

My daughter, Julia, now 12, has accused me of gross exaggeration of the distance I claim to have walked when I was attending school in Fort Edward. Would any of you who went to school with me please confirm my memory that we did walk 35 miles each way to school, every day, and that in the winter we did have to dig down through the snow to get into the school once we arrived?

All right, all right. So, perhaps my memory has stretched the figures a tad. The truthful reality is that the kids in my family did walk four miles a day to school from our house in the lower part of the village: a mile to school in the morning. A mile up and a mile back for lunch. And a mile on the afternoon return home. Just out of curiosity, I clocked that distance on the odometer a few years ago.

And how about snow? Help me out here, but wasn't I right when I told my daughter that when we were kids it used to snow so hard that we had tunnel out into the yard to play?

All right, all right. So, perhaps my memory has stretched that a tad. But, seriously, that is a difficult question, for while you remember the snow being over your head as a child, you were only half your present height. Did it really snow more then, or was it relative?

Well, last year, when it snowed so hard, the issue came up again, for I heard so many people say, "Oh, that snow's no big deal. It's just like old times." Was it? I cast a thought back to more recent times, the early 1980s, when we lived on Harrison Avenue in Glens Falls. I remembered Julia going up to play with her friend Amorette on Lincoln Avenue and, according to my memory, the snow banks seemed incredibly high.

Then I thought back even further, into the Jurassic age, to my own childhood. It seemed as if it snowed from late November onward...and the snow stayed! I was sure that I correctly remembered the Village crew working day and night to remove the enormous snowbanks from in front of my family's pharmacy on Broadway, but (and this a big "but") could this have been only my memory playing tricks? I knew that I could not rely on memory alone, at least not mine. A good historian needs proof!

And what better proof than photographs? Normally, I could go to the Chapman Museum or the Old Fort House, but in this case, they wouldn't have what I needed: photos of my family in winter. So, I dug out my old family photo albums. Yes, there were winter shots of us in front of our pharmacy and another in front of our house. The snow was high, but the question nagged me: was it the camera angle? Still photographs can be deceptive.

Coincidentally, my wife, Sara, solved the problem with something special from her family, the Cutshalls (now my family, too). By chance, she happened to play some home movies from the time when her family lived on Harrison Avenue in Glens Falls.

As we watched, there on the sidewalk in front of her family home stood 12- or 13-year-old Sara, in a classic Doris Day 1950s shot, waving at the camera (her mother, Edna, being the Cecil B. DeMille of the family), with the un-shoveled snow in the yard being belt-high to a tall lumberjack.

Did you capture that important information? That the snow in the yard was just as it fell from the heavens: pure, white, untouched – and about three feet deep? As the camera moved and cars sped by, you saw that the snow really was deeper on the other side of "the Memory Zone."

My daughter literally gawked as she watched the film. "Was that in front of Grandma's house?" she asked, flabbergasted. Indeed! There in living 1950s color was proof: the snow WAS deeper when we were kids. Ah! My daughter was a believer from that moment on. (And, you know, she never once asked if the images were computer-enhanced.)

I bathed in the glory of that moment and – just casually – happened to mention how difficult it was to shovel that snow, what with all the other work that I had to do. I simply said that in addition to going to school, and doing homework, and shoveling snow, I also maintained a 35-hour-a week job in my family's pharmacy.

What? Oh, all right, all right. So, perhaps my memory has stretched things a tad.

Maybe it was only 30 hours a week.

"PASSED TIMES" COLUMN; SPRING 1994 VOL. I, NO. 2.
Water a big part of city's history

With little, if any fanfare, the City of Glens Falls passed through its eighty-sixth birthday on March 13, and ironically *The Post-Star* has been filled with news of the one thing that brought into being, and could well bring the end to, the City of Glens Falls. The news is about water.

In one article, *The Post-Star* reported a task force had looked into a municipal electrical system. In another article, there was news about the possibility of the city's giving up its watersheds and reservoirs, something over which Glens Falls has had control since 1871.

It was water that made Glens Falls, a fact evident from the word "Falls," the Hudson River falls that in 1763 first supplied the founder of Glens Falls and Queensbury, Abraham Wing, with power for a sawmill, located where Finch Pruyn is today.[i]

Water powered the lumber, lime, and paper mills of a tiny village and carried its products to markets to the south via the canal. Abe Wing's little hamlet changed names to "Glens Falls" and grew to a village that incorporated in 1839. By the end of the Civil War, Glens Falls was ready to boom.

Now another "water" played its part: reservoirs. When all downtown burned in the Great Fire of 1864, a movement began to create a "municipal" water system. In 1871, a "water company" was formed and in 1873 the Wilkie Reservoir in western Queensbury began sending its clear gold to the village.

The system was gravity fed and, according to reliable sources, on the day it opened a group gathered on Ridge Street (near present-day M.C. Scoville's)[ii] to – what else? – jeer.

"There'll never be any pressure!" they taunted. The group was invited to hold a fire hose attached to a hydrant, and as the water shot through the hose with unbelievable power, it rose snake-like in the air, shaking off the disbelievers and flailing about, crashing through store windows. Fortunately, there were shut-off valves up the line.

The new system promised more adequate fire protection, and the controlled – and forceful! – pressure was exactly what textile mills' steam presses needed. Shirt and dress factories sprung up like mushrooms in a cow pasture and the little village grew at a staggering rate, adding more reservoirs and watershed area in the mountainous area of western Queensbury.

Though the issue was a little contentious, still, the citizens of Glens Falls were Town of Queensbury citizens, too. The town's hub was growing, and it needed water.

By the early 1890s, the perspective in that hub was changing. There were those among the ruling elite who saw the village as an entity unto itself. Its boundaries had expanded several times, and, after all, they reasoned, the village had the industries which made the town: lumber, paper, textiles, and lime. And it had its own school system and library, plus hotels, theaters and opera houses, a trolley system, and more beautiful homes of up and coming wealthy people than you could shake a stick at. And it had water. River water power, as well as reservoir water piped into homes and businesses. Water that, virtually overnight, had made Glens Falls grow.

That part of that water – the reservoirs – was not in the village, but six miles away in the mountains at the west of town. Well, that was a ho-hum issue.

Besides, the watershed was a source of pride for all in the town, with prominent citizens like Egbert West, chair of the Glens Falls Insurance Company, leading the movement for reforestation of the watershed and contributing to the beauty and serenity that that land possesses today.

As early as the late 1880s, but definitely by 1896, a movement was at hand to separate Glens Falls from Queensbury. Movers and shakers led by newspaper publisher A. B. Colvin and others got up a petition and things began to move in the direction of municipal incorporation and separation. After all, they reasoned, they had everything. And they had water. That ticklish problem, water.

To cut to the chase, in 1908, in a move not wholly celebrated by everyone in Glens Falls, but definitely not celebrated by anyone in the Town of Queensbury who lived outside the village, Glens Falls became a city, separating politically from Queensbury and taking with it its economic, cultural, and historic heart.

In that separation, though, were the seeds of trouble. Open space for one thing. Only half-developed in 1908, within thirty years most of the city's land would be laid out for streets and homes. And there was the car. In 1908, the auto was a baby. Within thirty years, it would be king, and people inside and outside the city would be seeking ways to by-pass congested city streets.

The present Northway and Quaker Road were first proposed in 1937[iii] and, when completed in the early '60s, the gradual movement of retail stores, industry and homes to Queensbury – a movement started in the 1920s – became a land rush.

And then the very source of the birth and growth of Glens Falls – water – became a problem. The reservoirs' maintenance costs and the land taxes paid to Queensbury began to add up as city revenues shrank. Environmental regulations increased, adding millions in potential costs.

So, the talk that was a trickle in the 1960s has now become a torrent: should the city invest in – or divest itself of – its reservoirs? Should it sell the land and merge with the Queensbury water system? Or should it tap into the Hudson? And while that discussion goes on, conversely another city group looks at generating hydroelectricity from the Hudson to keep, and to attract, business.

It is but one opinion, my own, but allow me to say that if the City of Glens Falls divests itself of its watershed lands, it will cease to exist as "a city" within one or two decades at most. This is not a judgment upon the possible reincorporating of Glens Falls into Queensbury. That's for the people to decide. Rather, this is based on the historical observation that at the heart of every political entity – city, town, state, whatever – there must be a source of power. In Glens Falls' case, it is water. Trade it away and, essentially, the heart is traded away. Trade away the heart....

But the obligation for consideration of this rests also on the Town of Queensbury. For if the city watersheds are dissolved, broken up into just so many lots for building, the Town will lose one of its most precious resources: open land that is at once a state-certified watershed, as well as an animal habitat, potential recreation area, and place of exquisite beauty.

Having lost its public access to Lake George, Round Pond, and Lake Sunnyside, the Town of Queensbury could do well to contemplate history. As certainly could the City of Glens Falls. These cousins share much in their common heritage.

Water, water everywhere. And you thought history a dry topic.

"OVER MY SHOULDER" COLUMN FOR NOVEMBER 21, 1994
"Current" events in the region

*T*he *Post-Star* is filled these days with news of the City of Glens Falls investigating a municipal electrical authority. And electricity has a long history here.

From Oct. 21, 1879, when Edison demonstrated the first incandescent light bulb, the idea of electricity caught on with the people of Glens Falls, then only a tiny village, but advanced in its thinking. By the time Edison installed the first central power station in New York City in 1882, Glens Falls had already advertised in the *Glens Falls Messenger* for proposals to light the village with electric street lamps. By 1884, it was being advertised that electric lamps were already lighting the stores downtown with a light far brighter than that provided by kerosene or by gas, which had been manufactured near Finch Pruyn since 1854. The new electric lights were so bright that the whole business area was lit up in a way that people had never experienced before. (What a great business gimmick that must have been: "Peruse our winter fashions under our new electric lights!")

According to what I have been told, the first electricity generated in Glens Falls was at the Finch Pruyn mill in 1880. Not surprising. This was a progressive business in a progressive village. Why, people in Glens Falls got the phone shortly after it was invented. (Though, because they had children, they immediately regretted it.)

Electric lighting took off in the 1880s and 1890s. The trolleys, started in 1885, were electrified in 1891. Everybody wanted to be electrified. Well, almost everyone. There were still those who thought that the electricity could leak out of the walls like gas vapors and electrocute them while they were lying in bed at night.

By the end of the 1890s, it was apparent that electricity was here to stay. (Christmas tree lights had been invented by that time, so there was no choice.) A man named Eugene Ashley cast an eye on the abundant water that flowed down the Hudson River and decided to build a hydroelectric plant on a part of the Hudson just above (to the west) of Glens Falls. In spite of the love for the new-fangled electricity, and in spite of Ashley's success at generating hydroelectricity at Kane's Falls in Fort Ann, some thought Ashley was a little round the bend.

Not everyone, however. In 1899 Ashley was joined by Elmer J. West and a group of associates in creating the Hudson River Water Power Company. In 1900 they began some serious construction work. As will happen in any construction, problems erupted. Storms, flooding, and bursting cofferdams cost money...and workers' lives. Many were Italian immigrants newly arrived in the United States who poured their talents into the project. Several died doing so. (In fact, Ashley adopted the child of one of the laborers who had died on the job.)

Amidst all the trouble, including a surprise depression in the river bed that was 65 feet deep, money ran out. Ashley and company were faced with ruin. In stepped a wealthy lumber baron, William E. Spier, who, according to printed history, gave Ashley a $150,000 personal loan with no interest and no security asked. Today this amount would be the equivalent of several million dollars. (Where is this person when we need him now?)

You might have guessed that the dam, completed in 1903, is known today as "Spier Falls," named in honor of that wealthy lumber baron. What Ashley and West had managed to build was, in 1903, the fourth largest dam in the world AND the largest dam ever created for the sole purpose of generating electricity. Subsequently, the Spier Falls plant was expanded and two other plants closer to Glens Falls, the Sherman Island and Feeder Dam plants, were built. Through mergers, Ashley's company became the Adirondack Power and Light Company in 1911, expanding its service northward as far as North Creek. In the 1930s the company merged with the New York Power and Light Company and that, in turn, became a part of what is today Niagara Mohawk.

So, there you have it. A bit of history about electricity to keep you "current." Sorry. Couldn't resist it.

"OVER MY SHOULDER" COLUMN FOR DECEMBER 5, 1994
Downtown memories

At each Christmas shopping season, I think of downtown Glens Falls, which is natural, as so many of my childhood memories of the 1950s are associated with shopping there. But others who remember the Christmas season in downtown as adults, recall a place of excitement, beauty, bustle, music, variety and, above all, service. Service: personal attention to your needs. A desire to please you, the customer.

This was Christmas shopping in downtown Glens Falls, before shopping plazas, malls, and strips. No matter where you lived, you simply had to shop Glens Falls. Envision this scene: streets crowded with cars and people and strung with decorations from lamppost to lamppost. Store windows decorated exquisitely, bursting with merchandise. Music in the stores, on the streets and the Salvation Army, out ringing and ringing and ringing. Looking up Glen Street through a canyon of buildings, you'd see all five stories of the Glens Falls Insurance Company building decorated in an extravaganza of lights and garland. I always thought it looked like an enormous cake with lights.

My friend Father C. Michael Abraham recalls walking over from South Glens Falls, up Glen Street hill and past the Hotel Viaduct. At about the corner of Berry and Glen he'd enter "downtown." He said he'd shop at the Economy and the Outlet, where you got good quality for lower prices. Places like the Fashion Shop on Ridge were too expensive for him at that time.

Of course, if you wanted "upscale" stores downtown Glens Falls had them: Erlanger's, on the corner of Exchange and Glen, Fowler's just up from it and Merkel and Gelman's two doors up. Honigsbaum's was in the carriage barn by City Park[iv]. There were all kinds of specialty shops, including furriers like Faxon's in the Rogers Building on Maple. There were stores for every need, every desire, and every pocketbook. There were four department store chains: Grants (where Hudson Avenue now meets Glen) and Newberry's a few doors above it, and then across Glen Street, Woolworth's and Kresge's. How good they smelled!

Regardless of how much money you had, it was exciting to shop downtown, going in and out of the stores, crossing and re-crossing the street, crunching through the snow, seeing friends and being seen, the fun of shopping at night and, yes, the thrill of entering each store. Going into Erlanger's was like entering a glass tunnel of show windows filled with exotic goods and decorations. Of course, you went into every store, regardless of its price tags, for you were always treated like a Rockefeller. My friend Marge Januszkiewicz recalled when her son Andy, then a little boy, went into Achenbach's with only a few dollars. An elderly gentleman waited on Andy, treating him with all the courtesy he would have given a customer with a few thousand dollars to spend. That was the essence of downtown.

My father would drive Mom and us kids up from Fort Edward but wouldn't stay. Frankly, neither Christmas nor shopping were his forte. But for my mother? Lord! Christmas was THE holiday and shopping was like champagne to a bon vivant: intoxicating and essential. Up and down the streets we'd go: Woolworth's, then the Fashion Shop, then the Outlet, then Erlanger's....then and then and then. "Mom!" we'd cry, "Can't we stay here after Santa and play with the toys?". But Mom, invigorated by every store, moved like Sherman marching to the sea. An ardent reader, she always made the pilgrimage to the Ridge Book Shop. (Though I wondered then, "Why's the 'Ridge Book Shop' on Glen?")

Even Mom tired and we'd decadently eat supper at, say, the Kong Chow or the Kansas Restaurant on Warren Street. The stores were open late, so, revived, we'd go back for another fitting or a last drool over some toy. Waving to friends, we'd visit Braydon and Chapman's to sit in one of their booths to preview the Perry Como or Elvis records or just browse in the stores before it was time to end our Christmas shopping visit; to pack up our bags, tired, but so sad to have to go.

Then we'd head homeward – homeward from that crowded, wonderful, long ago and faraway place called "downtown."

"OVER MY SHOULDER" COLUMN FOR JANUARY 2, 1995
Heartfelt wish for a company

I f you look in the phone book for the Glens Falls region, you'll notice under the "G's" a listing for "Glens Falls Insurance Company."

The recent news about the merger of Continental Insurance has those who know that name and its history wondering: Will the "Glens Falls Insurance Company," the "Old and Tried," be around after the merger dust settles? A stranger in town may not readily connect the 10-story white marble Continental Insurance building on Glen Street[v] with something called a "Glens Falls Insurance Company." Ironically, the building itself was constructed as a part of the terms of merger between the Glens Falls Insurance Company and Continental in 1968.

The Glens Falls Insurance Company began in 1849, 10 years after the Village of Glens Falls incorporated. In fact, in reading its founders' names, you are also reading many of the same people's names who founded the village, the first volunteer fire company in Glens Falls and Queensbury, the present-day Glens Falls National Bank and Trust Company, the present-day Evergreen Bank[vi] and ... I think you get the picture. Yet, it was a humble beginning for a company that would be international in scope by the 20th century.

It started as the Dividend Mutual Insurance Company, selling fire insurance. Now, fire insurance companies in the mid-1800s had the longevity of houseflies and about the same reputation. But fire insurance was a necessity.

The company's founder, the Rev. Russell Mack Little, had lost the ability to preach loudly, as was custom then, because of a throat ailment. With the zeal he would have put into his sermons, he spread his concern for fire protection in the little, but growing, village. Fires were commonplace in the closely knit, wood-framed buildings. The volunteer fire company was virtually ineffectual because the municipal water system consisted of horse drinking troughs.

Little galvanized town leaders to start the company, which changed its name in 1863 to the Glens Falls Insurance Company. Little was everything from agent to CEO in the beginning. The first offices were spartan, and Little, Yankee thrifty, promptly moved the offices when the first landlord tried to raise the rent. In later times he refused his pay being raised above $3,000, because "no man in the world is worth more than $3,000 a year."

Newt Gingrich would have loved Little.

The company grew while others folded, because of good sense and ethics. In 1864, when downtown Glens Falls was incinerated, the insurance company was in the streets, paying claims immediately.

In 1870 Little went to Chicago and promptly wrote all the company's agents: Do not underwrite Chicago property. In 1871 Chicago burned and the competition went bankrupt. The company began to be known as the "Old and Tried." After the 1906 San Francisco earthquake and fire, while other companies backed out of paying the claims, the Glens Falls Insurance Company stood by every policy, because it was right.

And it grew.

By 1912 it had built a third, and enormous, home headquarters at the intersection of Bay and Glen streets, where today a park stands next to the Church of the Messiah. It became a major employer in the Glens Falls area and soon spread throughout the United States and to other countries. Following Little's precepts, it could be a stern master. Ced Traver, who worked there for years, told me that one did it the company's way or one left. Period. But this company also started providing employee health coverage as early as 1918.

In 1968 the Glens Falls Insurance Company agreed to merge with Continental Insurance. As mentioned, a new office building was constructed, I assume to insure the company's remaining here, and the transition was heartbreakingly completed in 1976, when the five-story 1912 building was razed. Change had its price.

Now the "Glens Falls Insurance Company" faces another change, and the question is raised, for the sake of community pride and history, will the name remain? Also asked, for the sake of the jobs in it, will the building remain?

My New Year wish is that 1995 will see both the Glens Falls Insurance Company and the insurance employees at 333 Glen moving forward, in Glens Falls, toward a prosperous 21st century.

And a Happy New Year to each and every one of you.

OVER MY SHOULDER COLUMN FOR JANUARY 16, 1995
Skiing not new to Glens Falls

Going skiing? While some of us consider the cold from an open refrigerator to be excessive, there are those whose eyes simply sparkle with the. thought of snow.

My friend Bruce Adams in Glens Falls is like that. But you'd expect this from a man who was in the 10th Mountain Division, serving in the ski troops in World War II.

Each winter I think of Bruce and am amazed again by how long a history skiing has in this area. I don't know the exact date when people first started skiing in the Greater Glens Falls area.

Of course, they skated and snowshoed from early times, but by the 1920s skiing was well in place. In the mid-1920s Lapham's Sporting Goods Store on Glen Street was selling wooden skis.[vii]

According to the history *Bridging the Years*[viii], in 1927 when the Outing Club began, it created "skating rinks, toboggan slides and ski jumps" in Crandall Park. The 1932 Winter Olympics at Lake Placid started a ski fever and the first commercial ski area in the East was established at Gore Mountain in North Creek in 1933.

The Glens Falls Recreation Commission, started in 1924, set up ski trails in the late 1930s on West Mountain, five miles to the west of the city. There were four major trails ranging from "novice" to "expert" in difficulty and you drove to the mountaintop in a truck or your own car. West Mountain was "privatized" in 1961 (I think) and the Brandt family operates it today.

Bruce has spoken of skiing in Greater Glens Falls at other spots, including Bolton Landing at the Sagamore Golf Club on Federal Hill. He worked at the Sagamore Hotel as a sports instructor.

There were also trails and open slopes at French Mountain, a few miles from Lake George Village and the open slopes were lighted. Lake George Village itself was a hot spot, pardon the phrase, with 27 miles of trails on Prospect and Cobble mountains. (Cobble had a ski-tow!) There was "Langlauf" (cross-country skiing) on the Still Pond Trail, though cross-country wasn't as popular as now. Definitely overshadowed by downhill.

Like Bolton Landing and Glens Falls at Crandall Park, Lake George had tobogganing, hockey, and skating, and like Bolton Landing, ski-joring (being pulled in a sled by a horse or dog), harness racing and ice-boating, all under the aegis of the Lake George Winter Sports Club.

Lake Luzerne offered skiing at Stone Mountain and Warrensburg had skiing on lighted trails with a ski- tow.

North Creek's Gore Mountain was "ski capital" of Warren County in the '30s and '40s with 50 miles of trails, a ski school and sports club house, built in 1941. Gore was the first to introduce the electric ski lift in 1947.

And what did all these ski and winter sport areas have in common? They were served by snow trains. The Delaware and Hudson ran snow trains through Fort Edward up to Glens Falls and Lake George, serving Glens Falls, West Mountain, Lake George, and Bolton Landing. The other line ran from Saratoga north and served Hadley-Luzerne, Warrensburg, and North Creek.

Trains would come loaded with skiers and equipment (and some skiers loaded with "antifreeze"). The ski fashions from the '30s and '40s may not have included spandex, but they were chic.

Imagine Garbo in ski gear or something out of Bing Crosby's 1942 movie "Holiday Inn." I have this image of pre-war Garbo wannabes plunging down the slopes at Gore or playing it safe by lounging around the huge fireplace in the lobby of the Queensbury Hotel. (That's where I would have been—lying about my skiing!)

Last fall when the state was debating bringing back the snow trains to the Adirondacks, the thought occurred to me that snow trains are what I call "sensible nostalgia:" an older, very sensible concept, that no one is willing to pay for.

Sadly, then, snow trains are probably a thing of the past. But I think it's safe to say that skiing is here to stay.

So! My good luck wish for the ski season: break a leg. Oh, that's right. You're supposed wish that to actors going on stage.

Sorry.

"OVER MY SHOULDER" COLUMN FOR FEBRUARY 13, 1995
Living proof of his beliefs

Help! I received a call from Mike Brandt concerning the January 2nd column, in which I stated that the Glens Falls Recreation Department had begun a skiing facility at West Mountain in the mid-1930s and that, in 1961, it was sold to the Brandt family, which opened it as West Mountain Ski Center. Actually, the Brandt family bought private lands to open West Mountain, which is still offering fine skiing in western Queensbury. Thanks, Mike!

Where, then, did the Recreation Department have its ski slopes? Obviously on the city's extensive watershed, but where exactly? Help!?

And speaking of skiing, in that same column, I had mentioned Bruce Adams of Glens Falls, who served with the famed 10th Mountain Division in World War II. Bruce's heroic stint in "The 10th" began with his family's love of sports and skiing. In fact, during winters before the war, Bruce had taught downhill skiing at the Glens Falls Country Club.

As a professional teacher, Bruce's abilities naturally led him to join the Army after the outset of World War II to serve with the 10th Mountain Division, itself established only a few days before Pearl Harbor. Starting with a small, highly dedicated group of skiers, this corps included refugees from Hitler's Europe, American college and Olympic skiers, professionals like Bruce Adams, plus loggers and foresters. By 1943, the corps had 15,000 soldiers and was named the "10th Mountain Division."[ix]

Bruce and thousands of others were sent to the newly created "Camp Hale," 8,000 feet up in the Colorado Rockies not too far west of Denver. There, Private Second Class Adams was a professional trainer of ski troops – from privates to Brigadier Generals. In winter, training was intensely rigorous, cold, and unrelenting, especially for the uninitiated learning to ski and shoot at the same time. In summer, the troops climbed mountains!

After Camp Hale, the 10th was sent to the Aleutians Islands to drive out the Japanese. Attu Island was taken by heavy fire, but, as Bruce said, they reached Kiska three days after the Japanese had snuck away. Later, the 10th Mountain returned for a short visit to Camp Hale before shipping out to Italy's Alps, the Apennines, in November 1944. There the 10th earned its fame and Bruce, though he would not admit as such, became a hero, along with other ski troopers like Senator Robert Dole.

Two months before war's end, in March 1945, Bruce was felled in a massive attack and left for dead. When the next day's sun rose, he was found alive, although horrendously wounded, barely able to speak or move. Through the successive months, the athlete in Bruce demanded that he rise and attempt to get on with living. On board the transport ship bringing him home, he practiced taking steps. As he told me, "I fell down and got up, fell down and got up, fell down and got up," over and over and over again. It is the story of the best of the human spirit embodied in one person.

Bruce came home to recuperate with his parents, Mr. and Mrs. Claude Adams. He says that in 1948, they opened their own ski center on Bay Road, Queensbury, just south of Sunnyside. It was a single trail center on five acres, but it had trail lights for night skiing and a ski tow – actually, as Bruce said, a tow rope powered by a 1931 Ford. Mr. Adams had removed the car's tire and looped the tow rope over the wheel. You simply hung on!

Well, Bruce spent many years recuperating, but eventually came to be able to ski at his parents' Ski Hill, using a conventional ski on one foot, while hand-guiding the other ski by means of a pole outfitted to it, allowing him to whiz down the open trails. I've never heard him boast of his valor nor complain of his injuries, and he deflects compliments by simply saying, "All things are possible." He's right. Because, fifty years after being left for dead in the snowy Alps, he is here: living proof of his belief.

So, on this special anniversary, please join with me in offering a heartfelt salute to Bruce Adams, a most special man.

"PASSED TIMES" COLUMN; WINTER 1995; VOL. II, NO. 1
Our area is rich in baseball history

NOTE: Here's a column I was pleased to read, as it mentions the possibility of the return of semi-pro baseball to the City of Glens Falls. Happily for baseball fans, East Field is alive with it today.

In the dead of winter, many people's thoughts drift toward one thing. Baseball.

While the City of Glens Falls' deliberations over the reintroduction of a semi-pro baseball team at East Field may have had many recalling the more recent games played there, many others were probably casting a thought back a few decades to the earlier semi-pro baseball teams in this region, and to names like the Doblers and the Independents and the Greenjackets.

Baseball has existed in Glens Falls and the surrounding region since at least after the Civil War. By the 1880s, it was so entrenched that the various Glens Falls newspapers were giving the same intense coverage that has lasted to this day.

Within memory, particularly from the late 1920s through the early 1950s, there were a slew of semi-pro teams in our area. While I may be challenged on this, I think it was the heyday of semi-pro teams.

In the early 1930s Glens Falls had two teams that were bitter rivals: The Glens

Falls Clerks, managed by LeRoy Akins, Sr., whose son Roy, Jr. lives in Glens Falls today;ˣ and the Glens Falls Independents, managed by Roland "Wady" Rozelle. These two teams would play at Recreation Field in Crandall Park, providing excellent baseball, as well as a connection for local talent to the minor leagues and big leagues.

While the Depression's effects on local baseball are debatable, it's very certain the Second World War really put a crimp in it. Even the major leagues were decimated by the call to duty between 1941 and 1945. But with war's end, local semi-pro ball resumed with a vengeance.

By 1948, the Warren Washington Semi-Pro League boasted thirteen teams in New York and Vermont. The following is a listing of the teams, although, as you'll see, my information is incomplete regarding the names of the teams or managers, or even, in a few cases, the town in which the team existed: (1) Corinth; (2) Fairhaven, VT; (3) the Fort Ann Blue Sox; (4) Fort Edward; (5) the Glens Falls Doblers, manager Sarto Marcantonio; (6) the Glens Falls Independents, manager Wady Rozelle; (7) the Greyhounds; (8) Hartford; (9) the Hudson Falls Greenjackets; (10) the Iroquois; (11) Poultney, VT; (12) South Glens Falls; (13) the Whitehall Legion, manager Johnny Day. Any information to complete these would be greatly appreciated.

By 1948, LeRoy Akins had stopped managing at that point, but had taken on perhaps an even more grueling job in baseball, that of umpire, I presume in the Adirondack Chapter of Certified Baseball Umpires. In August of '48, Akins came out of "retirement" from management to reassemble the Clerks for a revival match against their arch rivals of yore, the Independents. Wady Rozelle was still the manager of the Independents.

J. Harry Wallace of *The Glens Falls Times* sports department, in writing of the famed rematch, made it sound as if sparks would still be flying between the two teams, with the players, the "boys of yesteryear," as he called them, "attempting to play as well as...in their prime" fifteen years before. Something tells me the rematch spurred Absorbine sales a bit.

Of course, the semi-pro teams did play outside teams. The Doblers, for example, on August 1st of 1948, after playing a double header against the Fort Ann Blue Sox, followed with a second game with the Troy Negro Athletic Club.

While baseball was "king," there were two men's softball leagues, the Men's Industrial League and the Men's Open League, each with eight teams. Also, there was a Playground League in the City of Glens Falls. It was divided into six divisions, two for boys 12 and under, two for 15 and under and two for 18 and under. In addition to the Junior League softball teams for teens, there were great high school hardball teams playing during the school season. In the early 1950s, Little League would start.

The semi-pro teams filled a need for those craving to play baseball, but unable to move into the minor or major leagues for whatever reason.

Times may have changed, and baseball may have, too. But this spring the baseball diamonds will be cleared, and we will still hear those words "Play ball!"

When you do, reflect a moment on the Warren Washington Semi-Pro League and the wonderful legacy of baseball in the Glens Falls area.[xi]

"OVER MY SHOULDER" COLUMN FOR MAY 8, 1995
The day old Glens Falls burned down

Next time you turn on the water, think of May 31st. It marks the anniversary of "The Great Fire of 1864" that burned downtown Glens Falls to the ground.

I'd like to try to describe the fire for you in terms of today's downtown, because it was so enormously destructive! Even worse than Urban Renewal! Standing at the intersection of Glen, Ridge, Hudson and Warren, you'd be at the epicenter of The Great Fire, which burned just about everything within about two blocks of that intersection.

It started the morning of May 31st, in the huge coal-fired stoves in the kitchen of the new Glens Falls Hotel, which stood exactly where Hudson Avenue today intersects with Glen Street. The wooden inner structure of the four-story brick-faced building ignited and the fire "went to town," pushed to adjoining wood-frame structures by a good wind. There was no water system at that time. The only thing the poor volunteer fire companies were equipped with were two wonderful hand pumpers, plus private wells and cisterns of water, all virtually useless as the fire burned several stories above their heads, sending out walls of flame that could have literally incinerated horses and humans alike.

Fire raced in every direction. Westward toward Elm Street, where it burned with ease the mostly wooden structures. North along Glen. South, racing toward Park Street, engulfing buildings as far down as present-day R.G. Landry's,[xii] then, horror of horrors, jumping Park Street.

But the horror had just begun! The sheer intensity of the heat now coming from the solid blocks of burning buildings was magnified in its lethal potential by the wind: the fire jumped Glen Street at many spots! Over it went to somewhere just below present-day Lapham Place, careening down to today's M.C. Scoville's,[xiii] igniting everything in between and sending the flames gushing through to the west side of Ridge Street, then vaulting Ridge and burning from around the area of today's "Back Door Cafe"[xiv] down to the present-day Cowles Building on the corner of Ridge and Warren Street.[xv] The brick facing of the four story building then located there wasn't any match for this fire and its wooden inner structure must have nearly popped into flames, even though it had only been built in 1849.

Fed by new fuel and the ever-present wind, the fire chewed its way along Warren Street's north side as far east as Center Street, the sole building saved being the Rosekrans house (today St. Mary's Rectory) on the NE corner of Warren and Church.

Are you with me so far? Well, meanwhile, on the west side of Glen Street, the fire, now burning a block wide, had crossed Park Street with no effort and raged as far south as where J. E. Sawyer's is today, burning down the mansion there that had been built by Sidney Berry in 1836. Calvin Robbins' little stone blacksmith shop was probably spared because of its being tucked in under the hill.

Now the fire jumped Glen and ignited from where today is the Civic Center all the way northward to today's Burger King at the intersection of Glen and Warren. Then it raced eastward in a solid wave over to Church Street, but not crossing it.

In spite of gallant efforts from volunteer fire companies from Glens Falls, South Glens Falls, Hudson Falls and Fort Edward, the Great Fire burned into the night. Miraculously, in the tiny village of approximately 4,500 people, no-one died! However, all the business district was consumed, except for three stores. In all, 112 buildings burned, including three churches, two hotels, sixty stores and two banks (but not the money in vaults).

Now, the Great Fire is a great example of how people don't always learn from history. While most of downtown was rebuilt within a year, rebuilt entirely by 1867, under a new fire law mandating brick buildings and brick firewalls between them, for some reason people rebelled against the notion of installing a water system! It would take until 1872 before a gravity-fed water system was created, even then barely squeaking through, so intense was public sentiment against it!

Facts like that are enough to drive you to drink! Water, of course.

"OVER MY SHOULDER" COLUMN FOR MAY 22, 1995
Monument still causes controversy

The Civil War Monument dedicated to the fallen soldiers of Queensbury stands at the intersection of Bay and Glen Streets in Glens Falls: beautiful and disintegrating.

To many of us, then, the call by Chris Heidorf and members of the Adirondack Civil War Round Table for the monument's restoration comes not a moment too soon.

The monument's original symbolism honoring those who died serving in the Civil War has gradually expanded to honor the forging of the "United States" into a single country and to acknowledge the Civil War's role in the eradication of one of humankind's most horrible institutions, slavery.

Like the war that spawned it, the Civil War Monument was fraught with controversy and scandal, both in its making and in its subsequent care. According to Holden's *History of the Town of Queensbury*,[xvi] when the Civil War broke out, the Town of Queensbury established a war committee, whose job it was to insure a supply of troops for the Union Army. Money was raised as bounty for soldiers' salaries. At the end of the war, enough was left that the Town resolved, at the annual meeting of 1866, to build a "soldier's monument" to those of Queensbury who "fell in battle or died from wounds received or disease contracted in defense of the Union" and in memory of two war committee members, who had died at sea while doing committee work.

Eight thousand dollars was committed, with the "five thousand two hundred and sixty-four dollars and thirty-nine cents" of the war fund to be used; the balance, I assume, to be raised. Therein began the controversy. The next issue was the placement of the monument at "an appropriate place...in or near the Village of Glens Falls." While there's no recorded contention over that, Glens Falls' emergence as the center of power, if not the geographic center, in the Town was "an issue."

An R.T. Baxter, a local marble dealer, set about the job, as Holden wrote, "con amore" – "with love," a phrase used charitably by Holden to signify that Baxter went overboard.

Beginning in the spring of 1867, Baxter hired expensive artisans from other cities and commissioned a foundation of local marble, quarried from near present-day Finch Pruyn, atop which was placed a base of Sprucehead granite from Maine and atop that Dorchester freestone from New Brunswick. On it were inscribed the names of the dead and the major battles of the war. By the time the monument was completed in 1868, it had cost twelve thousand dollars! Poor Baxter departed town, as Holden wrote, "left to...make up an unprovided deficit of four thousand dollars"! By 1872, things had calmed sufficiently to have a proper dedication ceremony and the monument, one of the earlier to be erected by any community after the Civil War, quickly assumed the affections of the townspeople.

In 1908, the Village of Glens Falls separated itself from the Town of Queensbury and with it, among other things, went the monument. In my opinion, shared by others, which governmental entity now owns the monument is, at best, secondary to the issue of those whom the monument honors: the dead who fought to save the Union and to eradicate the slavery of African American people. Those dead were, back then, citizens of either or both Glens Falls and Queensbury. They were then, are now and will be for all times citizens of the United States.

This monument, regardless of its location, is the joint responsibility of both the present City of Glens Falls and Town of Queensbury. Its function was and is to respectfully acknowledge the highest price those listed on the monument could give in the name of freedom: their lives. To relegate the care of this symbol of "these honored dead" to partisan politics and jurisdictional squabbling is roughly equivalent to spitting on the causes for which they fought and died: the freedom of a whole race of people and the unity of this country.

May I suggest that the citizens represented by both the Town and City governments join with those who advocate the repair of this symbol, so that it may continue to honor those dead and the freedoms for which they fought.

"OVER MY SHOULDER" COLUMN FOR JULY 31, 1995
Theatre Dreams

NOTE: A preservationist at heart, I often championed the restoration or adaptive reuse of historic structures, in this case The Empire Theatre building. The happy ending for this column came several years after with the creation of The Wood Theatre on Glen Street and the revitalization of the Park Street Theatre on Park Street, Glens Falls.

Post-Star Editor's Note: In this column Cutshall-King subscribes to the old-time practice of using the "theatre" spelling to refer to live performances and "theater" to refer to movie theaters.

Charles Adams' proposal for a legitimate theater in the old Clark Silk Mill on Elm Street, Glens Falls, is the 1990s version of a decades-old proposal with more lives than a cat.[xvii]
As early as the 1850s, "legitimate theater" was being offered at the Apollo Hall just above where the Civic Center is today. The rich post-Civil War era gave birth in 1871 to the Glens Falls Opera House on the south side of Warren Street, near Glen. After burning in the Fire of 1884, it was rebuilt at the start of what I think was the true era of "legitimate theater" in Glens Falls: from about the late 1880s through to the early 1930s. During this time there were two major legitimate theaters built, the Glens Falls Opera House and the Empire Theatre on South Street. Movie theaters opened from 1902 onward. Including the two legitimate theatre's being used for movies, there were in all nine theaters for movies.

The grandest legitimate theatre in this entire area was the Empire, built in 1899, and the grandest movie theater was the Paramount, the last movie theater constructed in Glens Falls. It opened January 22, 1932. Both, plus another former movie theater, the Park, played significant roles in recent efforts to revive legitimate theatre in Glens Falls.

To the best of my knowledge, the end of that first era of legitimate theatre performances in Glens Falls came in the early 1930s at the Empire, after which the word "theatre," connoting live performances, virtually disappeared and "theaters" (movie-style) were all that remained. Urban Renewal removed the State and Rialto movie theaters on Warren in the late 1960s, and until 1978 the sole operating movie theater was the Paramount on the northeast corner of Ridge and Maple Streets, the Empire having ceased altogether as a theatre/theater in 1950.

From the late sixties on, a desire grew. Organizations such as the Lake George Opera Festival[xviii] and the Glens Falls Community Theater, both performing in high school auditoriums, sought to create a legitimate theatre. In 1975, the old Glens Falls Insurance Company Building across from the Crandall Library was to be demolished. Plans were offered to convert it to a complex of legitimate theatre, not-for-profit offices, and City Hall. That particular dream is buried with the building's remains up along Quaker Road.

In 1975 or `76, the Opera Festival had the architect who designed the famed Wolf Trap performing arts, McFadyen,[xix] do a preliminary study of the Empire Theatre, in its prime an acoustical wonder that hosted the Barrymores and others of equal fame. Even though the interior space was filled in with floors of offices, the original hickory stage and building remained. He proposed renovation to make a modern theatre of 800 to 900 seats, but the Empire plan never came to be. Frankly, that broke my heart.

In 1978, the 2,000 seat, gilded plaster Paramount closed as a movie theater and was eyed for office space – or legitimate theatre. Hopes soared, then were dashed with the wrecker's ball in 1978.[xx]

Early plans for the Civic Center that had called for a theatre facility, by 1979 had gotten a slap shot out the door. In the early '80s, the City toyed with a theatre/museum complex north of the Civic Center, in the urban renewal site at the corner of Glen and Warren. Burger King is playing that site right now.

I haven't touched on them all, but there have been dreams galore. At one point, a smaller movie theater was eyed, the Park, on Park Street, just west of Glen. Built in 1911, the city's first movie theater, the Park attracted the Glens Falls Community Theater and others with considerable theatre know how, including producer David Eastwood, creator of the famed Lake George Dinner Theater. Like those before, and some since, that dream came...and went. It has been like Quixote's impossible dream, this hope for a legitimate theatre for downtown.

And so now there's a proposed project on Elm. I do wish it luck, for it is nearly a century since Glens Falls' last legitimate theatre, the Empire, was built. And even dreams of empire fade.

"OVER MY SHOULDER" COLUMN FOR NOVEMBER 6, 1995
Holmes' visit in 1894 left few clues, my dear Watson

Sherlock Holmes was in downtown Glens Falls in 1894. On Warren Street. Really!

Go ahead, scoff. But one hundred eleven years ago this month, on November 23, 1894, Arthur Conan Doyle, spoke at the Glens Falls Opera House.

Let me backtrack momentarily to a meeting of the "Baker Street Breakfast Club" I attended in September. It was a dark and stormy night. Dark, at any rate. Our society (one of hundreds in the world) meets to discuss anything about Sherlock Holmes, Dr. Watson, and their "creator" Arthur Conan Doyle. Many "Holmesians" regard Holmes and Watson as real-life people, with Doyle being merely the "literary agent" who brought Watson's stories to public attention.

The leader of our society, Sally Sugarman, gave me a wonderful book, *Welcome to America, Mr. Sherlock Holmes*, published in 1987 by Christopher Redmond. The book details Doyle's two-month speaking tour in the northeastern United States and Toronto, Canada in 1894, including a stop in Glens Falls!

By the time Doyle reached Glens Falls, he had (he thought) stopped writing about Sherlock Holmes forever, having "killed off" Holmes in his famous fight to the death with the fiendish Professor Moriarity at Reichenbach Falls. When Doyle arrived in Glens Falls, he of course had no idea that in 1903 he would resume the Holmes stories (or, if you prefer) that he would resume being the "literary agent" for Dr. Watson and publish Holmes for years to come.

Doyle's tour from Boston to Milwaukee was certainly oddly scheduled. He had already spoken in Saranac Lake, New York, and Milwaukee, Wisconsin, before arriving in Glens Falls, with which he was familiar from boyhood. Doyle was enthralled by James Fenimore Cooper, especially his *Last of the Mohicans* with its vivid description of the falls and the cave at Glens Falls which would become a centerpiece of the novel. Doyle's visit, then, was a pilgrimage in a way.

He arrived by train in Glens Falls at the old station, where *The Post-Star* stands today. His talk would be at the Glens Falls Opera House on the south side of Warren Street, not quite midway between Glen Street and Church Street. For those whose memories include the 1960s, you will remember this building as the Rialto Theater. The Opera Block was built in 1884 as replacement for the original that had burned in that year. Presumably the new Opera House had at least the same seating for 1,600.

Redmond mentions that Doyle's presentation was part of the Union School Course of entertainment, a series begun by Superintendent of Schools, Dr. Sherman L. Williams. He doesn't mention that Dr. Williams, who came to Glens Falls to be the first superintendent when the Union Free School District No. 1 of Queensbury, was a brilliant and innovative educator who would go on to head the New York State Department of Education and spearhead the statewide movement to teach local history.

Doyle spoke about Holmes, the detective in fiction, and the influence of Poe on Holmes, among other topics. Sherman Williams was deeply gratified and the next day *The Glens Falls Times* declared "Conan Doyle Delightful."

So many questions abound. Where did Doyle eat? Where did he stay? The answer to both could be the elegant Rockwell House located where, today, Hudson Avenue meets Glen. Or perhaps he dined with Dr. Williams and stayed at the hotel. And there are questions about influences upon Doyle. He later became an ardent Spiritualist. In 1894, Spiritualism had a sizeable following among Glens Falls' movers and shakers. Spiritualist Russell Little, second president of the Glens Falls Insurance Company, ran "Psychical Hall" downtown. Did he have contact with Doyle? Influence him?

Did his visit to Glens Falls have an impact upon Doyle? Therein is a mystery. Redmond noted that Doyle's personal papers had been sealed off for decades from the public because of legal disputes. What would they tell us about Doyle's visit to Glens Falls, the impressions he took with him and the influence the visit had upon Holmes?

It could well be that an idea for a future Holmes' mystery sprung right out of that one visit. But we won't know until those private papers are released.

What agony. Talk about being clueless!

"OVER MY SHOULDER" COLUMN FOR NOVEMBER 20, 1995
Glens Falls Operetta, 60 years later

The 1955 playbill in front of me describes the 20th anniversary of the Glens Falls Operetta Club and the playbill itself is history.

Sixty years ago this fall, the Glens Falls Operetta Club – now the Glens Falls Community Theatre – was born. Looking at this 20th anniversary issue from 1955, the amazing thing is how many of the volunteers listed in the 1955 era could be found in playbills twenty and thirty years later.

Bruce Adams loaned me the playbill, dedicated in memory of his mother, Vina S. Adams, who had played piano for 16 of its 20 seasons. Part of the dedication, "Never did she fail to give generously of time and talent..." are the hallmark of the sixty years of volunteers of the Glens Falls Operetta Club/Glens Falls Community Theatre.

The Fall of 1935. Despite a Depression, there was good news. Swing was emerging, the Social Security Act had just passed and in Glens Falls, two teachers, Edgar Pitkin and Paul E. Bergan, co-founded the Operetta Club, with George I. Davis as its first president. Pitkin's and Bergan's first production, "H.M.S Pinafore," was performed in 1936 to benefit the Glens Falls Hospital Guild. It was a smash with over 1,100 people attending two performances, I assume at the old Glens Falls High School on Glen Street.

The Operetta Club provided a sophisticated outlet to a community with some very sophisticated artistic talent. To give a very small example, in addition to Bergan and Pitkin, the orchestra was filled with tremendous talent, such as Dr. Walter Garrett, Virginia DeBlasiis, Vina Adams or music teacher Dr. Maurice Whitney. Artists Douglass and Margaret Crockwell designed the sets. Volunteers did a little of everything. A. Carlos "Sparky" Johnson and Paul Woodcock, both later presidents, were in the production. Twenty years later, their names were to be found in the 1955 production "Song of Norway."

The success prompted other musicals. Then the Oratorio Society was formed in 1937 and, in 1938, a "Little Theatre Group," performing non-musical productions under the leadership of Mr. and Mrs. J. Thatcher Sears. Its first was "French with Tears," and the photo of that 1939 production shows, among others, Sidney Rosoff, Helen Gahimer (the club's first woman president in 1951) and John Van Der Voort. Their names, along with Sid's wife Elsa, would grace the 1955 playbill and playbills for decades to come. Names! I'd need two pages to list them! The whole town must have participated – and for years! Look, there's

Mary Brown, who sang, ushered, and did a zillion things from the 1930s through the 1980s. Today, her memories are still vivid, her support strong! Everybody wore two hats. Sparky Johnson had served both as usher and as Club president. Florence King sang and did costumes. It seems everybody doubled at something.

World War II eliminated productions between 1944-6, but in `47 the club rebounded with a bang and its fortunes soared with hits such musicals as "Brigadoon," Finian's Rainbow," and "Carousel," as well as plays such as "The Late George Apley" or Oratorio performances of Handel's "Messiah."

By 1955 the club was a community fixture with tremendous leadership: Tessa Squire, president; Tony Forcucci, vice president; Faustina Smith, recording secretary; George Smith, treasurer; Murray Prouty, assistant treasurer; Emily Hamell as secretary; and Dorothy Tucker as historian. Her history was great. Over there is the 1955 photo of Hugh Allen Wilson, whose mark on music in this area is legend. Or there's a great shot of Helen Gahimer and John Van Der Voort as the romantic leads in the 1940 production of "Our Town." So many names, so little space!

Consistency and dedication can be seen in the names listed as having served between 1935 and 1955. Twenty years later, in 1975, so many of those same people were still serving in some capacity, whether in costumes, chorus, ticket sales or publicity.

Now it's 1995 and names from 20 years ago and more can be found in the playbills. May this too brief history, that sadly cannot mention the hundreds of people that it should, be taken as a sincere tribute to the history of the Glens Falls Community Theatre. May its curtain rise forever!

OVER MY SHOULDER" COLUMN FOR MARCH 11, 1996
Remember the old "Y"?

Lee Brown of Adirondack Community College set off a chain reaction of memory when he said he had worked at the YMCA in Glens Falls.

"The old `Y' or the new `Y'?" I asked.

"Both," he replied, and we performed the "Do you remember...?" routine. Many of you who use the present YMCA don't know about the original YMCA, today Godnicks' chic furniture store on Glen Street. I thought I'd share a personal memory or two about the old `Y' building in its latter years.

The old `Y' occupied the second, third and fourth floor of its first building, built in 1891 and occupied by the YMCA until 1969, when director Ray Bennett convinced everyone to build a new one. There was a gym and a pool, and the upper echelons had rental rooms, for the most part occupied by single, usually older, men.

Part of the flavor of the old `Y' was its general handyman, a `Y' resident named John Snyder. "Big John" he was called, and he was! He'd come to Glens Falls in 1925 from Rhode Island to work on the roof of the Glen Street Presbyterian

Church. He had a thick Rhode Island accent, a love of talking and a powerful physique.

My favorite Big John story took place when John was in his early seventies. He was on South Street, now quite trendy but then just damn tough. Two young men decided to attack John, who instead seized them, one under each arm in a headlock, and proceeded to rhythmically thunk their heads together, as he bellowed in time, "You shouldn't pick on senior citizens!" The police rescued the young men.

But I digress. The Kiwanis, Rotary, and Optimist Clubs held their meetings at the old Y. It was a central meeting place, for males. Nothing like it exists now because it combined so many functions and because times have changed. At 14, I was invited to participate in the Optimist Club speech contest designed to build confidence in young people.

My "coach" was a local attorney, whom I'll just call Jim, to save him embarrassment. Jim truly lived up to his club's credo to be optimistic. In fact, he was a raving Pollyanna to think that the club's speech contest would build my self-confidence. At fourteen, I knew that only a deeper voice and ten years more years of life would give me that.

I traveled up from Fort Edward each week to meet Jim at the `Y' – of course, at my parents' insistence. So, I was already depressed when I opened the YMCA's heavy doors to trudge up that long and creaking stairway, imbued with an aroma blended from seventy years of basketball sweat, tobacco smoke, floor wax, old woodwork, and age. Sometimes some of the residents would overindulge when their pension checks came in, and their reeking breath would flavor the air.

Slowly over the weeks Jim and I practiced, Jim encouraging, me forgetting every word of my talk, "What is Optimism?" However, as the weeks went by, I began to look forward to the `Y' and to cherish seeing kids running around, screaming, and snapping each other with towels, the older men sitting quietly reading a magazine and the important business men in well-tailored suits combing their wet hair after a basketball game or getting ready for their club's meeting.

The day came for my speech. We contestants addressed the club members in an upper floor front room that looked out over Glen Street. I remember wishing I could jump from one of the large windows. I took fourth place out of four speakers. A minister's son had risen and with a self-assured forcefulness that made him envied and hated by the rest of us, gave the prize-winning talk. I rose and found that, in the time it had taken me to stand, a frog had grown in my mouth and someone had performed a lobotomy on me.

Yet, I lived to tell this tale. I even have spoken to the Optimists again. So, I guess, in the end, Jim won his battle. But I still can't pass by the old `Y' without hearing a small "burr-reep" in my throat.

"OVER MY SHOULDER" COLUMN FOR FEBRUARY 27, 1995
1860s newspaper reveals temper of the times

Several years ago, I learned a history lesson while researching in the 1860s issues of a newspaper called "The Glens Falls Republican." In issues from the Civil war period there were vicious attacks upon Abraham Lincoln that make today's sideshow of sick and tasteless name-calling seem tame. Throughout the 1860s the paper spewed the kind of racism that today would be found in "polite" neo-Nazi and Klan literature. "The Republican" was a violently radical hate-paper. It hated African Americans, Abolitionists, Lincoln, and Republicans. Given its name, ironically it was the organ of the minority Democratic Party.

Such attacks on Lincoln were no surprise. That it took place in a Glens Falls newspaper was. That racism existed here during the Civil War was no surprise. The ferocity of it was. What surprised me even more was the name of the subscriber to the paper: Dr. Austin W. Holden, the first man in all of Warren County to respond to Lincoln's call for volunteers for the Union army. Holden led the region in recruitment of soldiers. Holden, later to write the History of Queensbury, was a Union patriot.

Please understand that the paper did not represent everyone in this area, the majority of whom were Republican and a large minority of whom were anti-slavery. But it revealed the sizeable minority that either did not care what happened to African Americans or who actively supported slavery by supporting the status quo.

On the good side, the Abolitionist cause, especially in Washington County, was powerful. This region played a strong part in the Underground Railroad.[xxi] Also, free African Americans lived here, owning businesses and farms. The local white population protected runaway slaves. Abolitionist rallies were common events and ones in Fort Edward featured such greats as Frederick Douglass. This is heritage to be proud of and not enough research on this has been done.

On the bad side was the kind of racial hatred voiced by "The Republican." Racial purity and the horrors of miscegenation obsessed "The Republican" during the war and long after the war's end. The "mildest" article I saw about race was from a December 1863 edition. It told an apocryphal story about the quill pen used to sign the Emancipation Proclamation. The pen was in a Chicago museum, but the woman who owned the goose that supplied the quill pen refused to sell the goose for a million dollars, saying it "had caused enough trouble already."

Right up to Lincoln's assassination, the paper foully abused Lincoln, his family, his party, all Abolitionists and African Americans. Then Lincoln was assassinated. The paper "mourned" for about an issue, then got back to business as usual. "The Republican" supported President Andrew Johnson, a Democrat and racist, and by 1868 was denouncing everyone who supported Grant and the Republican Reconstructionist efforts as "Radicals."

The April 1868 paper quoted a politician who railed against the taxes paid by "the poor white voter" for the support of "five millions of n-----s." The paper used the horrible "n-word." It loved any of those words that tore down African Americans.

My lesson was to reread history. My trouble with understanding Holden's subscription to that paper was that I had mistakenly wed Holden's (and Lincoln's) desire to save the Union with the Abolitionists' desires to end slavery and promote equal rights. It didn't work that way. Lincoln had started the war solely to save the Union. Holden responded solely to that cause. Lincoln moved closer to the Abolitionist goals as he went along. That's what got him killed. By mid-war, he was signing an Emancipation Proclamation to free slaves, although only in the Confederate states. By war's end I think he was at a point of believing in what we today would call "separate but equal."

Disappointing by today's standards, but that is exactly my point. What was, was. In history, the good and the bad need to be seen for what they were, otherwise we perpetuate a lie. As long as we are forthright about the racism that existed here, we can also be proud of the work done to combat it. And that Lincoln was not "perfect" by today's standards does not negate ideals he put forth, ideals that need be applied in the present if we are to survive as a nation in the future.

"OVER MY SHOULDER" COLUMN FOR JULY 14, 1996.
Saving more than just an old house

NOTE: My Editor had vetoed this for the book, but I thought it important to show how historians often tilt at windmills and lose.

Recently I was quoted in Mike DeMasi's article in this paper about the Norris House on Center Street in Glens Falls.[xxii] It sits directly in back of Genpak, a company on Warren Street that received permission from the City of Glens Falls to raze the house.

This is a complex issue and I'm not without my opinions. But I'm going to try to achieve a balance. First, about Genpak: the company needs parking and, in all honesty, looking around where it's headquartered, it's not hard to see why they would look toward demolishing the Norris House. The downtown parking situation leaves a lot to be desired.

However, as I also worked with the City and the DAR [*Daughters of the American Revolution*] to save the Norris House in 1980, I have a slightly different take on the house's worth. For the record, I DO believe it's worth saving. If not on that spot, then somewhere.

Ever since the article appeared, I've heard the same comments I always get concerning old buildings. So, I would like to answer those questions. Bear in mind that I'm writing this about a week before publication, so a lot may have happened. Nonetheless, similar comments and similar answers will come up again, as more old buildings are slated for demolition.

The comments I got (and always get) were of three kinds. The "esthetic" comment: "I mean, look at it! It's going to fall down anyway."

The "age-bashing" comment: "It's just an old house."

And, finally, the two "who-gives-a-damn-about-history?" comments: "Can you justify saving every old building?" And: "What difference does it make who was born there?"

Regarding the "esthetic comment," I went to look at the building. I've seen far worse rehabilitated by talented carpenters. In the Norris House, I saw a plumb roof and walls. It's a post and beam house, what carpenters call "overbuilt" – built like a tank. Could this one have hidden problems? Absolutely. But if it doesn't and it's demolished? That brings up my answer to the "age-bashing" comment: it's sad that, in this day and age when people are begging for houses, old ones like this are flattened simply because they are old.

The last comment was the saddest: "Can you justify saving every old building?" Translation: Is it historical enough to justify saving? Honestly, I cannot justify saving every old building. But this one is historically important. First, it was built by Alonzo Morgan in the 1840s as a part of the first housing development ever in the Village of Glens Falls and the Town of Queensbury. In 1840, Morgan built his home on Maple, widened the lane in front of it and called it Center Street. He built homes on it, including one for the Norris family.

Captain William T. Norris died a hero at the Second Battle of Bull Run in 1863, while giving aid to a wounded soldier. The house was the birthplace of his daughter, Helena Norris Whitney, co-founder of both the Glens Falls Women's Civic Club and the local Red Cross, and an ardent Suffragist.

Lastly, it was the birthplace of Robert Porter Patterson. During World War II he was Undersecretary of War to Roosevelt and Secretary of War to Truman. After the war, Patterson and James Forrestal designed the present Department of Defense. After his death in a freak accident in 1952, Felix Frankfurter said of him, "The manner of his life ought to become a part of our national heritage." Like those who lived at Number 13 Center Street before him, he truly was a great person. It matters who lived there.

The Norris House is only a symptom. The disease is a lack of planning for adequate parking. Since 1946, at least four major parking plans, including parking lots and parking structures, have been created. All have died. In the meantime, side streets full of old structures have been decimated for inadequate parking and the problems worsens.

Friends, you can knock down every "old building" for parking. And in the end, you'll have wiped out your heritage, eliminated structures that had potential for rehabilitation and beauty and tourism – and have one hell of an ugly city that nobody will want to come to.

[**Postscript:** the Norris House was demolished.]

"OVER MY SHOULDER" COLUMN FOR MAY 20, 1996
Recalling "The Ri"

In a recent Elvis special on WCKM, Kip Grant said that when Presley's movie "Jailhouse Rock" opened at the Rialto Theater in Glen Falls on Thanksgiving Day of 1957, The "Ri" played the movie six times.

Listening to Kip, it occurred to me how many Post-Star readers are clueless as to where the Rialto was or how absolutely different movie watching was in those times. (Yes, wiseguy, we did sit in seats and watch the screens, but we didn't listen to the soundtrack for five other movies coming through walls thinner than toilet paper.)

First: where the Rialto was. Stand on the corner of Warren and Glen Streets in front of Burger King and look east to St. Mary's. The Rialto was about halfway in between.

By 1957, there were two movie houses left in Glens Falls: The Rialto and the Paramount, the latter on Ridge Street across from the Queensbury Hotel. Both had that imitation European opera house design of Silent Era "movie houses," with balconies, box seats and plaster moldings that gave the illusion of pomp and wealth. The Paramount was the high price spread of the two theaters.

But back to "The Ri" – always "The Ri" – and those differences. The Ri, being amid other four and five story buildings, had more of a "city feel," as opposed to the strip mall experience of today. If it was a popular show, like Elvis or "Godzilla" (though our parents sarcastically said they could NOT tell the difference) you got in a long ticket line on Warren Street. How thrilling to stand there as the traffic whizzed by.

I saw "Jailhouse Rock" with friends when I was ten. That day we surged through the large plate glass doors, past recessed, ornately framed glass boxes containing "Upcoming Attractions," clutching our 25 cent tickets, the smell of popcorn and candy assaulting us. We pushed up the sloping lobby floor, through exiting crowds of mostly teen-age girls, screaming about how "neat" Elvis was. We fought our way to the strategically placed candy counter, all the while screaming for popcorn, Raisinets, and soda. The smell of grape soda makes me sick to this day.

Everything was jammed with people. The restrooms, mobbed. The phone booth, a wood structure built into in a recess in the lobby and designed for one person, now holding four teens. They were sticking a pin in the telephone cord, touching it to the metal rotary dial (no push buttons then), and getting a dial tone. A free call! The cord was riddled with pin holes.

Juggling food, we went through a set of padded doors down carpeted floors to the seats. There was a huge curtain before the screen. The projectionist always started to show the film as the curtains were being drawn and the beginning credits of the first of two cartoons flowed like waves over the parting curtain.

Ushers escorted you to your seats, usually tall high school boys recruited from the football team who wore uniforms making them look like members of an occupying army. They had long flashlights for illumination. They used these as weapons, casually crushing kneecaps of those who dared to put feet on seats or in the aisles. In those "pre-lawsuit days" ushers could scream at you to be quiet, hit you or throw you out of the theater with impunity. They were terrors.

The Ri had a balcony with a curving brass railing the length of it. Sitting there was a thrill, especially in the first row. You could innocently drop popcorn down on those below, protesting to the usher that it was someone else. You could also sit up in the back and surreptitiously watch the teenagers neck.

And "Jailhouse Rock"? A hit. Everybody screamed. (Screaming was "cool" then.) Girls screamed and ran at the screen (ushers body-blocked them) or screamed and fainted (ushers hauled them out). Guys, thinking themselves too cool to scream or faint, made total asses of themselves by coming out of the johns with their hair combed like Elvis.

Ah, but you could do that at The Ri, because it was a theater: designed as a fantasy to show fantasy.

And to give you two cartoons and a double feature – which you don't get today.

"OVER MY SHOULDER" COLUMN FOR JUNE 2, 1996.
Movie memories and more

NOTE: This was the first "Over My Shoulder" Column to run on a weekly basis. I celebrated by getting the name of the New Way Lunch wrong. It is correct in this printing.

While doing the last column on movies, several friends, including Mary Pissare Deep and Rev. Father C. Michael Abraham flooded me with questions: "What about Ray LaFarr, the organist at the Paramount?" "What about the gum under the seats at the State?" "What about Kay Bushman?" Obviously, my research was not done!

The answer to the third question was provided in my having a wonderful conversation with Kay Bushman herself. Born in this city as Katherine O'Connor a few movie seasons ago, Kay was the ticket seller at the Rialto Theater from 1926 to 1943.

Kay remembers well her 17 years as ticket seller at the Rialto, on the south side of Warren Street, midway between Glen and Church Streets. When she started in 1926, silent films were in their glory. "The Ri," located in the 1884 Opera House Block, had just been rebuilt after the disastrous fire of 1925 and was a full-fledged "movie palace," also featuring vaudeville. Kay said that there was a five-piece orchestra made up of the entire Smaldone family. The Smaldones would play the background music for the silent films and music the vaudeville acts.

She would open around 6:45 p.m. to sell tickets, which cost 40 cents and 25 cents, children under 12 only a dime. (Imagine!) The movies started at seven

with a newsreel, then cartoons and then the main feature. Double features began
to be shown more in the 1930s. On Thursdays, Fridays and Saturdays, the Ri had
vaudeville, five live acts of singing, dancing ("hoofing"), magic, comics, and so
on, followed by a movie.

Kay remembers the vaudeville performances lasting to about 1940. She says
she got to meet all the vaudeville people, as the performers always stopped in to
visit her at the ticket booth. During the Depression, theaters began trying to
attract people with giveaways and bingo games. Kay remembers refrigerators and
such being the prizes.

She worked under a variety of managers: B. F. Keith, Gerald Sullivan, and a
Mr. Fitzgerald. (Keith later ran the Hudson Falls Strand Theater. The building
still stands on Main Street and is now home to the Kingsbury Town Offices.)[xxiii]

Did she ever get to watch a movie? Yes, she usually watched right after the first
night's showing. This means that Kay got to see first runs of Buster Keaton and
Charlie Chaplin films. Not to mention "It Happened One Night" or "The
Maltese Falcon." Be still my heart!

Mary Deepe and Father Michael Abraham have reason to remember so well
that area of Warren Street, too. Both of their families were in businesses there.
Mary's family, the Pissares, owned the Sugar Bowl on Glen and Father Michael's
father worked at Alex's vegetable market on Warren. Between Kay, Mary and
Father Michael, I have put together this sketch of the south side of Warren Street
in the 1930s and early `40s together: as you walked from Glen toward St. Mary's
Church, you started at Shulte's Cigar store on the corner, then Boxer's Drugstore
(with entrances on both Warren and Glen); next was the Palace Diner; the Red
Cross Shoe Store; Alex's Fruit Market); then a tailor shop; over a driveway; then
Wiley's shoe shop; the Postal Telegraph; the Rialto; the Karmel Korn (where had
been a men's clothing store before); Steiner's wallpaper, paint and toys;
Schulman's lady's hat shop; the Kansas Coffee Shop; State Theater; Cowie's
optometrist shop; Mohican Market, and two other businesses that I need help
on. One was a gift shop at the corner of Warren and Church.

Here's the east side of lower Glen Street, but I really need your help here!
Starting at the southeast corner of Warren and Glen there was Shulte's Cigar
Store on the corner, then Boxer's; the Sugar Bowl; Johnny Dever's restaurant;
Stein's clothing store (had been a barber shop); the Economy Store; then Louis
Silverman's (later Cohen's Outlet); the New Way Lunch (now on South Street);
Fitzgerald's Restaurant (burned in 1945); Mesnick's Meat Market; the Rochester
Furniture store; Berry Street; then Shapiro's men's clothing store and the Viaduct
Hotel.

I know it's not complete. Can you write me care of *The Post-Star* and help me?
Thanks! And thanks to Kay Bushman, Mary Deepe, and Father C. Michael
Abraham.

See you next week.

"OVER MY SHOULDER" COLUMN FOR JUNE 9, 1996
A walk through history

D on't forget the LARAC festival in downtown Glens Falls today! You'll be walking through history.
    Twenty-five years ago an "arts and craft festival" was held in City Park and its success spurred the creation of LARAC: the "Lower Adirondack Regional Arts Council."

LARAC's Executive Director, Pat Cary Joyce, was recently showing me the LARAC scrapbooks, started in 1971 by LARAC's first historian and an original LARAC steering committee member, Sister Dominica Joseph, known lovingly as "Sister D.J." Her wonderfully thorough scrapbooks are "the" history of the arts in this area. Let's browse those "old" news clippings, okay?

In December of 1971, the festival's organizers held their first formal meeting at the home of Sunny and Paul Buchman in Queensbury. They had decided to organize an arts council for the Greater Glens Falls region and had invited the director of an arts center in Albany to speak. An ad hoc committee was formed: Sunny Buchman, Robert J. Kafin, H. Wayne Judge, Joan Aronson, A. Morton Raych, and Martha Pugh of North Argyle, who had been a longtime advocate of an arts council.

By March of 1972, they'd written by-laws and were incorporating – these folks wasted no time! The first board of directors was composed of seven people. Sunny Buchman was president. Mrs. Marcella Dodge, who herself was president of the Fort Edward Art Center, was vice-president. Gary Walrath, the first paid curator of the Chapman Historical Museum, was secretary, and Martha Pugh was treasurer. The other three directors were Bob Kafin, Joan Aronson, and H. Wayne Judge. In October at the first annual meeting, Sunny Buchman was elected president; Sally Millman, secretary; Marcella Dodge, vice-president; and Brenda Italiano, treasurer. Many more directors were elected.

There were 11 founding organizational members in 1972: the Adirondack Arts Center from Blue Mountain Lake; Adirondack Community College's Cultural Affairs Committee; Crandall Library; deBlasiis Chamber Music Series; Fort Edward Art Center; Glens Falls Concert Association; Glens Falls Historical Association (now the Glens Falls-Queensbury Historical Association); Glens Falls Operetta Club (now the Glens Falls Community Theatre); the Hyde Collection; the Lake George Opera Festival; and the Glens Falls Shutterbug Club. That diversity has been LARAC's key to success.

Others quickly joined. Today's Voluntary Action Center, then the "Volunteer Service Bureau" had just started and helped provide volunteers for the arts and crafts festival the fledgling LARAC planned. LARAC hoped for 50 participants. It had over 100! Art abounded: music, dance, paintings, sculpture, crafts. Music? Opera from the Glens Falls Opera Festival. Broadway music from the Operetta Club. And folk singing Lucille Tasker brought over from the Frame coffeehouse, a part of the Fort Edward Art Center.

Oh, and those photos from 1972! Everybody looks like a hippie. There's a great shot of Queensbury art teacher Paul Chapman with hair down to his shoulders. "Hey, wow, man," as we said back then in the dark ages.

There's also a great publicity shot of Bob Kafin posing with Robert Cronin, the flamboyant and wonderful mayor of Glens Falls, with Cronin in an artist's frock.

The festival became an instant tradition. LARAC started a regional calendar of events, began a radio arts program, hosted by Paul Buchman, and in early 1973 held a winter arts carnival at the Glens Falls Armory. "Behind the scenes," it also assisted young arts organizations with fundamental things, like bulk mailings. It was a uniter, a helper. It still is.

Within a few years LARAC hired its first Director, Scott Clugstone, who served a year. Next was Joyce Smith, who served four years. Third and most recent is Pat Cary Joyce, now in her fourteenth year! Congratulations, Pat!

Time has robbed LARAC of many people, including Sister D.J., who passed away in 1990. Still, I have this vision of the celestial gates being draped each June with a LARAC festival banner.

And now we arrive at 25. This too brief history of LARAC's beginning is my way saying thanks to LARAC's founders, whose vision was based on a timeless message: the arts, like water, air, and food, are essential. Without the arts, we are not really alive.

So, be alive! And say, "Happy 25!" to LARAC today at City Park.

"OVER MY SHOULDER" COLUMN FOR JUNE 16, 1996
Valentine to a diner

When I say this column is an unadulterated fan letter, I do so to reassure you that I'm not advertising when I say "Happy 35th Anniversary" to Peter's Diner on South Street – the Street of Dreams – in Glens Falls. My friends Peter and Helen Demas have achieved something of a record on South Street, not an easy feat on a street where business longevity is almost expected, much less taken for granted. Tell someone on South Street you've been in business ten years and you get "Just started, huh?" for a reply.

For a moment, let's pull the camera up and away from Peter's Diner, the way they do in those older movies. There's a long shot of South Street and a warm voice says, "Yes, South Street. Street of Dreams. Where family businesses have run for decades and where dreams come true." Then the camera slowly zooms on Peter's Diner.

Well, perhaps not everyone has made a dream come true on South Street. But for the Demas family, South Street has been, I think, more than just a place where their business is. I'd say it's been a way of life.

Peter came to America as a young man from the Peloponnesian area of Greece and was working in a restaurant in Saratoga when Uncle Sam extended "the invitation that cannot be refused." So, he joined the United States Navy and, for the next four years, he saw the world.

And he got married, in Greece, in January of 1961, while still in the Navy's Sixth fleet. Yes, true to his roots, he married a young Athenian girl named Helen. (Can one ask for a name more fittingly Greek than "Helen," the name immortalized by Homer in the Iliad and Odyssey?)

Pete had to leave his Helen in Greece, while he served out the rest of his tour. Returning stateside, he filled out all the essential paperwork and Helen came here in the fall of 1961.

In the meantime, twenty-three, married and just out of service – "Just a boy," Pete always says – he had returned to Saratoga. But he itched for his own business and looked around the region. His gaze fell on South Street. He bought a restaurant business from George and Ann Constantine, who owned "Rancho Bill's." In June of 1961, he opened for business. "Peter's Diner" was born.

Many years ago, I wrote of Pete Demas as being "the new kid on the block." In 1961, Peter's Diner was a baby compared to Kaulfuss' Empire Billiards, started in 1919; K Locksmith (1936); Marcantonio's barbershop (1929); Collotti's Shoe repair (1928); and New Way Lunch (which started in 1916). The first two are gone, but the rest remain, and Peter's, the new kid, has become one of "The Street of Dreams" institutions.

Over the years, Pete and Helen ran the restaurant and managed to find time to raise three children: Antonia, Anthony, and Olga. At one time or another, all the kids worked in the restaurant.

They extended that sense of family to their "dedicated customers," as Pete referred to them the other day, adding, "Most became my friends."

So, what makes the diner "an institution?" Good food and a cross-section of humanity: judges, truckers, librarians, and the guy stopping off for a lunch in between some heavy action at OTB. And news! You want to know what goes on this region? Pick up a Post-Star and eat at Pete's and you've got your news covered. Of course, you may have to listen to Pete talk about horses or politics, but, hey, what can you do?

South Street's heritage is stored in Peter's, just waiting to be written. Like the history of the shooting of Joey Green in `32 or the histories of people like "Egypt," a gentleman from Birmingham, England, who served in Egypt in WW I. And so many, many more.

Pete said that when he and Helen were first married, they had no time for any extended honeymoon. Maybe, in a way, they've been honeymooning for 35 years on The Street of Dreams.

To Peter Diner's, a happy 35th! And to Pete and Helen: "Ehf karee-stoh!"

That's the phonetic spelling of the Greek for "Thank you."

"OVER MY SHOULDER" COLUMN FOR JUNE 23, 1996
Ask and you will be told

Answers have come in regarding businesses on Warren Street, surrounding the Rialto. Max Tupper and Sue Traver wrote. Sue wrote that one of "the two businesses you need to complete the south side of Warren Street" is "Salvatore's Shoe Service, operated by my grandfather, Salvatore Pepe, my father, Andy, and my uncles Newie, Tony and Joe." Thanks, Sue!

An anonymous caller remembered the gift shop on the corner of Warren and Church as "Slaters" and reminded me that Knobby's Record Store was there in the late forties and fifties.

Max Tupper's enormous letter brought the thirties alive as it described a bustling downtown with hundreds of businesses. Max, now living in Fort Ann, has been a sign painter in this area since...well, I'll let his letter start the story: "I worked at the Rialto Theater from 1934 to 1937 in the sign shop down the alley, in back under the stage and behind the orchestra pit. Joe Draxl was the sign painter and I was hired as his helper for $13 a week, when the Schine chain took on the Strand in Hudson Falls." He adds that around the corner on Glen he "bought $15 suits at Steins."

Just graduated from Glens Falls High in 1934, Max had been working for Erlanger's, a carriage trade clothing establishment on the corner of Glen and Exchange Streets. Bill Heiss, who was the manager from 1934 to `40, offered a job with more excitement and future. Draxl taught Max the trade, making him keep a notebook, that with his art scrapbooks now keeps alive memories for us to share.

His letter continues, "We did all the lobby displays, big false fronts for major shows and stage shows. Also signs and lobby displays for the Empire on South Street and the Strand," in Hudson Falls. "Also, down the alley, under the Walk Over Shoe store, was George Roby's sign shop. He was quite elderly at the time and took in Hubie West as a partner for a while. His biggest client was the Mohican Market."

Roby had done all the major theater sign work before Draxl, major stage decorations for traveling vaudeville productions and other major legitimate theater productions.

Top acts such as burlesque queen Sally Rand, of fan-dance fame, had appeared there. (Very daring, then. Today she'd be on daytime soaps.) Max recalled a young high school boy working at the Ri, who came upon Rand as she was readjusting her fans. Instant education! Max laughed, "The boy nearly fainted."

The Schine chain bought the Rialto, Empire, and the Strand in 1936, the year Max signed up for the newly created Social Security. They rebuilt the Ri, with a new marquee, new supports under the balconies, and so on. The need for major art work diminished during the renovations. Moreover, the Schines decided to limit the scope of live productions. The last major show was in 1936, not really vaudeville, according to Max, but a Ziegfeld style review: "the Marcus Review, with 97 people."

During reconstruction, Draxl went to a Schine theater in Lockport and Max was given a doorman suit. That he did not like. Around the time of the reopening of the refurbished theater in 1937, Max said, "I went into business for myself in a shop in back of the Empire." Bill Heiss let him continue to work in the shop at the Ri, too, and Max did signs, marquees and other major art for the Ri, Empire, and the Strand.

This year, 1937, was pivotal at the theater. The remodeling helped attract patrons as did the bank nights, bingo nights, and give-away nights. Win a refrigerator or a car! Smaller live acts continued into the late thirties. Name bands like Art Moody's Orchestra played. Swing was in and the Battle of the Bands featured local groups, who aspired to be Ellingtons and Goodmans.

As the thirties ended, live theater ended at the Rialto. An era was gone. A new decade and a World War would eradicate the Depression, but also would forever change a way of life.

Thanks, Max for sharing memories and "painting pictures" of a time past, but not forgotten.

"OVER MY SHOULDER" COLUMN FOR SEPTEMBER 29, 1996
Of news, trolleys and cows

O ver the years I have adopted certain historical people and events as my "pets," my favorites, for any number of different reasons.

One of my favorite characters is Addison Beecher Colvin, known as "A. B. Colvin." Had Charles Dickens been an American, he would have invented Colvin, whose life epitomized the nineteenth century, small-town self-made man.

Colvin was born in 1858 in Glens Falls. His mother died early in his life and his education was, as he confessed, spotty. His family was not well-to-do and like many self-made people, he was an enigma. He was a physically large man who was bombastic, self-centered, and class conscious; and generous and loving as a husband, father and friend. The relics of his empire are many, usually scattered about with little to indicate their creator. Whatever contributions he made to the area have faded, although his most lasting contribution is to me his most ironic.

You hold his most lasting contribution in your very hands: this daily newspaper. At age 21, Colvin founded Glens Falls' first daily newspaper on June 21, 1879: *The Glens Falls Daily Times*. Later called *The Glens Falls Times*, it was purchased by *The Post-Star* in 1927. His paper was, like Colvin, hard hitting and blunt. I think in his early days he had a messianic streak that may have been the result of his taken a pledge of abstinence from alcohol when only a child.

The irony of Colvin starting the paper, the foundation his business career, was that his English was horrible. While his basic reporting was fine, when he attempted something "literary" he failed grotesquely. He would, for example, write obituaries that were almost gibberish – half sentences and poorly connected thoughts that still leave one gasping for breath. It was if he were taking English as a second language but didn't have a first one.

And yet he had power. Although five libel suits were brought against the paper within its first six years of existence, none succeeded. That in a day when lawsuits were far rarer. Colvin built his paper's printing shop just off Glen Street in 1882. When that burned in 1902, he built the present Colvin Building on Glen Street with a new print shop to the rear of it. The print shop is now a parking lot.

In a short period of time he amassed a powerful fortune, which some maliciously attributed to his having married a wealthy woman from Northville. Whether or not true, Colvin's own ability to make money cannot be doubted. He came of age at a time when Glens Falls was doing the same. He became involved in the trolley business, becoming a partner in the Hudson Line in 1891. (It would involve him in the most famous strike in Glens Falls' history, but that story for another time.)

And speaking of the trolley reminds me of his home on Glen Street. Around the time when Glens Falls expanded its village limits in 1886, he built a princely home on the southeast corner of Glen and Chester Streets, in the then up and coming part of the village. It stands there to this day. His wealth brought – and bought – enormous influence and power in those days of unfettered capitalism. A possibly apocryphal story told of him was that, in spite of a public ordinance prohibiting it, he had a cow in his carriage barn to supply him with his gallon-a-day ice cream habit. But a tale that is absolutely a matter of record regards his trolley. Each morning the trolley stopped in front of Colvin's home at precisely the same time. He boarded and was summarily deposited in front of his business on Glen Street. And the reverse was repeated each evening.

Well, it was his trolley, wasn't it?

Next week I'll finish my Tale of Colvin and give you a sampling of classic Colvin English.

"OVER MY SHOULDER" COLUMN FOR OCTOBER 6, 1996
Of vanity, humanity and good memories

Last week I was relating "The Tale of Colvin," a brief history of A. B. Colvin, self-made business entrepreneur of nineteenth century Glens Falls. This complex man would have made for a classic Dickens character. Born in Glens Falls to a family of little means, he had launched his business career in 1879 when he founded Glens Falls, first daily newspaper, *The Glens Falls Daily Times*.

Throughout the 1880s he amassed a financial, political, and social fortune. It would take this whole page to describe his business dealings in the Northeastern United States. He was an ardent supporter of the Prohibition Party, which contained some of the most influential of Glens Falls citizens. He sought to be with the "right" people and do as they did, including wintering in Florida, a new fad.

His ego grew with his power and influence, although sometimes the amount of power and influence he imagined he had did not match reality. When in 1894 he was appointed New York State Treasurer, an office of no real importance, Colvin and his family arrived at the Capital building as if he were being sworn in as governor. The Albany papers sarcastically described his triumphal procession to the capital building, although I am sure he interpreted the papers' accounts as glowing praise. Later, he would hire his minister, the Rev. Charles McKay, to transcribe all the news clippings about him in a book, now in the Chapman Historical Museum.

But make no mistake: he exerted tremendous power, both through his paper and outside of it. After becoming State Treasurer, he started banks in, among other places, Hudson Falls, Argyle and, of course, Glens Falls. The Glens Falls Trust Company began in 1897. He built the Empire Theater in 1899, to his credit hiring top flight New York theater architects to create a jewel. He was among those who started the Glens Falls Country Club.

For reasons unexplained to this day, Colvin, a devout Protestant and Republican, became good friends with Al Smith, the devout Roman Catholic and Democratic Governor of New York in the 1920s. Once it fell to Colvin to introduce Smith at a speaking engagement in Glens Falls. According to the memories of the late Frederick Bascom, Colvin rose and nearly put the crowd to sleep with a long-winded introduction. Colvin, as he often did when at a loss for conventional words, invented one, describing Smith's involvement in the "congalorious" affairs of state. I think their friendship grew from a kindred understanding of having been poor and on the outside.

When he "retired" in 1906 at age 48, he printed a booklet recapping his life, containing testimony from friends and colleagues and setting forth what he would do in his retirement. It would have been just vanity if were it not for the sadness he expressed over the recent death of one of his daughters. That moment of heartbreak revealed the very human Colvin.

By the mid-1920s his empire was unraveling, the complexities of post-war American finance overwhelming the Victorian entrepreneur. By 1932, when the National Bank of Glens Falls took over the Glens Falls Trust Company to become the Glens Falls National Bank and Trust Company, he had lost most of it.

Bereft of his companies, his fortune, and his pride, he was given a small office on the top rear floor of the Colvin Building, overlooking his former printing plant. There he spent his last days publishing pamphlets railing against the "socialism" of Roosevelt. If not a hell, it must have been a purgatory. He died in 1937 and was buried from his home.

To those who may think that I look down upon or mock A. B. Colvin, let me dispel that notion. I find him a fascinating ingredient in our local history. He was human, and vain, as are we all. May he be remembered with charity for the good things he left behind.

"OVER MY SHOULDER" COLUMN FOR DECEMBER 15, 1996
Downtown during the holidays

R ecently I met two women who were in their early forties. One observed that there's a dwindling number of us who can remember the downtown Glens Falls of the fifties and sixties.

And then she said, and I think I'm quoting correctly, "If I could just go back once to downtown as it was then." There was in her voice a combination of nostalgia and the reality that things have changed forever. I understood her.

Now, malls and shopping centers are fine and for all the memories that I write about, I am anchored in the present. We are where we are, and the only the constant in life is change.

Still I confess to a love of a "downtown" – perhaps the product of having lived in Manhattan – and understand the feeling they were missing, that certain "something" about walking the streets of downtown Glens Falls at Christmas. We "Alumni of the Downtown Club" remember the excitement.

In the 1950s, my mother would bring us kids to "the falls" on the bus. We'd get off at Warren and Ridge and head north. I loved the decorations strung along the lampposts. The buildings on Warren, Ridge and Glen formed mini-canyons that trapped the sounds of Christmas shopping: a mix of people's voices, crunching feet, cars, trucks and buses and Christmas music piped through the air. Oh yes, and the Salvation Army bell ringers. I always wanted to give them every penny I had.

Hundreds of shoppers staggered under the shopping bags and bulky coats, bumping one another as they passed, but not minding. It was hard to when blinded by the beautiful displays that so gorgeously decorated the windows of Erlanger's, Merkel and Gelman's, and the many other stores.

Up until about eleven, my focus was upon toys, so the trip was not a success until we had gone to Grants or to Kresge's and Woolworths, on Glen Street, just south of the YMCA. Mom's sights were usually set on buying a lot for a little, so the department stores were her target, too. Thank God!

Crossing Ridge, you looked north on Glen at the Glens Falls Insurance Company building, decorated like a huge five-layer Christmas cake, with enormous garlands and lights. An incredible sight! We passed by Fanny Farmers and took a moment to smash our faces up against the window. Mother, on a mission, dutifully hustled to Kresge's. The indignity of shopping as a little boy was having to stand still while your mother tried about five hundred pairs of "dungarees" on you, seeing if they would fit.

While there, we'd get to tell Santa our wishes, perhaps more importantly to show Mom every toy we wanted. We knew she was connected to Santa in some mystical way. The aisles seethed with toys and kids. "Mom, look! A Davy

Crockett hat, Mom!" ("That's nice," she'd murmur.) "Mom! A chemistry set!" ("Mm-hmm," she'd murmur.) "Mom! A Daisy BB gun!" ("You'll shoot your eye out," she'd murmur. Case closed.)

Out into the cold air. Leaving a building and threading up a crowded street to the next building was so thrilling, too. Upward to the Woolworths the King Army marched in heavy boots, laden with packages ("Don't you dare look in that bag!" the ominous Mother's Voice said.) You jingled and crunched and pushed your way into Woolworths. Ahhhh. It smelled right, too. A combination of candy, wrapping paper, lunch counter goodies and floor wax. I can see that heavenly place now.

We'd hit every store: Englander's, Erlanger's, the Outlet, the Ridge Book Shop, Van the Shoeman – you name it – and always found everything we wanted. We'd eat at the Kong Chow or the Kansas or the Palace or...well, there were so many, weren't there?

Finally, exhausted we'd head homeward from downtown Glens Falls, which will always be a special place for the Alumni of the Downtown Club.

Happy holidays to you.

"OVER MY SHOULDER" COLUMN FOR FEBRUARY 16, 1997
Pondering a murder mystery

Being a mystery buff, I find the prospect of an unsolved murder in our area grimly fascinating.

Relax. The murderer is dead by now, as the crime, as described in Dr. A. W. Holden's 1874 "History of the Town of Queensbury," took place August 1, 1873. Holden described Morgan's death as "mysterious, sudden and horrible." Holden never states it was murder but wrote that "it would always be enveloped in doubt and uncertainty." Murder's my interpretation. In a moment, more gruesome particulars to demonstrate my theory.

First a bit of background on "the deceased." The victim was James Morgan, 59, a prominent lumber baron and esteemed citizen of Park Street, Village of Glens Falls, Town of Queensbury.

Morgan was born into a very poor family in Bolton in 1814. In 1834 he moved to Glens Falls at the moment when the tiny village was beginning to prosper from building the feeder canal. Morgan, Holden wrote, possessed "rare business abilities, energy and perseverance." Starting at the Cheney lumber mill, Morgan bought a grocery in downtown Glens Falls in 1837 and by 1839 had started a second, even more successful grocery.

Around this time, he entered the lumber business, which was also thriving from the canal connection. Everything Morgan touched made money. By 1841 he was wealthy enough to win the approval of attorney Martin Eastwood to marry his daughter, Olivia. They had two daughters.

By 1873 Morgan also had controlling interests in two huge businesses, the Morgan Lime Company and the Glens Falls Paper Mill. His mills ran day and night. Holden wrote Morgan had "two year's stock of logs, worth two fortunes, constantly afloat on the Hudson."

He also had enemies. Holden gently brushes them away, stating, "An unfortunate infirmity of deafness no doubt contributed largely to isolate Morgan from his fellow men," but that "beneath his crust of reserve" Morgan had "a kind heart."

Holden also described him as "a bitter and unrelenting opponent." But let's call it for what it is (or was): Morgan clawed his way to the top and more than a few of Glens Falls citizens would have been glad to do him in. I think someone did.

It was in the wee hours of August 1, 1873 that Morgan met his end. (I've got to stop reading mystery books.) Mrs. Morgan and her daughters had gone to Saratoga to stay for the season. There were none of the usual servants at the residence, only a boarder who had been living for some time in the home. According to Holden, a passerby awakened Morgan to tell him "that his horses were making a disturbance at the barn." Morgan dressed and went to the barn with a kerosene lantern. "That was the last he was seen alive. In less than half an hour an alarm of fire was given, and the barn was found in a bright blaze, and when the building was burned down, his charred remains were found lying beneath one of the dead horses."

Accident? Could a horse have kicked Morgan and his lamp have started a blaze? If so, why in a residential neighborhood did it take so long to sound an alarm for a fire company only a few hundred feet away? Why was the blaze so disastrous when a fire hydrant on the village's brand-new water system stood directly in front of Morgan's house? Who was the passerby and how did Holden know of that passerby? How did Holden know that it was about a half hour before the alarm was sounded?

Perhaps more to the point, why was a deaf man left alone without servants? Where was the boarder who had been living in the Morgan home for some time?

Accident? Murder? Morgan's wife remarried shortly after his death, inheriting a fortune we'd all be happy to have today.

Oh, and by the way. It was said that she married the boarder.

"OVER MY SHOULDER" COLUMN FOR MAY 11, 1997
Memos from a former publisher

In the pantheon of the newsroom, above the editor sits "The Publisher," the person with whom, in terms of the newspaper's responsibility, the buck stops. A while back, Florence McIlvaine sent me a sheaf of memos from the desk of Arthur P. Irving, a priceless few of the thousands Irving issued in his many years as publisher of *The Glens Falls Times* and *The Post-Star*.

Florence had gone to work as a writer at *The Post-Star* in 1938 and her husband,

Leonard "Mac" McIlvaine, was a proof reader before going into the service. After the war, Mac decided to be a printer and eventually became the head of the composing room. Mac had saved these memos from when they had been posted on the Composing Room door. Florence very rightly thought they would be nice to share.

The memos date from between October of 1942 and February of 1946. At that time, the Glens Falls Post Company owned the only two dailies in Glens Falls, the morning "*The Post-Star*," with a Democratic editorial page and the evening "*The Glens Falls Times*," which was Republican.

Publisher Arthur "Art" Irving was a Glens Falls native who had worked his way up through the paper. As Florence said, Irving loved to call himself a "newspaper man." He never lost interest in the most minute aspects of the paper and read each edition thoroughly, sending off lightning bolt memos of correction to the various editors, proofreaders, and copywriters. And by the way, the word printed at the top was "Memorandum," not "memo."

The memos are treasures. On October 10, 1942, in the depths of the Second World War, Irving sent a memo to "Messrs. Knight & Fox," his two editors. It began: "Dorothea Clarke, the singer, called at the office to see me this morning and very sweetly and graciously explained that, while she does not want to appear too fussy, she is most anxious that anytime our newspapers refer to her professionally we do so by referring to her as Dorothea Clarke – not Mrs. Dorothea Clarke." Otherwise, "the correct name is Mrs. Robert S. Clarke." The editors were to have the staff "read and initial this memo and then have it posted where it can be observed from time to time as a reminder." A carbon had also been sent to the proofreaders!

Florence said that Irving was a Rotarian and each week his fellow Rotarians would roast him royally over the slightest mistake in the paper. Here's one that involved Irving himself! On February 2, 1943 he wrote: "I wonder what we must do to have editorial staff members and proofreaders understand the difference between single possessive and plural possessive?" In that very morning's Post-Star, he (Irving) had been referred to as the "Bishops' representative in scouting," and patiently explained why it should have been "Bishop's." Plaintively he asked, "What could be simpler?"

To no avail, for on Mar 11, 1943 he was asking "proofreaders to bear in mind that…in the case of the plural possessive…the word should end with the apostrophe after the letter s, instead of before it." He asked the Editorial and Advertising Departments "to first assume responsibility for having such words correct." (The split infinitive is Irving's.)

A January 28, 1946 memo chastises the editors about "the unfortunate and embarrassing mistake in the lead story on Page 2," regarding the misuse of the word "affect" instead of "effect." After advising them to have "all members of the staff convince you they know how to use these two words," he ends "…I feel sure that with this memo of caution, no more such mistakes will be made in the

Editorial Department."

Oh, sure. I mean, surely.

My thanks to Florence McIlvaine for sending these memos, which, combined with other memories, could be a most wonderful book.

I'll send that thought in the form of a memo to the editorial department.

"OVER MY SHOULDER" COLUMN FOR JUNE 1, 1997
A jewel in the school crown

The news that the Salvation Army headquarters, on Chester Street in Glens Falls, will soon be transformed into a Baptist school was proof of the adage "what goes around comes around" – but in a very happy way.

That building was originally the second home of the Glens Falls Academy, which for almost 100 years was one of the jewels in the educational crown of Glens Falls and the surrounding region.

The Academy started in 1841 on Warren Street in the Village of Glens Falls. That building today comprises part of Warren Tires. The Academy was one of the many private schools, such as the Elmwood Academy or the Fort Edward Collegiate Institute for example, that would flourish in the climate of the pitiful public schools that existed until the late 1800s.

The Academy's trustees were the real movers and shakers of the region. Because of space, let me sketch three of them as examples. William Caldwell was the son of James, who was founder of the Village and the Town of Lake George, formerly Caldwell. William, an aggressive business person, built the post office and the Mansion House, among other important businesses and buildings, and was always involved in everything new. Caldwell was a Congressman in the 1850s. Likewise, the brilliant and mercurial Halsey Rogers of Moreau, was a lumber baron and a merchant, having built a stone store in Lake George Village. At one time a Warren County Judge, Rogers was elected a state Assemblyman in 1842.

Third is Alonso Morgan. A land developer par excellence, Morgan is credited with the first subdevelopment in Glens Falls and Queensbury. With his house standing at the head of Center Street (as it does today), he laid out Center, Maple, Oak, Cherry, and many streets in that area. It's no coincidence that the first Academy building sat on Warren Street adjacent to Morgan's lands. These three men were among the very far-sighted group who tried to organize a railroad here in 1832 – only one year after the first American railroad was created in Schenectady!

Its four officers were similarly extraordinary. President Billy J. Clark of Moreau was founder of the first temperance society in America. Russell Mack Little of Glens Falls was founder of the Glens Falls Insurance Company. Attorney Enoch Rosecrans served for years on the New York State Supreme Court. His home, the present St. Mary's Rectory, was just down the street from the Academy.

George Sanford of Sanford's Ridge in Queensbury had been a state Assemblyman and, among his many accomplishments, founded the Plank Road Company in 1847.

The Glens Falls Academy started in a brand-new building. Its first students were male, but almost immediately females were included, the first "preceptress" being a Miss Dora Wilson, who worked with the first five principals.

Everyone equally received a state-of-the-art education, and I stress "equally" because the female students took the same courses as the male students, including biology, advanced mathematics, and chemistry, for example, a radical departure from the Victorian traditions of prose and poetry, and domestic sciences for females. The quality and equality of the Academy's education were evidenced by the fact that the first three New York State Regents diplomas ever awarded were to Academy students – three female graduates in 1880. The very first Regents Diploma was awarded to Isabelle Selleck. That is now in the archives of the Chapman Historical Museum. And here's something to ponder for those of you who, like my daughter Julia, are about to take your Regents Exams: kids have been suffering through those Regents Exams for well over a century. It's awful, isn't it? I still get nauseous thinking about regents.

Time's up. Will you join me next week? We'll follow the Academy through its golden years to its end in 1937 and explore the legacy of its alumni.

"OVER MY SHOULDER" COLUMN FOR JUNE 8, 1997
Academy's final days

Last week, we had come as far as 1880 in the history of the former Glens Falls Academy. The Academy's second home, formerly the Salvation Army headquarters on Chester Street in Glens Falls, will soon be converted for use as a school.

Although the Academy had predecessors that existed from 1803 to 1841, the formal founding of the "Glens Falls Academy" on Warren Street, is accepted as 1841. Never a large school, on the scale of Dr. Joseph King's Fort Edward Collegiate Institute, which opened in 1854 with 500 students, the Academy was, however, an educational leader.

The first academy building underwent several expansions at its Warren Street site, still standing at 92 Warren Street. An 1870 rear extension doubled its size. Under the energetic and very talented headmaster, Dr. Daniel C. Farr, the Academy again expanded, this time in 1892 with a three-story brick and terra cotta addition to the front, very reminiscent of the architecture of first YMCA, now Godnicks on Glen Street. If you face the first academy building today and look beyond the single-story structure added in 1925, you will see the huge addition. Look closely and you can still see the faint traces of the words "The Glens Falls Academy."

It would be unfair to assign a particular period as "the golden days" but certainly under Dr. Farr, principal from 1878 to 1905, the Academy was very vigorous. Ironically, during this same period, the Glens Falls public school system, established in the 1880s under Dr. Sherman Williams, would become a powerful competitor, and eventually a factor in the Academy's demise.

The graduating classes averaged about ten in size, small enough to afford each student individual attention, but large enough to have a good theatrical society, language clubs, baseball, basketball, track, tennis, and fencing. By the late `teens, girls would be included in everything except baseball and track.

The students represented many of the leading families of Glens Falls, Queensbury and surrounding communities – Wing, Pruyn, McEachron, Robertson, Paris, Cool being among the many. Skimming through the Academy's 1937 yearbook, its last, we see an 1884 photo of Mary Pruyn Hoopes, daughter of Samuel Pruyn of Finch, Pruyn & Co. A later 1920 photo shows her daughter, Polly Hoopes Beeman, perhaps one of this region's greatest, yet most silent, benefactors. The 1906 class photo includes Frederick Bascom, son of the powerful attorney O.C. Bascom of Fort Edward. Frederick would achieve his own fame in publishing and the law in Glens Falls.

Its students made their mark both here and afar: John A. Dix, Governor of New York State (1910-1912); Rev. Thomas Goodspeed, credited with saving the University of Chicago from financial and intellectual bankruptcy; Major General Daniel Sickles, Civil War hero; U. S. Commissioner of Pensions John Bentley; and Harriet Bentley, John's sister, a local artist and historian whose historical map of this region is still being sold. The Bentley homestead is today the headquarters of the Moreau-South Glens Falls Historical Society.

A fire in 1913 destroyed enough of the rear section of the building to prompt the board, under direction of its president Daniel Robertson, to build an entirely new school on Chester Street. It must have helped. Yearbooks from the period show more students and more activities. The faculty remained consistent, which was a strength, a classic example being Professor C. L. Williams, who taught biology and other sciences from 1887 to 1937 and served twice as principal!

From 1917 to 1937, Headmaster J. Thatcher Sears and his wife Katherine ran the Academy as a team, but their dedication and brilliance could not overcome two powerful forces: The Depression and the long-term growth of the Glens Falls Public School System. Not having expanded in the way many other private schools had in the decades before the Depression, the Academy was, perhaps, too lean to survive and it closed in 1937.

"OVER MY SHOULDER" COLUMN FOR JUNE 15, 1997
Readers respond to Academy

Although I risk putting off readers by writing too much about a topic, I simply must respond to the many people who have contacted me regarding my first column on the Glens Falls Academy. By the time they had reached me, I had already written the second column about the Academy and I felt compelled to answer them.

The ripple effect of the Academy and its teachers upon the many students and the community at large, as is true with any school, is history-making in itself. A letter from Florence McIlvaine, an alumna of the Glens Falls Academy class of 1933 illustrates that point beautifully. She wrote about a Professor Williams, who, when she was there "was still teaching physics and chemistry on the third floor." Williams (whom I never heard called anything but "Prof") had started teaching at the Academy in 1887. I had first heard of him from Gwen Perceval, who taught at the school until its closing in 1937, and from Ralph and Dot Lapham. Ralph, one of the co-founders of the Chapman Historical Museum and its first Curator, was a graduate of the Academy. Lining the walls of the Lapham's home were frame after frame of beautiful hand renderings of various plants, all done by Williams.

Florence remembered that Williams had bequeathed "his extensive mineralogy collection" to Elmer Rowley. Many of us today remember that Mr. Rowley greatly expanded that collection and subsequently, in an act of supreme generosity, donated it to the New York State Museum. What started as Prof Williams' mineral collection is today one of the most important to be found in any museum. That is certainly a legacy.

So, too, is the connection Florence draws between the Academy and the Glens Falls Community Theatre. She writes that the Academy's annual play, directed by Headmaster J. Thatcher Sears and his wife Katherine B. Sears, "was a community event of some importance. It was presented every spring in the K. of C. Hall to large audiences." After the Academy ended in 1937, the Sears directed "plays for the Outing Club and later for the newly formed Little Theater Group of the (Glens Falls) Operetta Club," later to be the Glens Falls Community Theatre.

She wrote of the Academy's "basketball prowess under Coach Alexander `Bay' Robertson and the spirited rivalry of the City Series among the high school, St. Mary's and the Academy." The City Series basketball games are a part of our regional sports histories, waiting to find an author to unite them into a book.

As for "Coach" Robertson, Alexander P. Robertson went on to be a Warren County Judge and Surrogate Court Judge. Interestingly, the Robertson family played a significant role in the Academy. Daniel L. Robertson, Judge Robertson's father, was president of the board of trustees of the Academy from 1908 to 1931. At the time of the school's closing, Alexander P. Robertson and his mother served on the executive committee and Judge Robertson's son, Daniel, was among those who were attending the elementary classes, or "lower school," as they were called.

Perhaps the greatest irony of the Glens Falls Academy's history has to do with the Glens Falls Public School System. Founded well after the Academy, the Glens Falls Public Schools became the Academy's true competition under its first Superintendent Dr. Sherman Williams. Yet among the founders of the Glens Falls Public School System were Jerome Lapham and Samuel Pruyn. Lapham was a trustee of the Academy and Pruyn a major donor. Many of Pruyn's family would either attend the school, such as his granddaughter, Polly Hoopes Beeman, or serve it, such as his son-in-law, Louis F. Hyde, president of the board from 1931 to 1934.

For all their help, my thanks to William Woodward, Daniel Hall, Florence McIlvaine, the Robertson Family, Albert Fowler of Crandall Library, R. Paul McCarty, and the many others who wished to remain anonymous.

"OVER MY SHOULDER" COLUMN FOR OCTOBER 12, 1997
Glens Falls Hospital's progressive founders

We've been celebrating it since July 1. However, the State of New York State would probably prefer October 15.

Nonetheless, as both dates fell in 1897, both are perfectly acceptable for observing the 100th anniversary of the Glens Falls Hospital. Confused? Well, the founding board of the Glens Falls Hospital met in the old Glens Falls Insurance Company Building (on the northwest corner of Glen and Bay) on July 1, 1897. However, the New York State Board of Charities did not approve the application by the hospital's founding board until October 15, 1897. Without that approval, there would have been no Glens Falls Hospital. (One can't fight the state!)

But, locally speaking, there would have been no Glens Falls Hospital without the people who created it, by and large physicians who brought the newest in medical theory and practice to the Glens Falls region.

Before we discuss them, please consider what had occurred in medical science almost up to 1897. Not to be disgusting, but to be honest, even though Dr. Lister had developed the "antiseptic" method in 1863, down into the 1870s and 1880s, surgeons in the most prestigious hospitals in Boston and New York never disinfected nor sterilized their instruments. They even wore the same suit of clothing at every operation – street clothes caked with the blood and gore of their past patients. However, by the time the Glens Falls Hospital opened, it began with the "aseptic" method, that is, the use of sterile equipment and facilities. What a difference!

This was because of those progressive physicians, backed by enlightened lay people, who worked to start the hospital. The acknowledged founder, Dr. R. Jerome Eddy is a perfect example. Born in Vermont, Dr. Eddy graduated from

Middlebury College, then took his medical degree from the New York College of Physicians and Surgeons. He then worked at Bellevue Hospital, as it was emerging as a true modern hospital, helping to shape Eddy as a medical progressive. In the 1870s as a dedicated physician he nearly sacrificed his life caring for the smallpox victims in "the pesthouse" on Sherman Avenue, near today's Northway. (At times he even dug the graves and buried the victims!) He started the Glens Falls Medical Society in 1880 and, in 1896, drew together those who would charter our hospital in 1897. I cannot think of a finer model for the hospital's "first founder."

Another co-founder was Dr. Dudley Hall of Stony Creek, and a graduate of the University of Maryland. He was the first health inspector in Glens Falls and succeeded in getting all milk delivered in the city to be placed in sterilized containers. Fellow founder Dr. Fred Fielding, a native of Queensbury, was a graduate of Columbia College of Physicians and Surgeons in New York. He was a major agitator in the creation of the city's present reservoir system, promoting on the basis of its providing clean water.

All the 12 founders were true progressives. Eight were from Glens Falls and Queensbury: Dr. R. J. Eddy, Dr. Fred Fielding, Dr. David J. Fitzgerald, Dr. Dudley Hall, Dr. Thomas I. Henning, Dr. William J. Hunt, Dr. William M. Rapp, and Mr. Joseph A. Kellogg, (the only lay person, a Glens Falls attorney originally from Hudson Falls). From Hudson Falls: Dr. Henry C. Monroe and Dr. James T. Park. From Fort Edward: Dr. Silas Banker and Dr. William B. Mellick. (Though not a charter founder, a Dr. James S. White, an eye surgeon of South Glens Falls, was among those who was on the committee, which in 1896 did all the preliminary work. He also was among those who approached the state Charities Board for certification of the hospital.)

In next week's conclusion, I'll show you how medical history was made at the Glens Falls Hospital and I'll relate how one of its first surgeons employed "Dracula" in his crusade against a medical fraud!

"OVER MY SHOULDER" COLUMN FOR OCTOBER 19, 1997
Hospital's success tied to its workers

During the first year of its founding, 1897, the Glens Falls Hospital really wasn't a hospital at all, but a name.

However, Dr. R. J. Eddy, its founder and first president, was in secret negotiations with a patient who had a home on Park Street, a Mr. Solomon Parks.

In early 1898, Parks — whose name bore no relationship to Park Street — announced to the hospital board that he would donate his home for the first hospital building. For next two years workers would convert the three-story mansard-roofed home into a hospital. Sadly, Parks died just months before the building's official opening in 1900.

Parks mandated that the hospital be called "The Parks Hospital," which it was for ten years until a new building was constructed on Park Street. Parks' home then became a nurses' facility.

In 1898, the hospital's board began to change composition. While it took on other physicians, and its first dentist, Dr. Thomas Foulds, for whom the laboratory would subsequently be named, it also included more lay people, including publisher A. B. Colvin and Glens Falls Insurance Company head, E. W. West, a son-in-law of Parks.

The early hospital survived, thrived, and made medical history because of its medical personnel, both board and staff members. For example, a new board member in 1898 was Dr. Howard Paine, the first surgeon ever to perform cataract surgery outside of Montreal and Manhattan. This new surgery brought him into conflict with Dr. Edward Bemis, an optician who had built up a huge eye sanitarium in Glens Falls, so large he was considered to be a mini-industry by many.

Paine had assisted a Dr. Jamison in an operation to remove the eye of James Pettys, who had been treated for glaucoma by Bemis. In the treatment, Bemis had used his "Magnetic Eye Vaporizer," a secret device he had invented. Paine was so enraged that he assisted Pettys' physician in mounting a lawsuit against Bemis. In a March 1898, letter to Jamison, Paine wrote of "destroying the influence and power of this vampire," not only an unflattering reference to Bemis, but a current one, as Bram Stoker's "Dracula" had only been published in 1897.

There is no record of whether the suit succeeded, but the attack on Bemis had begun. Bemis died of coronary in 1901, taking the secret of the "Magnetic Eye Vaporizer" to the grave.

Ironically, Paine was a physician of the homeopathic school of medicine, which itself was under severe attack at that time. Paine was not the only homeopathic physician on the hospital staff who would bring the newest medical advances to the hospital. Another was Dr. Stephen T. Birdsall, who first introduced radiology to Glens Falls in 1904, only nine years after Roentgen's discovery of the X-ray. He became the hospital's first "roentgenologist" in 1910.

Until 1916, the hospital used Birdsall's own radiological equipment, located in his Glen Street office in the Colvin Building. That year Dr. Birdsall established the hospital's first Radiology Department. Patients needing x-rays were shipped to his office. As the late Stephen Birdsall, the doctor's grandson, told me, the elevator was not meant to accommodate patients lying down, so often stretchers were placed in an upright position!

Those are only two of many examples of the innovative medicine of the early Glens Falls Hospital that laid the foundation for its survival and growth over 100 years.

But one factor must not be ignored in that success: the people who work at the hospital. For those of us who, like myself, have been patients there, or have had a loved one cared for in the last days of cancer, or have experienced the joy of seeing our new baby born there, "the hospital" is really the people who work there in every capacity.

To them and to the institution also affectionately known as the "Park Street Hotel" – a happy 100th.

"OVER MY SHOULDER" COLUMN FOR NOVEMBER 2, 1997.
Red Cross chapter is formed

I'm either one day late or ten days early, but either way, happy 81st anniversary to the Adirondack-Saratoga Chapter of the American Red Cross, possibly the only chapter ever to begin with a potential disaster.

The chapter has certainly undergone some changes since its founding, not the least of which is the name. The chapter's first public organizational meeting was on November 1, 1916. In just a half a year, the United States would be drawn into the war raging in Europe and the founding of the chapter actually foresaw that eventuality.

Of course, before November 1, 1916, there was plenty of activity, primarily by a far-sighted group whose contributions to this region were many and substantial, however are all but forgotten: the Glens Falls Women's Civic Club.

The club was founded in 1907 by an incredible leader and person of vision, Helena Norris Whitney (who, coincidentally, was daughter of Lieut. William T. Norris, who died in the Battle of Bull Run in 1862). Since 1914, the club had been meeting in the old Glens Falls Academy Building on 92 Warren Street. Mrs. Whitney was the leader of a trio of women who were the "founders" of the chapter. The other two, also Civic Club members, were Estelle Palmer and Josephine Demarest.

Not coincidentally, Helena Whitney was at that time the president of the Glens Falls Hospital Guild, of which Estelle Palmer was a member, too. Knowing that makes it easy to understand why the hospital's Superintendent Florence Wetmore, its board president, Maurice Hoopes, and vice president E.W. West, among others, ended up on the founding board of Directors of the Red Cross.

I don't know when the National Red Cross was first approached, but I know that throughout October of 1916, the Civic Club had held public meetings at their headquarters on Warren Street. On October 26 and 27, two meetings were held at the Civic Club headquarters with Neafie Adams, a representative of the national Red Cross, to formally discuss creating a chapter to be called the "Glens Falls Woman's Club Red Cross Chapter."

The Post-Star of October 31 appealed for the public to attend the first public meeting for the chapter, held the next day at the First Presbyterian Church, then located a few doors west of St. Mary's Church on Warren Street. Edward Moree, a representative of the National Red Cross, spoke both in the afternoon and night. The directors were chosen and a name, the "Glens Falls Chapter of the American Red Cross" was settled on, instead of the originally suggested name.

The first board elected that night consisted of Glens Falls Mayor Edward Reed as Chairman, Helena Whitney as Vice Chairman, Estelle Palmer as Secretary and Mrs. T. C. Fowler as Treasurer. Reed's position was nominal, although he was very active. The Chapter was truly run by the other three.

About our chapter possibly being the only one to have started with a potential disaster? On the night of November 1st, Moree had given an absolutely rousing address about Red Cross work in such disasters as the San Francisco earthquake and fire, and the sinking of the Titanic, among others. Then, just as everyone was leaving the church at 9:20 p.m., an earthquake struck Glens Falls! Houses shook. People fell out of their beds and, horrified, ran into the streets. Moree rushed to *The Post-Star* (just around the corner at that time) to be in immediate contact by wire with national headquarters.

No serious damage occurred, but the next morning the paper was filled with stories about both the earthquake and the Red Cross. Could one have asked for better publicity?

As the Chapter's charter was signed on November 11, 1916, today its official anniversary is November 11. And now you understand my being a day late or ten days early.

Next week: the chapter moves full circle – almost.

"OVER MY SHOULDER" COLUMN FOR NOVEMBER 9, 1997
Red Cross chapter expands its territory

The Adirondack-Saratoga Chapter of the American Red Cross, originally called the "Glens Falls Chapter of the American Red Cross," was founded on November 1, 1916. However, the chapter's charter was given by the National Red Cross on November 11, making that its official birthday.

The chapter had its first headquarters in the Glens Falls Women's Civic Club building on 92 Warren Street, where it was founded. However, chapter founder Helena Whitney was busy behind the scenes and on November 13 the Glens Falls Insurance Company announced that it was making available Room 505 for the chapter's headquarters. (Didn't hurt that the company's Vice President, E.W. West, was on the Red Cross board, too.) Until 1919, the chapter would be located in the insurance company building at the northwest corner of Bay and Glen Streets.

From Room 505, the chapter rapidly expanded into other communities by the creation of branches and auxiliaries. Mrs. Preston Paris formed the very first branch in Hudson Falls in February 1917. Dozens followed, and every one providing supplies for Pershing's troops in Mexico, "war relief supplies" for England – in essence, preparing for war. Nurses were trained, and ambulance corps established. From the US entry into war on April 4, 1917 until war's end, the chapter supplied millions of dollars in goods and services – clothing, bandages, sanitary items, nurses, and money – to field hospitals, orphanages and other institutions serviced by the National Red Cross.

The war over, the chapter returned to providing this country emergency disaster relief, rural nursing services, and health and welfare programs. When the former home of Jerome Lapham on the southwest corner of Ridge and Maple Streets became available for public use in 1919, the chapter moved in, along with the Crandall Library. Both would call it home until 1931, when the Crandall Library building was completed.

Sadly, the Lapham home was razed, and the chapter moved its headquarters to the Rogers Building on Bay and Maple Streets, where it stayed nine years, essentially the duration of the Depression. During those years, many of the dozens of auxiliaries and branches of the Red Cross either merged with other local Chapters to the north, west and south, or they disappeared, economic casualties.

In 1940, the Chapter returned to the Glens Falls Insurance Company building, once again providing relief to Europe and, again, preparing for war. In 1941 it moved into the former home of the Glens Falls Academy on Chester Street, where it spent World War II, doing everything it learned in WW I, but also becoming involved in one of its greatest and noblest roles, the collecting and saving of blood in blood banks, which continues to this day.

In 1946, the chapter moved to the Kreiser Building on 222-224 Glen Street and then moved again in 1949 to #2 Bacon Street, where it would remain for 40 years! In 1949, the chapter began the first of several name changes, each reflecting its growing territory. In 1949, it became the Warren Washington Chapter; in 1964, the Southeastern Adirondack Chapter and in 1967, the Adirondack Chapter. That last name held for 29 years. Then on July 1, 1996, the Chapter merged with the Saratoga Chapter to become the Adirondack-Saratoga Chapter of the American Red Cross.

I purposely did not mention the Chapter's last headquarters' move until now. In 1989, our chapter moved to its present location on the corner of Warren and Center Streets, placing it only a few doors to the west of its very first home in the Women's Civic Club building at 92 Warren Street. While our chapter's headquarters have come almost full circle to its place of origin, the chapter itself has expanded its territory to serve about a tenth of our entire state. Helena Whitney and her fellow co-founders would be very proud!

Happy 81st anniversary to the Adirondack-Saratoga Chapter of American Red Cross.

"OVER MY SHOULDER" COLUMN FOR NOVEMBER 23, 1997
Floating the logs changed everything

In last week's column I urged that there be celebrations to observe Glens Falls' 90th anniversary of incorporation as a city (in 1998) and its 160th anniversary of incorporation as a village (in 1999).

Despite its vigorous beginnings, the little Quaker hamlet of Glens Falls was severely stagnating by the War of 1812. The fact is just not stressed enough that other Queensbury settlements – at Glen Lake, French Mountain, or Sanford's Ridge – could have eclipsed Glens Falls. Sanford's Ridge lacked the disease bearing mosquitoes that plagued Glens Falls, located on the Hudson, and it had a thriving potash industry, based upon an availability of trees.

THAT was Glens Falls' problem: though it had plenty of water power and sawmills, it had cut down its available trees. Then two wholly coincidental things happened: (1) logs started floating down the Hudson and (2) the Champlain Canal opened between Waterford and Whitehall.

Somewhere around 1813, Alanson and Norman Fox of Chestertown, got the idea to drive their logs down the Hudson River to market. Later, their partner Abraham Wing III of Glens Falls perfected the idea with a system for booms and sluiceways and in time others joined them, all hammering unique marks upon the cut ends of their logs to identify them. (The British pound symbol atop Finch Pruyn is an example.)

With log drives, Glens Falls sawmills suddenly had more lumber than markets! Then, in 1823, the canal opened a cheap, direct route to Troy, Albany, and New York. Well, almost direct, for it was still necessary to haul the lumber from Glens Falls to Sandy Hill by wagon, as the section of canal running through southern Queensbury was only a "feeder" (feeding water to the main canal) and not navigable by boat.

In 1832 it was made navigable and the economic race was off! Initially, Fort Edward and Sandy Hill had been in the lead, but gradually, over the next three decades, Glens Falls went ahead. Why? Here's one clue: by 1836, Glens Falls had a "Lime Street." Using scrap wood from local lumber mills, Glens Falls limestone was burned to make lime, an intrinsic building tool. Keyes P. Cool (later a Queensbury Town Supervisor) became the first to ship that lime on the canal. Lime, limestone, and lumber fueled the state's building boom. When those products went south, money came north.

Glens Falls became a central outlet for the many river-based sawmills in Queensbury, fed by logs from upper Warren County. It also became a transportation hub, as the canal intersected with the main road, now US Route 9, right at a new "free" (non-toll) bridge that spanned the Hudson at Glens Falls. Add a new industry, "tourism," and you had a boom! (Remember, Lake George was already emerging as a destination, attracting people like James Fenimore Cooper, who stayed in Glens Falls in 1825. His visit to the cave in the island beneath that bridge inspired the famous "cave scene" in "The Last of the Mohicans.")

Hotels for business people and tourists sprung up, as did associated businesses, churches, schools, a library, an opera house, a stagecoach company, and a volunteer fire department. The population, approximately 300 people in 1809 (my estimate) was 1,289 in 1839, one-third Queensbury's whole population.

Economically, politically, and socially, the town became centered upon Glens Falls, as did much of Warren County, in turn, upon Queensbury.

On December 8, 1838, the state was petitioned to make Glens Falls an incorporated village and on April 12, 1839 the Village of Glens Falls was born. Interestingly, among the first village officials, James Ferris, William Peck, and James Sisson would also serve as Town Supervisors and the mix of town and village politics kept the two entities united. By 1896, that was all changed.

Next week, I'll bring us to 1908 and the founding of the city – and a possible flaw that was embodied in its beginning.

"OVER MY SHOULDER" COLUMN FOR NOVEMBER 30, 1997
The city deserves to celebrate

When the Village of Glens Falls incorporated April 12, 1839, recession ruled, but Glens Falls seemed immune, the canal fueling the village's roaring economy. Over the next 69 years, until becoming a city in 1908, Queensbury's hub went from about one square mile and a population of 1,239 to four square miles and about 15,000 people.

Since it's impossible to condense 69 years of history in even several columns, let me show how fortunate circumstances and a philosophy where "new" and "progress" were the key words, led to the formation of the city.

Creating businesses and financial institutions ranked high among the village people. By 1849 they started the famed Glens Falls Insurance Company and, subsequently, numerous banks, including two still headquartered in Glens Falls: Evergreen Bank (in 1851) and the Glens Falls National Bank and Trust (in 1853).

Lumber "boomed." In 1851 132,500 logs arrived. By 1877, 12,309,500 had, the equivalent of almost 2,500,000,000 ("billion" with a "b") feet of finished lumber. The spin-off industries of paper and wallpaper emerged and created new fortunes. Alongside lime and limestone, brickmaking, silver processing, and more industries emerged.

Attempts to imitate the public works of larger municipalities accidentally led Glens Falls to create a climate for more business. Expanding the water system for fire protection and clean water failed until 1864, when most of downtown accidentally burned down. The result inspired the village: downtown was rebuilt by 1867, a reservoir-based water system was completed by 1873 – AND the system attracted a new industry, textile mills!

In 1854 the village had a gas manufacturing plant for street lighting. By 1881 it was generating electricity and in 1882 electrically lighting the streets. By 1891 it was electrically powering its streetcar line (started in 1885). By 1903, it had funded the fourth largest hydroelectric dam in the world.

The 25 streets and 2,717 people in 1850 blossomed to almost 80 streets and 5,000 people by 1880.

The rich got richer and many others were becoming upwardly mobile. Several times the village would officially expand its boundaries, in 1856, 1874, and again in 1886. The wealth did more than multiply homes of the wealthy. It created schools, commercial buildings, churches, opera houses; and the train, 1868; paved streets starting 1877; telephones, 1878; a daily newspaper, 1879; Crandall Library, 1892; a sewer system, 1893; Glens Falls Hospital, 1897; Crandall Park, 1898; then, cars and movies and more. From 1880 to 1900, population went from 4,900 to 12,613 and the village fathers (no mothers being allowed to vote) had decided to split from Queensbury to become a city.

From the idea's inception in 1896 to March 13, 1908, the day Glens Falls' native son, Governor Charles Evans Hughes signed the City Charter, everything had been thought of except three. First, space. Although there was vacant land in the city in 1908, by 1938, it was practically all used. Second, the city's watersheds were not within its boundaries, which has led to today's "water wars" with the Town of Queensbury.

Third, few deeply considered how pulling out the economic guts and true center of Queensbury would make the town feel – in a word, bitter. My late friend, Minnie Jenkins Bidwell, a native of Queensbury, who passed away residing in Glens Falls, epitomized this in an angry, if debatable, accusation: when Glens Falls left the Town, it never paid for Village Hall that Queensbury helped fund in 1900.

Oh dear. Have I brought up another problem to add to the Civil War Monument hassle and the "water wars"?

Sorry. My intent was to say that a tremendous good came from the growth of Glens Falls, and that Glens Falls' government and people should celebrate those two upcoming anniversaries and use them as a time to set up a forum with Queensbury's government and people to discuss their common past – and, perhaps, a common future.

SECTION 2: AREA HISTORY

"OVER MY SHOULDER" COLUMN FOR OCTOBER 24,1994.
Memories of a mill town

NOTE: This was the first ever of the "Over My Shoulder" columns, originally published bi-weekly. It began weekly publication in June 1996.

W hether we're 25, 55, 105, or anything in between, we remember parts of our childhood far better than where we set our last coffee cup. I call them "today memories."

For me, the whistle at the Scott Paper Mill[xxiv] in Fort Edward is a "today memory": as fresh today, as when I heard it as a child, swimming at the beach summers or working in my parents' pharmacy on Broadway or going to school; or whatever. I believe that Scott Paper is a part of the today memories of anyone who's lived in that town at any time in the last fifty years. The news of its closing may now be "old news," but to our memories, it's still fresh. It's still hard to accept.

When my family was new to the Village of Fort Edward – forty plus years ago – I was a very little boy and the mill's whistle was a strange thing, even a bit frightening to me at first. But I soon came to rely upon it as everyone did, for the time and for the news. I got up by it, went to lunch by it, lived my life by it. It was like a modern-day version of the medieval clock towers in Germany. The whistle would blow, and people would pause, sometimes right in the middle of Broadway while crossing the street, to look at their watches. Or to listen.

Just to listen. They listened to hear if the whistle would blow more than just the long blast for the time. They'd listen to hear if the whistle were going to tell them of a fire. There was a number code that had been worked out: longs and shorts, each blast for a certain section of or something special in town. I remember when I was six learning what the whistle really meant, the night the lumber yard next to the railroad tracks caught fire, out on East Street. The whistle blew and blew and blew. Little and afraid, I listened from our apartment window and I watched. Fire trucks came in from all over and the nighttime sky was orange with the light.

One special code would cause everyone to stop, then to run, even if they didn't work at the mill, even if weren't a volunteer fire fighter. The code was for the mill itself. God, what a fear came over people's faces when that particular whistle blew, for the mill was so special.

By the way, it always seemed to be "the mill" to anyone who lived there. There were other mills. The Decora. Or General Electric. But they were always referred to by their names. "Where you working now, Ed?" my father would ask the fellow just returned from the service. "The mill." A smile. A funny grin. It was a good job. Secure. Hard work, no doubt about that, but a good job.

Oh, yes, and there were other whistles, too. The Durkee Hose had a fire whistle that could blow the paint off a car at a hundred feet. At least it felt like it. But the mill's whistle was THE whistle. It seemed to be a sound of life.

It's important not to romanticize the mill. The jobs were hard. Paper mill jobs are. It was not a romantic place; most mills are not. It spewed a lot of junk in the river. We swam in that junk. But, then, the other mills spewed a lot of junk in the river, too, and we swam in that. Our beach was at the north end of Roger's Island, pointing into the stream, so to speak. If the mill made hard demands upon the people and the environment, it did upon the village, too. A share of lower Mechanic Street and a part of Eddy Street were eaten up in the expansion of the mill. Older homes, lovely things, that were a part of the heritage of Fort Edward, taken down in the name of progress, not to mention the actual streets themselves. All gone.

But that being said, it's important to say that it was a place that produced jobs. What an important word, "jobs." Though the Depression to me was ancient history, a time before I was born, for most who worked at Scott Paper, the depression was a vivid memory, a today memory. It was damned good to have a job. Damned better to have your neighbors have jobs along with you. Also, the mill produced a product people could measure the quality of and speak with pride about. Making paper is that way.

Funny thing is, I never was in the mill itself, so you could wonder, "How does he know all that about paper mills?" I know because, when I got older, I worked summers in the International Paper (IP) mill in Ticonderoga. Ironically, some of the older machines I worked on in Ticonderoga had been at Fort Edward until the forties, when IP left, and Scott moved in. And before that, those same machines had been at the IP mill in South Glens Falls, where they began their life. Would you like to know something funny – and sad at the same time? The mill I worked in is gone, torn down to make a new one outside of the village. But those machines that traveled from South Glens Falls to Fort Edward to Ticonderoga? They were moved out of the country, to Mexico I think it was, and put to work in a new paper mill, built with the bricks torn down from the old one.

I don't understand what's going on to cause it, only what has happened. I know the mill is history and that Decora and General Electric aren't what they were. I used to see history as something that had happened "back then" and be surprised at the coincidence when it occurred again. But I see a repetition of the same story that is bothersome. Since the early 1900s, new industries seem to have sprung up, become established and then, boom, they're gone. Look at the number of textile mills and clothing manufacturers there were from the turn of the century even into the 1950s. Most gone. That took many, many decades. Now it happens in a single generation. People who were in grade school in the 1970s can tell their kids about the "Old Days," when there were all these different kinds of mills around. Look at the recent closing of a certain catheter plant that's only one generation old and you'll see what I mean.

Few people in their twenties think of their lives in terms of history. But whether they realize it or not, those living in Fort Edward today have already joined an elite group of people who have a today memory embracing elements of a life gone by: speaking the language of the mill, such as "what shift you on?" or "broke" (for imperfect, rejected paper), or bringing home a roll of toilet paper in your lunch box – or listening to the sound of a whistle blowing on a fall morning, telling everyone that it was time, time to get up, time to go to work and school, time to live another day in a mill town.

"OVER MY SHOULDER" COLUMN FOR FEBRUARY 27, 1995
Lemuel Haynes preached here

NOTE: With the outlawing of slavery in New York State fully coming to completion in 1827, the Abolition Movement to abolish slavery grew feverishly. Our region became an integral part of that movement. Blacks had lived in this region for at least a century, most as enslaved people, but not all.

There needs to be a monument in South Granville to Lemuel Haynes, an extraordinary and brilliant man.

It would take a book to describe the life of Haynes, an African American who lived from 1753 to 1833. He was a Revolutionary War veteran, the first black American to take a college degree (from Middlebury College) and the first black Congregational minister. His renown in religious circles came from his defense of the traditional Calvinist thinking in the many articles he published, and in speeches he gave from little chapels in tiny hamlets right up to Jonathan Edward's Blue Chapel at Yale. Haynes was so renowned, that over fifty years after his death, different towns in New England, such as Rutland, Vermont, and in New York State, such as Granville, went out of their way to claim him as their own. Not unlike "Washington slept here," except it would be "Lemuel Haynes preached here."

Born in 1753 in Connecticut, Haynes began his career as an indentured servant. Upon earning his freedom, he joined the Minutemen in 1775 and was with Ethan Allen at the capture of Fort Ticonderoga. An ardent Patriot, he believed that the power of the Revolution that freed people from Great Britain would eventually free black slaves from their chains, something he did not live to see.

He started his Congregationalist ministry in 1776, a staunch defender of the Hopkintonian brand of Calvinism.[xxv] He attracted considerable attention with his published speeches and became a leading spokesperson of traditional Congregationalism. By the turn of the century he was embroiled in a debate with a Rev. Hosea Ballou, who represented Congregationalism's more liberal

Unitarianism. One of Haynes' pamphlets, *Universal Salvation*, won such critical acclaim that it was reprinted without authorization for decades and was being reprinted long after Haynes' death.

But Haynes was a preacher of the people. He traveled and lived in communities, especially along the New York/Vermont border, where Washington County, New York, meets Bennington and Rutland counties of Vermont. He arrived in West Rutland in the early 1800s and eventually became legendary in the Rutland-Granville area. In 1822, Haynes became minister of the First Congregational Church of South Granville, where he ministered until his death in 1833.

Even though Vermont had prohibited slavery from its inception and New York had abolished it in 1808, acceptance of Haynes was not automatic, and prejudice was intense. As brilliant in his wit as in his defense of his faith, he was able to survive and thrive in a climate hostile to Blacks, as well as to preachers of any color. Stories of his wit spread far and wide and remained popular long after his death. In Haynes' day, Northeastern New York and Northwestern New England were frontier. Drunkenness, fighting, and general lawlessness were common. People drank alcohol then like we do soda today. Once Haynes went into a store and asked how everyone was. The owner, being humorous, replied, "Oh, not more than half drunk." Haynes shot back, "I'm glad that there is reformation begun."

In Haynes' day, people were far less likely to belong to any church or subscribe to any faith. Ministers had their work cut out for them. Once Haynes was taunted by two men who told him that they'd heard he was out of work because, they said, "the devil is dead."

In a flash, Haynes put his hands on the men's heads and said, "Oh, poor fatherless children! What will become of you?"

Haynes overcame prejudice and won love and respect through his love for his fellow humans, through a sense of humor, and by his fairness in his search for the truth. That fairness spared no one, not even fellow clergy and I'll close with an anecdote that illustrates Haynes' use of his incredible wit in search of the truth. A young minister told Haynes that he believed ignorant ministers were more likely to succeed than learned ones. Haynes replied, "Won't you tell me, sir, how much ignorance is necessary to make an eminent preacher?"

The time is ripe for a well-written biography on Lemuel Haynes, this African American preacher who contributed so much to the history of the Granville-West Rutland area – and New York and New England.[xxvi]

"OVER MY SHOULDER" COLUMN FOR MARCH 13, 1995
Women's suffrage: its time had come

This year we celebrate the 75th anniversary of the ratification of the 19th Amendment, which gave women the right to vote in 1920.

In New York State, women had been voting since 1917 and, indeed, this area of upper New York State saw many battles waged in the war for Suffrage. One of its champions, Susan B. Anthony, had her early education in women's suffrage on her family's farm in southwest Washington County in Easton.

Coincidentally, the 19th Amendment was ratified on her 100th birthday.

From its heavily Quaker roots and its influx of Methodism in the early 1800s, this region had grown to be a hotbed of abolitionist activity, along with which grew suffragism. While the cause of women's suffrage would not tear the community apart, as did abolitionism with its deep hatred based on race, those who promoted suffrage were treated to an almost equal hatred.

"What? A woman vote?" was the standard "know-nothing" cry.

In the decades after the Civil War, the suffrage movement began to gain force and by 1900, women and men alike were joined in the cause.

Just as in the 1850s and early 1860s before the Civil War, when famous Abolitionist speakers such as Frederick Douglass came to Fort Edward to speak, now the Greater Glens Falls area saw famous Suffragists come. In late October 1900, Anthony and Senator Chauncey Depew spoke at a large suffrage meeting in Glens Falls.

The crowd was enormous, enthusiastic, and ready for change, charged by the then 78-year-old Anthony.

But why did it take so long for the movement to gather greater steam in this area, and elsewhere? A very deep resistance, of course. But another "problem" was the distraction of some success: women from the Civil War onward were achieving greater freedoms and greater opportunities to be outside the home.

In the 1870s, women gained the right to own property in the state and they began to go to work in new textile factories. Then inventions such as the typewriter and the telephone opened careers for "secretaries" and "operators," among others. Jobs became the "thin edge of the wedge!"

Also, from the late 1860s, the pre-Civil War reading and sewing clubs, and church circles would multiply by the first decades of the 20th century into organizations such as the Eastern Star, Catholic Daughters, Hadassah, the Hospital Guild, the DAR, the Women's Christian Temperance Union (which had strong links to the suffrage movement), the Women's Civic Club – and on and on!

Then, too, from the renewed fight for women's suffrage in the early 20th century new organizations emerged, representing competing philosophies on how to win the vote.

While a branch of the National American Woman Suffrage Association (NAWSA) existed in the Glens Falls area, other groups, such as the Political Equality Club emerged. The chapters of Warren and Washington Counties of NAWSA had their own newspapers, and the Hudson Falls and Fort Edward members were absolute firebrands.

In March 1917, the "Hudson Falls Political Equality Club" ran a "suffrage school" and 1,049 women enrolled.

In Glens Falls, the names of prominent women who had done so much to found or build women's organizations can be found in the suffrage movement: Eva Austin Judkins[xxvii] (the first woman President of the Glens Falls Board of Education), Helena Whitney, Estelle Palmer, and Josephine Demarest, all founders of the Glens Falls Chapter of the Red Cross – and so many more that I beg forgiveness for the names not presented.

Interestingly, though Glens Falls had a tremendous number of women and men supporting suffrage, Warren County as a whole was less supportive. In the state vote on suffrage in November 1917, Glens Falls voted "yes," but the proposition as a whole in Warren County went down by 19 votes.

In neighboring Washington County, it passed overwhelmingly. It also passed statewide and the women of this area went on to fight for the victorious passage of the 19th Amendment in August 1920.

In future columns, I'll share more stories of local suffragists, as well as other women who contributed to the history of our area. Please share your memories with me.

Happy 75th!

"OVER MY SHOULDER" COLUMN FOR MARCH 27, 1995
Changes, they're a'comin'

C hange is inevitable for every generation, but few people in history have known the kind of radical change experienced by those who knew life as it was in the period from the mid-1880s to mid-1920s.

I was struck by this as I spoke with my cousin Cornelia Mahar, as she related how she and her sister, Mary, would drive to school from the family farm, just south of Cambridge, New York, in the mid-teens of this century. The girls "drove" in a horse drawn buggy. Mary, two and a half years older, did the driving, Cornelia said. Mary loved horses. Their father, Michael Mahar, had purchased a pacer named "Mabel" for them to use, when it was time for the girls to attend the upper grades in the Village of Cambridge.

They drove up the Owlkill Road to avoid what is now Route 22 with its motorized vehicles that could whiz by at speeds of thirty miles an hour. "Drove," by the way, is the correct term. You drove a carriage or other horse drawn vehicle. When autos came in, the term was kept, as were "dashboard" and "brake."

Along the way, they picked up a friend, Pearl Austin, who would complete the approximately five-mile journey into the Village of Cambridge. It took about one hour. Cornelia said that at lunch they'd eat then go to feed Mabel. Their other school pals would join them, as they got a kick feeding the horse.

In the winter, the girls stayed right in the Village of Cambridge with their Grandfather Mahar, who had moved into town from his farm nearby. Certainly, a difference between Grandfather Mahar's house on Washington Street and their own home was electricity. Like most villages of any size, Cambridge electrified fairly early on. However, Cornelia said that rural electrification for her part of Washington County did not come until 1926 or `27 and her father was among the first to sign up for it. It cost $5.00 a month, not including the cost of wiring your home!

But that was Mike Mahar. He had had telephone service installed around 1908 by the Granville Telephone Company. Cornelia remembers as a small child her father lifting her to speak into the hand-cranked wall phone to her aunt who worked nearby. There were seven or eight customers on the party line. For those of you unfamiliar with a party line, steel yourselves: you shared the line with other customers, each with his or her own number of rings. And, yes, eavesdropping, although strictly prohibited, was not uncommon.

The Mahars purchased their first car in nearby Bennington, Vermont around 1916 or 1917, a Maxwell, "a step above a Ford," Cornelia said. The salesman drove the car over to the Mahars, gave him a few tips on running it, and then Mr. Mahar drove the salesman to North Hoosick, where he got the trolley back to Bennington. Mike Mahar drove home alone!

By the time Cornelia Mahar attended her high school graduation at Hubbard Hall in Cambridge, a new age had begun. The countryside was being connected by telephone, the horse and buggy were being replaced by the car and electricity was at hand to power that new communicator, radio. And, in 1920, women throughout the United States began to vote. The roles of women were changing. Cornelia trained to be a teacher, certainly a job common to women in the nineteenth century, but ultimately, she became a school superintendent in Ballston Spa, something radically different from the previous century.

So many changes have occurred in Cornelia Mahar's lifetime. Insulin, penicillin, and the polio vaccine were discovered. Two of the world's worst wars, World Wars I and II, occurred. People landed on the moon. The countryside in which she grew up and the schools in which she taught are not only being served now by television but also by personal computers, which are being linked worldwide through the Internet. It's staggering.

But to me there is just one image which symbolizes this change the most: the image of two girls clippity clopping their way to school in a horse drawn vehicle in a time that is, really, only yesterday.

"OVER MY SHOULDER" COLUMN FOR APRIL 24,1995
Our Navy? Born in Whitehall?

How would you like to help solve a problem that involves the United States Navy and Benedict Arnold?
And Whitehall, New York?
I know it's morning and you need coffee, but read on, please.

For years, Whitehall, New York, has claimed to be the birthplace of the American Navy. If you're coming to this information for the first time, it's a bit shocking. Whitehall? Not Boston or Philadelphia, but Whitehall? The place on East Bay of Lake Champlain, where the lake meets with the New York State Barge Canal? That Whitehall? Indeed!

Many people have pooh-poohed this idea for many reasons. One is that Whitehall is the only community not on the Atlantic Ocean to make this claim. Two major contenders for "birthplace of the American Navy" are Beverley and Marblehead, Massachusetts. Being on the ocean, to their way of thinking, strengthens their respective claims. Also, Beverley maintains that the ship "Hannah," commissioned as a U.S. ship by George Washington, sailed from its docks on Sept. 2, 1775.

However, in 1991, historian Allen Hovey asserted the Hannah was "outfitted, armed and commissioned" (but not "built") three days earlier in a town near Beverley and Marblehead. In other words, an area ship was converted to a war vessel on August 31, 1775.

I say: Big Deal. On May 14, 1775, four days after he had seized Fort Ticonderoga with Ethan Allen, Benedict Arnold (later, the notorious traitor) took command of a schooner captured from Loyalist Philip Skene, founder of Skenesborough. Arnold renamed it Liberty and, after a raid on Canada, took it to Skenesborough (now Whitehall) where he refitted the ship with more armaments and also built new ships, including a large one called the Enterprise. Arnold also sent a recruiter to the Boston area and by May 24, 1775, had captains and seamen to serve on the ships! If that's not creating a navy, what is?

Arnold would have captured Canada at that point, had Congress allowed, but that wasn't to be. Instead, later that year he and General Sullivan led an invasion of Canada. Sadly, that failed, though not for want of bravery or leadership. Sullivan and Arnold made it back safely and by July 7, 1776, three days after the Revolution formally began, Arnold was at Crown Point, New York, telling his superiors, Generals Philip Schuyler and Horatio Gates, that the only way to keep the British out of northern New York was by a fleet on Lake Champlain.

Schuyler, Gates, George Washington and ultimately Congress authorized Arnold to build that fleet. According to my histories, until this time there was no United States Navy. Instead, each ship in use belonged to one of the individual states' navies. Arnold's navy set sail in mid-August and was soon engaging British frigates up and down Lake Champlain. By late October of 1776, Arnold brilliantly forced the cautious British General Carleton back to Canada. Arnold ultimately lost his fleet, either through direct hits or, in the end, by sinking the remainder to prevent its capture. But the British invasion was staved off until 1777, when the British would try again – only to lose at Saratoga. Arnold would be there, too.

My reading of history is that Whitehall rightfully is "The Birthplace of the American Navy." To me, the only question is whether the date of origin is May of 1775 or July of 1776.

So, let's review the problems surrounding Whitehall's claim, class. First: Whitehall is not on the ocean. Are we going to dignify that with a response? Second: there are competing towns with competing dates. My answer? Let's explore their historical claims and demolish'em! And here's a possible third: perhaps in the past no one wanted to admit that Benedict Arnold, the most infamous traitor in American history, could be the father of the U.S. Navy.

To that, my answer is: After 220 years, I think we could let a bygone be a bygone. Couldn't we?

Let me know what you think. Write me care of *The Post-Star*. Let's settle this once and for all. After all, it's the 220th anniversary of the American Navy being born at Whitehall.

Or, if you choose 1776, the 219th anniversary!

"PASSED TIMES" COLUMN; SPRING 1995 V. II, NO. 2; 1995
41 years ago, Storytown became a fantasy world

Many people who visit the "The Great Escape" today may not realize how it has changed since 1954 when Charles R. Wood started it as "Storytown, U.S.A." A generation of American children, and of American entertainment, has grown up and I thought we'd share some memories of those earlier Storytown days.

In 1954, Glen Lake was a sleepy little body of water with summer camps and some permanent homes. The Red Coach was then Alphonso's Restaurant and the Northway was six years away. Television, around since the late `forties, had just started to broadcast in color. Movies were still "big." Disneyland and the Mickey Mouse Club began a year later. Computers were a block long and didn't mean much to the average person.

Early Storytown was a fantasy world, originally based upon nursery rhymes and other childhood stories, and then expanded to include Ghost Town in 1957 and Jungle Land in 1960. In 1954, for 25 cents per child and 85 cents per adult, visitors could sail in Swan Boats and see the three pigs, Humpty Dumpty, the old woman who lived in a shoe (a magical boot-shaped house) and nineteen other storybook themes.

My wife, Sara, who worked at Storytown in 1961 and `62 and remembers it well, said the concept of fairy tales brought-to-life assumed that the kids visiting then knew their nursery rhymes. They did because they were taught them, both in school and at home. I don't think it's the same today.

Playing Bo-Peep was one of Sara's delights. Children would come up and see her little lamb and she'd say, "Oh! Can I tell you about my lamb?" and proceed to recite the nursery rhyme. Like legions of other kids employed there, she worked for ninety cents an hour, including care of the lamb and dealing with one major problem: the lamb's "waste by-products."

By the time Sara went to work in 1961, Ghost Town and Jungleland had expanded Storytown from ten to fifty-six acres. Behind all of these scenes, fashioning these wonderful creations, was the most talented artist, Robert Vorreyer. Bob took Mr. Wood's dreams and made them a living fantasy! You can't walk through the Great Escape today without experiencing Bob's talent.

While Jungleland had reproductions of a whole jungle scenario, with jungle plants and animals, Ghost Town was, to many, the hub! Here was a recreated mining town with a 241 foot "mine," the longest man-made tunnel in the east.

"Keeping the peace" was Sheriff Windy Bill McKay, whose decades at Storytown are legendary. The Dan McGrew Saloon with its can-can dancers and free stage shows attracted so many that by 1962 Storytown had to erect a 2,000-seat grandstand. That year, Storytown saw its two millionth visitor!

Like all the entertainers, my wife Sara also worked in the Dan McGrew Saloon. There were five shows a day and when the announcement for the show was made, entertainers from all over the park would race to Dan McGrew's, change into costume, and perform along with Bob Hungerford on player piano and Bonnie Morton on accordion.

With a Gay Nineties costume and extravagant make-up, Sara transformed herself from Bo-Peep into Diamond Lil. (At the end of one tiring day, she forgot to remove her make-up and went back to the sheep to play Bo-Peep looking like Mae West.) The show always ended with the "outlaws" shooting their guns and riding down the hill and Sheriff Windy Bill McKay gathering up the kids to help drive the outlaws out of town!

No Storytown memories would be complete without anecdotes about its creator, Charles R. Wood. Legendary for his work ethic, he could often be found out working on hands and knees among the plantings.

Once during a rare lull, the young man hired to give rides in an antique car decided to hot rod it around the lot. Mr. Wood looked up from his flowers and advised him to stop. The young man, absolutely unable to comprehend that his employer would be tending the flowers, advised the "gardener" what he could do. The next day, the car had a new driver.

When Mr. Wood arrived on the grounds, no one wanted to be caught slacking! So, when his car pulled up, a signal went from the parking lot attendant to the train engineer, who blasted his whistle. Within minutes, everyone knew to look sharp!

Things have changed and the Storytown of old is gone, along with its name. But its memories will live on as an endearing part of passed times.

"OVER MY SHOULDER" COLUMN FOR JUNE 19, 1995
The law with no teeth

In these amendment-crazy times, it may do well for our lawmakers to reflect upon two amendments to the Constitution, passed back to back and as different in effect as day and night. One is the 18th Amendment, passed in 1919 and the other, the 19th, passed in 1920.

The 19th Amendment, granting suffrage to women, I've already written about and will be again this August, on the 75th anniversary of its passage. What a perfect amendment! It righted a wrong and made our whole population a "part of the process."

The 18th Amendment, on the other hand, passed only a year before in 1919, was a loser from the word "go." The 18th was the glorious Amendment that brought us "Prohibition" – and bootlegging, speakeasies, and rum-running, all now portrayed as "romantic." However, they were serious problems, especially since they came to be largely controlled by the mob, which is still with us today.

In our area, Prohibition has a special meaning, for the first society solely dedicated to "temperance" was started in 1808 in the Town of Moreau by a physician, Dr. Billy J. Clark. While there were other societies that also included abstinence from alcohol as a goal, Clark's "Moreau and Northumberland Temperate Society" was solely dedicated to abstinence. Clark was responding to a nationwide problem of heavy drinking and drunkenness. Drinking had been commonplace in America since early colonial times. The Puritans, in fact, drank beer with breakfast. But in the early 19th century, drunkenness started to become rampant.

Clark's society was wise in its understanding of the fallibility of human nature and the desire of people to be given another chance. One pledged not to drink and if one did, then a fine was paid. The "fire and brimstone" kind of approach would come later.

Dr. Clark's society faded away, but was succeeded by others, who proudly acknowledged Clark's temperance society as their source, if not in fact, at least in spirit. (No pun intended.) Nationwide, an "American Temperance Society" was founded in 1826 and others followed, sweeping along with a new religious revival in the 1820s, `30s and `40s. But side by side with that, canals, railroads, and industrialization boomed, fed in part by new immigrant groups. While some headway seemed to be made against the tide of a public becoming saturated in hard cider, gin, rum, or whiskey, by the Civil War things were as bad again. In fact, the Village of Glens Falls had problem with the wee hour drunkenness of soldier-trainees.[xxviii] Hundreds of thousands of boys learned to drink in the Civil War and in the economic boom of the post-war era, towns, and cities grew at lightning speed. Saloons kept pace. While Glens Falls doubled in population in the 1870s, it added enough saloons to water most of northern New York.

The movement grew! A national "Prohibition Party" was formed in 1869, the

Woman's Christian Temperance Union in 1874, and the very political Anti-Saloon League (Carrie Nation with her hatchet) was established on a national scale in 1895. All favored total prohibition. So powerful in the Glens Falls area was the movement that the Warren County Prohibition Party fielded candidates for all offices. One unsuccessful candidate in 1891 was the renowned photographer Seneca Ray Stoddard, a member of the Billy J. Clark Division of the Sons of Temperance.

Having succeeded in getting many state and local restrictions on alcohol, after 1913 Prohibitionists fought for Constitutional change. The 18th Amendment was ratified in January 1919, but without teeth. The police chief of Glens Falls complained that saloons and hotel bars, along with their customers, openly flaunted it. In September 1919, Congress passed the Volstead Act, but this law was so poorly enforced that bootlegging and speakeasies virtually ran as openly as the old saloons, something I'll explore in another column.

In 1933, the 21st Amendment repealed Prohibition. The people's message: no matter how noble the goal, you can't fiddle with the Constitution if the majority doesn't really want it. Now new amendments are proposed to cover everything from balanced budgets to jaywalking. Perhaps it's time to take a breath and reread our history.

"PASSED TIMES" COLUMN; SUMMER 1995; VOL. II, NO. 3; 1995
Prospect Mountain's ups, downs

At 2,021 feet, Prospect Mountain, Lake George, may not be Mt. Everest, but climb it on foot and when you get to the top, you'll know you have lungs.

Until the 1870s climbing on foot was about the extent of human activity on Prospect Mountain.

Perhaps the famed Adirondack photographic artist Seneca Ray Stoddard had some influence over what happened next.

Stoddard, of Glens Falls, began taking shots of Lake George and Lake George Village from atop Prospect in the early 1870s. They sold like hotcakes.

Maybe Stoddard attracted extra attention to the mountain, maybe not, but in 1877 a Glens Falls physician, Dr. James Ferguson, purchased Prospect Mountain and built a hotel, The Mountain House, atop it. He also renamed Prospect Mountain "Mount Ferguson." (The audacity of these Glens Falls people!)

In 1880, a forest fire consumed the hotel and Ferguson sued a Lake George farmer, Frederic Hubbell, for negligence that caused the fire. The case, which went to the state's highest courts, was a *cause célèbre* (French for "hot stuff") in Warren County.

Dr. Ferguson lost, but rebuilt the Mountain House anyway. His son, Walter J., operated it for the next 15 years as a health resort (which then meant anything from getting serious medical attention to just sleeping all day).

In 1895, in steps another Glens Falls-ian, entrepreneur extraordinaire A. B. Colvin, publisher of *The Glens Falls Daily Times* (now a part of *The Post-Star*) and co-founder of the Glens Falls streetcar company (and friend of Seneca Ray Stoddard).

Colvin's Horicon Improvement Company built a 1.4-mile cable railway, "cog road," from Lake George to the summit of Prospect Mountain. ("Mount Ferguson" was retired.) It cost $150,000. The company also improved the hotel to the tune of $200,000. Extraordinary money in those days.

The cog road was the longest (7,392 ft. long) and steepest (about a 24 degree incline) at the time and for 50 cents you could take a round trip and for another $3.00 spend the night. The ride must have been fearsome!

In 1902, Colvin sold the railroad back to the Otis Engineering and Construction Company which had patented and built it. Otis operated it for a year and gave it up, either causing the hotel venture to fail or ceasing because the hotel had failed. At any rate, in 1903, it seems the whole operation ceased, and the site abandoned.

In 1917, the tracks were torn up for the war effort and by 1919 E. A. Knight's guidebook mentions all activity on Prospect as antiquity, just a sentimental note in the history of tourism.

But it was a lull, not an ending.

In 1925, philanthropist George Foster Peabody purchased the railway bed and the summit, turning the property over to the State. While Dr. Ferguson's old carriage road and various hiking trails allowed some visitation to the state fire tower erected at the summit, other people had grander ideas.

Influenced by the motor road cut up to Whiteface Summit in 1929, local groups began to agitate for the same for Prospect. From 1934 on, Warren County petitioned the state for money to construct the road. In 1953, State Senator Nathan Proller put a bill before the legislature requesting $2 million for a "Prospect Mountain Parkway." It failed, but the next year a similar bill was signed by Governor Dewey – authorizing $3 million. (Remember those days of money?)

The struggle wasn't over. Groundbreaking for the 5.6-mile Prospect Mountain Road would be twelve years away, April 14, 1966, and three more before completion.

On June 13, 1969, before over a thousand people, Robert Flacke presided over the dedication of the highway to the nation's war veterans.

[*The Post-Star* of June 14, 1969 lists several dozen "distinguished guests" among whom were many of the earliest advocates, including Arthur S. Knight, retired publisher of the *Lake George Mirror*, and former Senator Nathan Proller. Regrettably there isn't the space to list everyone.]

At last, the dream of over three decades had been realized and the "Prospect Mountain State Highway" was born. In 1974, the highway's name was officially changed to "Prospect Mountain Veterans Memorial Highway" – pathway to Prospect's summit and a view that has intoxicated travelers and artists since humankind first climbed it.

"OVER MY SHOULDER" COLUMN FOR AUGUST 28, 1995
A history of little Canada

Joan Hess Mullen of Fort Edward has written a history about a segment of Fort Edward that would be easily read and appreciated by anyone living from Rouses Point, New York, south to Albany, whether you were in Glens Falls, Ticonderoga, or Saratoga. The reason is that the fifty page booklet is called *A Little History of Little Canada*[xxix] and about the French immigrants to Fort Edward in the 19th century and their settlement along Frank, King, Chestnut and Ridge Streets, forming the community called "Little Canada." There is not a community of any size in Northern New York State or northern New England that has not had a "Little Canada."

As Joan writes, "Between 1866 and 1875, 50,000 people left the Province of Quebec, Canada, and crossed the borders into the United States. By 1900, half the population of Quebec had emigrated." Every community from Rouses point south to Albany received these French-speaking settlers, most of whose descendants today speak only English and have so intermarried that "pure" bloodlines are rarely to be found. If the history of our country has proved anything it's that biology transcends any human made barrier, such as language or ethnic considerations.

It's hard to say what is the best part of this well-done history. I loved the section tracing the anglicizing of Canadian French names into the names that I grew up with. Some, for example, are fairly understandable. Therrien became Terrio. Trembley became Trombley. If you pronounce "Therrien" and "Trembley" with a proper French accent, it is easy to see how that could have occurred. Some make no sense to me whatsoever. Why would the easily pronounced "LaForest" have been shortened to LaFarr? Why did Bujold become Bishop? Or Trottier become Trackey?

What's obvious from the name changes is that English was already having a profound effect upon the French community. The surge of immigrants into the upper part of the village caused another school to be built: School Number Two on Seminary Street, later be named the O'Donnell School, named in honor of Principal Margaret O'Donnell, one of the many teachers of Irish descent who taught there when the school opened. Joan notes that the children were largely bilingual and "today psychologists might label this a cross cultural conflict." In those days the issue of what language to be spoken was simple: you spoke what the teachers spoke. As all of the teachers at School Number Two were of Irish descent and all spoke English, and as every teacher in the 19th century ruled with an iron fist and total authority, what child in his or her right mind was going to charge in and demand to speak French? Case closed.

Language also affected church going. The original church of choice for Fort

Edward's Little Canada was St. Paul's, in Hudson Falls, with its French speaking clergy. The faithful walked two and a half miles (one way!) to its services. As English gradually supplanted French in the home, those of Little Canada switched to St. Joseph's Parish of Fort Edward.

"A Little History of Little Canada" covers the businesses and occupations of everyone in and around "Little Canada" so that you come away with a picture of a multi-ethnic society at work in the northwest area of the village starting near the present intersection of McCrea St. and Broadway and working toward the Hudson River. A list of occupations and businesses, then, shows among the grocers on McCrea Street alone, you had French names such as Etu, LaFarr, Boucher, Benware, and Hebert mingled with the non-French names of Baker, Mayhew, Ford, Balcom and O'Sick, among others.

Genealogically, the history does a tremendous service by listing the original families of Little Canada and their children. If you're looking for anyone from Arsenault to Weir, you'll find it.

Moreover, the booklet is just plain fun to read! Congratulations to Joan Hess Mullen for writing this wonderful history for the benefit of the Restoration Fund of the Fort Edward Library. You can purchase a copy of *A Little History of Little Canada* by contacting the library.

Must run. As they say in French: *À bientôt!*

"OVER MY SHOULDER" COLUMN FOR SEPTEMBER 11, 1995
Worth saving

My fascination with Whitehall, New York, and in particular Skene Manor, began when I was fifteen and my family was moving from Fort Edward to Ticonderoga. On each trip to Ti, we'd pass through Whitehall, stopping at the Silver Diner, listening to the accent changing as we entered the Adirondack region. Each time we'd see Skene Manor, perched upon a high hill overlooking the village of Whitehall, looking as if Bavaria's Mad King Ludwig had escaped to America and built a small castle. I was enchanted.

About a year later I met a Whitehall girl and, during my visits to her, she introduced me to Skene Manor, operating then as a restaurant. I went from enchanted to enthralled. I was amazed to learn that it had been built as a summer home in 1875 by New York State Justice Joseph Potter, a Gothic "cabin in the pines." After several owners it was purchased in 1946 by Pauline and Clayton Shear, who converted the first floor to a restaurant (which is how it was used until 1990).

For years afterwards, when I had moved to New York City and was returning home periodically to Ticonderoga on the train, Skene Manor stood like a beacon as the train pulled into the Whitehall station, letting me know I had arrived back in "God's country." The Manor was a symbol of stability, as unshakable as the rock it was built of, and on.

Recently, however, I learned from Mary French of Whitehall some bad news about Skene Manor: it had fallen on hard times and its future was looking bleak. But, she said, there was good news. A group of citizens had created a not-for-profit organization, the Whitehall Skene Manor Preservation Association, initially known as "Save Our Skene" or "SOS" – a nickname that connotes a down-to-earth group with high hopes and a great sense of humor. The group is filled with people volunteering time, money, legal aid, and other services. They are dedicated.

They need to be. The group's interim President, JoAnn Ingalls, appraised me of the daunting task they've taken on: to purchase Skene Manor for $110,000, retire its back taxes and run the Manor as a not-for-profit institution. A large enough task if the Manor were in perfect condition, which it isn't. The Gothic-style manor's elaborate stone and woodwork need restoration costing far more than the purchase price. But this group has vision and right now they are concentrating on purchasing the building. They have until October 1st to raise the necessary $30,000 down payment.

Impossible? No, for as the August 16th *Post-Star* reported, the Whitehall Chamber of Commerce has donated a magnificently generous $10,000 for the down payment in hopes of encouraging donations for the remaining $20,000. SOS is appealing to citizens both in Whitehall and beyond to help them match the Chamber's gift two to one.

Now, if you're a *Post-Star* reader in North Creek or White Creek or Hadley Luzerne, for example, you might say, "Well, good for Whitehall. Looks like a great building, well worth saving. But what does it have to do with me?"

The answer is this: there's a "Skene Manor" in every one of our communities. It could be a historic building or park or pond or wooded area that needs to be saved for the good of the community. But like most communities, Whitehall is small and hasn't got all of the money needed. Let's face it: times are hard. However, if we all helped Whitehall, then one day, when our own community's "Skene Manor" needs help, we could turn to Whitehallers for help.

It's the "many hands make the work lighter" routine – hands reaching into a wallet, writing a check to help save not just "an old building" but a symbol of a proud and lovely village. Ten here, twenty there and it's done.

And why don't you visit Whitehall? Actually, see Skene Manor. Only, beware! You'll probably end up a raving fan of Skene Manor. Even a member of "Save Our Skene."

You know, you could do worse!

"OVER MY SHOULDER" COLUMN FOR SEPTEMBER 25, 1995
Remembering the Suffragists

My father's mother, Ann Green King Fitzpatrick, turned thirty-six three days after the passage of the Nineteenth Amendment, which granted suffrage to women on August 26, 1920. Born in 1884, she cast her first vote that year in the Boston area, where she'd moved after her marriage.

Grandma would continue to vote every year, whether in local or national elections, for the next sixty-four years. When she died in March of 1985 at age 100, I had this image of her stopping at the Pearly Gates to ask where to register to vote. When she was ninety, I had asked her what it was like to finally get to vote after all those years. Her reply was sharp, still filled with indignation at having been denied the right so long: to vote was wonderful! Of Irish descent, at a time when the Irish were taking over politically, she loved politics, like her father who had been a union organizer and mayor of Mechanicville, New York. When her first husband died, she moved back to Mechanicville to raise her son. She continued to exercise her political rights. Even before she remarried, she was running a boarding house, raising a son alone and working hard for her political party. Later, she used her connections to get my father a job as page in the State Assembly, among other things. She had the vote and she used it. I think she could have been another Bel Moskowitz.

The story of my father's mother is symbolic of the freedom that the Nineteenth Amendment brought to women. By sad contrast, my mother's biological mother, Nina Cassedy Kalbaugh, died the year the Nineteenth Amendment passed, 29 years old and never to know what it was to vote in a national election. To many today this is unimaginable, but there is a lesson offered by the history of my two grandmothers: women's rights have been won at a cost and we need to remember who led the fight and what price they paid to win.

I am offering these thoughts about my two grandmothers now, rather than last month during the 75th anniversary of the passage of the Nineteenth Amendment, because I wanted to draw your attention to an exhibition that opened just this past Saturday, September 23rd, at the Chapman Historical Museum. Entitled, "Failure is Impossible: The Women's Suffrage Movement in Glens Falls," the exhibition was curated by Susan Jackson Karp and will run until December 30th. It is accompanied by some fine programs and lectures, some of which you know have already occurred this last weekend.

So, here's what you need to plan for. On October 14-15 there'll be an overnight bus trip to Rochester and Seneca Falls to visit the homes of Suffragists Susan B. Anthony and Elizabeth Cady Stanton. That is a must! I have always cherished the thought that Susan B. Anthony spoke at a rally in Glens Falls on October 27, 1900. Anthony, then 70, must have relished it, for she had traveled through this area innumerable times from her Washington County home, including once in the mid-1850s when she was ejected from a Lake George restaurant for attempting to dine in the "men's section." By 1900, women in New York State were permitted by law to own property, were working in factories and offices and, in certain areas like Glens Falls, voting in school elections. Though she did not live to see national suffrage, which occurred on the hundredth anniversary of her birth, Anthony did see several states extend suffrage by the time of her death in 1906. Wouldn't it be appropriate to have a plaque made to honor her rally in Glens Falls?

There's more. Still got your calendar? On Saturday, October 21st at the Chapman, Dr. Bonnie S. Anderson will present a lecture "Joyous Greetings to Distant Lands: International Connections Among Early Women's Movements." Then on Saturday, October 28 there will be a symposium "The Women's Movement: Looking to the 21st Century" at ACC's Dearlove Hall.

Right now, visit the Chapman for more information and to see the new exhibition. Please be sure to bring children, both girls and boys. This is history for the whole family.

"PASSED TIMES" COLUMN; FALL 1995; VOL. II, NO. 4; 1995
Do you remember your canal history?

Remember studying the early history of New York's canal systems in school? Singing the Erie canal songs ("...fifteen miles on the Erie Canal..."). Hearing about DeWitt Clinton throwing a pail of Lake Erie water into New York Harbor to symbolize the linking of the Atlantic Ocean and the Great Lakes. (Maybe the only clean water ever thrown in New York Harbor!)

The canal's effect in this area is profound, whether you grew up near the present Barge Canal, along its forerunner the "Champlain Canal" or along the feeder canal.

"Canal talk" is a part of every canal kid's life from Whitehall to Waterford. You knew "towpath" meant the path alongside the canal where the mules had walked as they towed the canal boats. A "lock" lifted boats up or lowered them down. "Dredges" dredged out the canal bottoms. And tugboats tugged. Even when some canals became landfills, the language and music of canals remained a part of our history.

What great news, then, that the state plans to spend $146 million dollars to rejuvenate its historic 524-mile canal system! And preserve and restore landmark areas along the canal, certainly music to the ears of the Feeder Canal Alliance, which led the way in its outstanding job of restoring the Feeder canal connecting Glens Falls with the Barge Canal.

Do you remember your canal history? The Revolutionary War had sidelined early ideas for canals in New York, but by the late 1790s Governor George Clinton had people out in Whitehall surveying for a "big ditch." Nothing transpired. (One French surveyor named Brunel, an escapee from Napoleon, moved on to England where his son built the world's first iron steamship.)

No, it took another Governor Clinton – DeWitt – to convince people they needed canals to connect Lake Erie with the Hudson River. In 1817 work began on the Erie Canal and in 1823, two years before its completion, Clinton convinced taxpayers to build the Champlain Canal from Whitehall to Waterford. (Silver-tongued politician!)

With the canal's completion, tiny places like Fort Edward and Whitehall were suddenly only days from New York City. Hamlets like Glens Falls, with a dwindling population, its forests cut down and sawmills languishing, saw the canal as life-giving.

In 1832 a "feeder" canal (feeding Hudson River water from Glens Falls to the Champlain Canal) was enlarged for boat traffic and, sha-zam!, Adirondack lumber cut at Glens Falls sawmills and locally produced lime was shipped south and money was shipped back. By the mid-1850s, you could ship a ton of anything from Glens Falls to New York for about a half cent a mile.

But railroads were developing even as the canals were flourishing and making New York State rich. Right alongside the Champlain Canal, the Delaware and Hudson Canal Company put in a railroad in 1842. Cheaper to build, railroads were put in everywhere from Manhattan to Marcy. Even with expansion and a little rerouting in 1912, the Barge Canal couldn't keep up with the trains, which themselves were falling prey to the car. Coincidentally, 1928 was the last year of the trolley and of canal traffic in Glens Falls.

By the 1950s, both canals and trains began to see to trucks take away freight hauling, the thing still cheapest to do by water – but who wanted to maintain the waterways? Especially when the only thing that ever seemed to use the canals on a constant basis were "pesky" pleasure craft. By the 1970s, serious talk of abandoning the canal system was being "floated" around Albany. By 1980, things looked bleak.

So, what happened? Well, what has saved the canals are the things we gawked at as kids sitting along the quay wall (pronounced "key" wall) in Fort Edward: those "pesky" pleasure boats. [Coming in all sizes, but every one narrow enough to accommodate the narrow locks, some were rather short for single families, others long and luxurious, all brass and mahogany with many staterooms and even a chef on board.]

The future of canals and canal communities is looking brighter because someone in Albany recognized that pleasure craft are "boats," playing the canals and bringing money, as did canal boats in days gone by.

[Somebody was studying their history.]

"OVER MY SHOULDER" COLUMN FOR JANUARY 15, 1996
Why Aviation Road

Ever wonder why Aviation Road in Queensbury has the word `Aviation' in it?

The answer involves the Glens Falls Chamber of Commerce[xxx], Floyd Bennett, the WPA... But, that's getting ahead of the story.

To answer the question, Aviation Road derives its name from a former airfield in that vicinity. Don't know where it was? Keep reading.

As William H. Brown's wonderful "History of Warren County[xxxi]" relates, the first notion of a local airfield probably occurred to people in 1919 when an "unidentified barnstormer" circled his aircraft around the City of Glens Falls and then performed an impromptu landing on the fields of Capt. C. M. Brownell, on Miller Hill in Queensbury. A photo of that aircraft can be found at the Chapman Historical Museum.

Capt. Brownell's proved to be a natural site because of its flat surface and good wind conditions and within no time his field was being frequented by pilots such as Clarence Chamberlain, who once flew his bi-plane down Glen Street in Glens Falls low enough to cruise right between the buildings!

In 1920, during a search for two lost Navy balloonists, the U.S. Army "discovered" the field. Use increased every year. In 1928, fresh from their recent success of creating the Queensbury Hotel, the far-sighted Glens Falls Chamber of Commerce leased 80 acres of Brownell's land for an airfield. It was named "Floyd Bennett Field" in memory of Admiral Richard Byrd's North Pole pilot. Born in Warrensburg on Oct. 25, 1890, Bennett was the first pilot to fly over the North Pole. In 1926, Congressional Medal of Honor winner Bennett piloted a plane nonstop from Spitsbergen, Norway, to the North Pole and back with the explorer Richard E. Byrd as his navigator. Bennett died in Quebec, Apr. 25, 1928, after contracting pneumonia during a rescue mission in the Gulf of St. Lawrence.

In 1929, the field was expanded to over 105 acres, a beacon installed, and pilot Ralph Pease hired as Manager. "Pop" Pease, as he was called, did just about everything, including giving rides and lessons.

In 1936, in the middle of the Great Depression, the Chamber of Commerce purchased the land and donated it to the City of Glens Falls. With $90,000 of WPA money, the city constructed concrete east-west and north-south runways and a hangar. On May 19, 1938, Ralph Pease flew the first air mail flight to Albany and Floyd Bennett Field officially became the Glens Falls Airport. On August 1, 1941, Canadian Colonial Airways initiated commercial flights with two commuter planes out of New York City – new, large twin-engine planes with 21 seats.

Ironically, it was Pearl Harbor pushing the U.S. into World War II only four months later that hastened the end of the airport. Canadian Colonial Airways closed down flight operations shortly after Pearl Harbor. The Civil Aeronautics Authority proclaimed the need for a national defense airport in Warren County, but Floyd Bennett Field was not able to support those larger warplanes that needed far longer approaches.

So, the present Warren County Airport was built in 1942. At war's end, Canadian Colonial began to fly into the new airport. Floyd Bennett Field/Glens Falls Airport now served only private planes. In 1946, it closed forever. A friend of mine, Gwen Perceval of Glens Falls, remembers Ralph giving her flying lessons around 1945, but cannot remember what later became of him. Perhaps you know?

So, where was Floyd Bennett Field? In 1950, Queensbury's one-room school houses were replaced by a new elementary school, enlarged in 1953 with a high school and junior high – all built on the former airfield. Drive up Aviation Road now to the Queensbury School campus. You'll find the hangar of the Glens Falls Airport – now the school bus barn! And the north-south landing strip? That is the road that will take you from the hangar to the elementary school addition of 1969.

May the children the Queensbury School District explore new worlds of knowledge in the same spirit as the famed Floyd Bennett and those other local pioneers, such as Ralph Pease and the members of the Glens Falls Chamber of Commerce, who fostered aviation – on Aviation Road.[xxxii]

"OVER MY SHOULDER" COLUMN FOR FEBRUARY 12, 1996
Cossayuna's history goes back to the Iroquois

When our family moved to Cossayuna last year we were graciously welcomed by our neighbors, especially Mr. Pat Johnson, who lives very near.

Knowing I was interested in history, Pat handed me a history of Cossayuna published in 1957 by the Cossayuna Volunteer Fire Department. Well, did I know I was in trouble or what! That's a lot of history. Pat's own family history would fill a book neatly. But he cautioned me, reminding me that Alan Lant's family history in Cossayuna goes back nine generations!

So, yes, I am going to tell you about Cossayuna, but certainly not in one article. Historically, Cossayuna is a feast. So, let's just say that this article is just the appetizer and periodically I'll be coming back to you with the soup, entree, and dessert.

What complicates things is that Cossayuna is a lake shared by two townships, Greenwich and Argyle. Cossayuna is also the community of residents around the lake. And Cossayuna, specifically, is a hamlet that sits at the southern end of the lake. Try to fit that history in one article!

If you look on a map of Washington County, you'll see Cossayuna Lake situated about midway between the Village of Argyle on Route 40 and the Village of

Salem on Route 22. These directions are for the benefit of my friends living in the arctic reaches of Washington County around Putnam.

Cossayuna Lake is about 3 miles long. "Cossayuna" is a corruption of "Quabba-yuna," the Iroquois phrase for "Lake of Three Pines," referring to three tall pines that stood on Oaks Point on the west shore. This area was a favored summer residence for the Iroquois who stocked their larder with the lake's bounty of fish and the deer and game birds on its shores. Later they would become role models for the summer tourists who began to flock to Cossayuna from the late nineteenth century on.

The lake flows south into the Battenkill via Cossayuna Creek. Originally, Cossayuna was a part of Argyle, the land grant by King George II to Scot Highlanders in 1764. Several of the original patentees settled around Cossayuna: Alexander McNaughton, Duncan McArthur, and Cornelius and Peter McEachron, whose farms on the northern end of the lake gave it its first name, McEachron Lake. (Later it was called Cowan Lake and then Big Lake.) After the Revolution settlers poured in, people of essentially English, Scottish, Scotch-Irish, and Palatine German stock. Their descendants can be found throughout this area today, with English names such as Pratt, Scottish names such as Robertson and Palatine names such as Bain and Lant. Until recently "Lant" was still pronounced as "Lahnt" reflecting the pronunciation of its original spelling "Landt."

People settled on the Creek, damming it for power, and a community was born. They simply called the hamlet "Lake." (Pioneer frugality: why waste words?) The dams provided power lumber, woolen and grist mills; all are gone now. Sometimes the dams supplied something unexpected, like the one built by an Asa Carter in the late 18th century. Residents complained of an epidemic they attributed to the dam. The sheriff, acting like the area's first Encon officer, tore the dam down and the epidemic stopped. Unlike today, Asa got off without a fine.

A hamlet was defined by New York State law as a settlement with a church and several houses. The first church to serve the area was a Presbyterian Church over in South Argyle. But the first church in the hamlet of Cossayuna itself was the Lakeville Baptist Church. (Did "Lake" become "Lakeville" at some point?) An offshoot of the Bottskill Baptist Church in the Village of Greenwich, the Lakeville Baptist Church was started in 1835 and still proudly serves the community to this day. In another article, I'll come back to the history of the hamlet of Cossayuna.

By the 1860s the railroads were making northeastern New York and Western Vermont a tourist destination. Anyplace with water of some kind became a magnet – including "the Lake." Which by this time, they decided once and for all, to call "Cossayuna."

Next, I'll tell you about how the 1880s brought Cossayuna farmers a new "cash crop" – tourists.

"OVER MY SHOULDER" COLUMN FOR FEBRUARY 26, 1996
Pease earned his wings

Before I return to Cossayuna's history, I have to respond to the calls and letters I have received about Ralph "Pop" Pease.

Let me acknowledge the many people with whom I've spoken about Pease: Francis Poutre; Henry Cady; Ralph Thurston, who worked at GE with him; and Pease's great-nephew, Andrew Szostak of Hudson Falls. Andy and his English teacher, Helen Cackener, co-authored an article for *The Post-Star*, a copy of which Francis Poutre sent, with Pease's flying diploma and his obituary. Those and the phone calls supplied me with excellent information. Finally, I had a delightful conversation with Pop Pease's niece Leonora Harrington of Hudson Falls, who flew several times with her uncle. Thank you all!

Now, some history! Pop Pease was born on March 29, 1894 on Fourth Street in Hudson Falls. He was one of six children and, as Leonora Harrington said, times were tough. Pease would sell popcorn his mother had made, earning him the nickname of "Pop" or "Poppy."

I am assuming, though it has not been stated, that as a young man Pease worked as a mechanic. My assumption is based on the fact that, when he enlisted in the Army in March of 1918, he was 24 years old, already a grown man with a job. He was sent to Houston, Texas, for aviation, so he must have already had mechanical training. He was stationed in England to work on the JM4D airplane. But, he never flew one.

That he started to do in 1925 and he received his diploma from Inter-Cities Airways Service in 1927, after 10 hours of dual flight and 30 hours solo. His commercial license number was 394, a very low number.

That year that Lindbergh flew to Paris, 1927, was some year for Pease. He married Anna Sweet, took his license, and bought a WW I Jenny bi-plane, a wreck of a thing he repaired and used for barn-storming, and giving lessons at an airfield on Burgoyne Avenue in Kingsbury.

If you read my last article, you'll know that Pease was hired as the first manager of the newly created Floyd Bennett Field in Queensbury. He and his wife moved there and lived at the airfield. Both "Pout" Poutre and Ralph Cady shared their reminisces of learning to fly with Pease at that airfield. Poutre remembers his childhood in the 1920s and `30s, going up to Floyd Bennett Field and meeting Capt. Brownell, whose fields had become the airport site. Cady remembers a lesson where they flew upside through the hangar at the airfield!

And since I have covered Pop Pease's life at the Floyd Bennett Field/Glens Falls Airport, let's skip forward to 1940, when Pease became an Aviation Defense Instructor. An anonymous letter informs me that the U.S. Army Air Corps (I assume as represented by Pease) conducted pilot training at Pease's facility. The letter states that the trainees stayed at the Rialto Theater on Warren Street.

When war broke out, Pease received his Captain's commission in 1942. At age

48 he went to Burma where flew over "The Hump" carrying supplies to China. In terse language, Pease's diaries tell of dangerous, heroic duty.

Home from the war, Pop and Anna bought the airfield on Burgoyne and Pease created his own airport in 1945. Because of its proximity to settled areas, the airfield was never given an official FAA status and he sold the site in 1954 to the Hudson Falls Central School system. And shades of Floyd Bennett Field and the Queensbury School, the hangar Pop Pease built for his airport is today the school's bus garage!

Pease went to work at General Electric as a Maintenance Supervisor. He retired in 1959 at age 65, one year after he relinquished his flying license. Until his death in 1973, he lived in Hudson Falls.

There you have a very slim biography of a very full and wonderful life. More needs to be done on Pease's history and on aviation history in our area. I hope that his papers and diaries will one day end up in a local museum and that Pease will be honored in the Heritage Hall of Fame.

Certainly, he deserves this. For, Ralph "Pop" Pease has indeed earned his wings.

"OVER MY SHOULDER" COLUMN FOR MARCH 25, 1996
Cossayuna Lake and the Golden Age of Tourism

To those who have awaited this last installment of Cossayuna's history, a thank you for your patience and an explanation. Knowing that I needed to learn more about the area, I thought it better to be late and right, than on time and wrong. In addition to published histories, I am indebted to Pat Johnson and Don Bain of Cossayuna for their help and the use of their photos.

Following the Civil War, trains made travel far more common and tourism grew, it seemed, wherever there was water. As larger lakes such as Lake George built tourism, residents along smaller lakes saw no reason they shouldn't share in this new industry.

Hugh Lant and John A. Lasher were the first to do so on Cossayuna Lake, converting their large farmhouses into boarding houses around 1880. Lant, on the west side of the lake, and Lasher, at the northern end, both built boat houses. Robert Morrow created a boarding house on the east shore, which the 1957 history of Cossayuna states was "less pretentious" – a bit of editorializing, I'd say.

The heyday of the boarding house and hotel on Cossayuna had begun. Duane Hall of Hartford, NY, built the famed Oaks Hotel on Macklin Point in 1889. Its fame is such that, even though it burned in 1915, it is still spoken of today as if it were only recently gone. It had a dance hall (a "casino"), bowling alley, and its own steamboat, used primarily to ferry its customers to the eastern, Greenwich shore. Then, as now, Argyle was "dry," that is it prohibited the sale of alcohol. The Town of Greenwich, on the other hand, was quite "wet."

Fishing was a large tourist draw. Many fishing establishments and boarding houses popped up. Here is an very incomplete listing of what existed between 1880 and the early 1930s: the White House where the former McIntyre farm was on the north end; Sunnyside, Jay Hill's tavern and the Four Horned Ram on the east; and on the west the establishments of Charles Bain and Jack Manning. Manning's two sisters also ran a boarding house just across the road.

People came from many places, especially from Troy, taking the train into Fort Edward or Salem and being brought to Cossayuna by carriage. In the 1920s, Lant's, by now Kincaid's, had its own Packard motorcar to pick up visitors.

Pat Johnson's family was among those who converted their homes into a boarding house, The Cossayuna House. Pat mother's parents bought the house in 1876 and began to take in boarders in the early 1880s. An early photo Pat has shows a nice story and a half Greek Revival home built around the 1840s. Another shows its 1901 conversion to two full floors with five bedrooms upstairs, all with their own door. Everybody shared the outdoor privy.

The Cossayuna House accommodated about ten boarders, a small boarding house by Cossayuna standards according to Pat. During the fishing season, family members vacated their rooms, the men sleeping in the barn, the women in the parlor and Pat's grandmother in her own room on the first floor.

From about 1880 to the late 1920s, the larger establishments reigned. However, individually owned cottages began to appear around 1910. Then came the automobile which made them even easier to own and commute to. By the early 1940s, the boarding houses were fast on the wane, the Great Depression only hastening what had started in the 1920s.

As cottages flourished, restaurants did well. The White House was a good example of this, thriving even after World War II. By this time, however, summer cottages were starting to be replaced by permanent homes. The 1957 history records these last businesses of an age gone by: Kincaid's; Clifford Norman's, originally Lasher's; the White House; the Billiken camp; and, "the fish and bait resorts of George Macklin and Arthur LeMaire." Over the last 39 years, all have ceased to operate. Cossayuna's Age of Tourism was over.

However, while change is inevitable, there is a shining piece of good news about something that is a constant. The same sense of community that was forged over 200 years ago is still alive and well, among both descendants and newcomers, in this place called Cossayuna.

"OVER MY SHOULDER" COLUMN FOR MAY 6, 1996
Traveling through the 19th century with Seneca Ray Stoddard

Over the last months I've been working on an exhibition of Adirondack Tourism featuring Seneca Ray Stoddard that will be going up next fall at the Chapman Historical Museum.[xxxiii]
My travels with Mr. Stoddard through the 19th century Adirondacks have led me to realize how pitifully ignorant I am of "The Adirondacks." But I salve that

wound with the knowledge that to know "The Adirondacks" is to know an area
of some 8,000 square miles, if you figure with Stoddard that "The Adirondacks"
is about 80 miles wide and 100 miles from north to south, approximately the size
of Massachusetts. Someday, perhaps, I'll be as knowledgeable as my friend Bruce
Cole, who has been such a help to me.

You'll note I've written it "The Adirondacks." In the mid-19th century, "The
Adirondacks" meant just the High Peak area around Mount Marcy. The
Chateauguay area to the north, Cranberry Lake area to the northwest, southwest
into the Blue Mountain Lake area and Fulton Chain area and southeast into the
Lake George region – none of that was considered "The Adirondacks." The
establishment of the Adirondack Forest Preserve in 1885 and subsequent
creation of the Adirondack Park in 1892 expanded the territory. But even
Stoddard's last "Map of the Adirondacks," published in 1912, showed the
entirety of the Lake George region being left out of the official Adirondack Park
blue line, as well as all lands running up along Lake Champlain. Yes, even
Ticonderoga. Sheer heresy.

Today, the Adirondack Park embraces those areas. The common sense of
geography and geology prevailed. Still, regional jealousies exist, and each region
of the Adirondacks claims to be "the true Adirondacks." Stoddard knew them
all. He was born in 1843 in Saratoga County's Adirondack foothills in Wilton,
though some say in Moreau, and spent part of his teens in the 1850s in the upper
Adirondack foothills in Franklin County, just northeast of Malone in the
Chateauguay area. By the time he published his first Adirondack guide in 1874,
he knew every inch of the Adirondacks.

The Adirondacks of his youth were absolutely wild in every sense of the word.
Even decades after the rest of New York State had been settled in the 1820s and
`30s, most of the Adirondacks were unmapped and virtually unsettled. New
York's highest peak, Mt. Marcy, was only named in 1837. It was only until after
the Civil War that the state hired Verplanck Colvin to survey the Adirondacks,
publishing his first maps and surveys in the early 1870s. Stoddard, who knew
Colvin and was with Colvin on his 1876-78 survey, had been sketching out his
own maps for inclusion in his first guidebooks in 1873 and 1874.

Stoddard's first maps borrowed heavily from those of Dr. W.W. Ely and
Colvin, among others, but by 1879, when he was ready to publish his own full
"Map of the Adirondacks," Stoddard had used many independent sources,
including his own surveying. He had now become a full-fledged cartographer and
would receive as much praise for his maps as he did for his photography. His
"Map of the Adirondacks" was adopted by the state as a standard shortly
thereafter. He also published a series of maps of Lake Placid, Lake Champlain
and Lake George, among many others. His last effort at map making began in
1911 with an auto map. The man who tramped the Adirondacks before trains
ran there, now was promoting auto tours!

In photos (around 10,000), guidebooks, maps, oil paintings and pen and ink, as well as in his lecture series and conservation work, he was – and I defy anyone to disprove it – the person who defined "The Adirondacks" in the 19th and early 20th century. While others may be credited with starting what we call Adirondack Tourism, from the early 1870s to the early 20th century, Stoddard Ray Stoddard was "The Adirondacks."

Almost forgotten by the time of his death in 1917, ignored by major historians of the Adirondacks, S.R. Stoddard has now been rediscovered by those in the ivied halls in Cambridge, New Haven and Princeton, in the art galleries of New York, Boston and Washington.

Isn't it time that we, in "The Adirondacks," welcomed him home?

"OVER MY SHOULDER" COLUMN FOR JULY 21, 1996
Don't let a heritage disappear

NOTE: In another column in 1996, I had joined the fight to save the Norris House and we lost. There were other battles I helped win. This column sparked the creation of the Italian Heritage Committee of the Fort Edward Historical Association and the publication in 2001 of *Con Amore – The Italian History of Fort Edward.*xxxiv

*P*arlate Italiano?
Translation: Do you speak Italian?
I don't, but as a child in Fort Edward it was certainly not uncommon to hear it spoken, especially over by the "Y" around Taylor Street. Most words I knew have faded from me, except most foods and some choice swearwords I won't repeat.

The other day as I was sitting in the Old Fort House Museum talking with Andy and Louisa Esperti and Mary Smith an old concern re-emerged: what will happen to the history of the Italian community as time, intermarriage and assimilation erase the Italian culture's distinctive features in our community? Cielo! – Heavens! – What a thought! Well, I have a challenge for you, so read on!

It wasn't until I moved that realized how many people of Italian descent lived in Fort Edward. I went to school with kids with names like Arcuri, Aurelia, Catone, Cicero, DelSignore, Munoff, Quattrocchi, Zeno…

And Esperti. Andy and Louisa are actually rarities, as both are full blooded Italian. She is first generation, that is, born here of Italian parents from Italy. Her father, Antonio Gabriele, and mother, Maria Gabriele were from Arpino, Italy. Louisa said that as her mother's maiden name was the same as her married name, it caused it no end of problems. In Arpino, Gabriele was as common as Smith.

Andy is second generation, son of Andrew J. Esperti, Sr., and Angeline Sofia Esperti. Andy's Esperti grandparents came from Portafino, Italy, near Naples.

Now, here it gets really interesting, because Antonio and Concetta Besogano Sofia were from ElFurno, Sicily. Naples and Sicily – Napoli and Sicilia in Italian.

Why, you ask, is it interesting? Because the rivalries between those from the different parts of Italy crossed the ocean with these immigrants. Romans could look askance at Neapolitans. Neapolitans at Sicilians. And all three at those from Firenze – Florence, in the north. There were different accents and people looked different: black hair, brown hair, red hair, blond hair, blue eyes, brown eyes, and everything from pale to deeply rich olive-colored skin.

They came from all over. Such as Mary Casini Smith's father, Jerome, from Fabrizia and her mother, Mary Aurelia Casini from Naples. Thousands came 1890s and early 1900s to work on the railroad, the canal, or to build the Spier Falls dam. They bought homes and recreated their Italian neighborhoods, with the street festivals for the saints, and the arbors covered with grape vines. Like Mr. Sarchioto, to whom I delivered prescriptions for my father. I told Andy my first taste of wine was from Mr. Sarchioto. I was about 12, I think. Andy's eyes sparkled. "Did you have the red or the white?" The red, I answered. "Ah, that was good. But the white, ohhhh...."

Italian families added their culture to the one they found. Anita Catone's family had our family over for Thanksgiving one year. Homemade pasta by the yard, eggplant Parmesan and other succulent treats poured out of the kitchen. We ate ourselves silly. Then Mrs. Catone came out with the turkey! We sat stunned! We hadn't realized that all the other foods were simply the beginning courses!

Today the grape arbors are gone. Only a few people speak Italian, such as Frank Williams (whose family name was Guglielmini, meaning "belonging to William") or Frank Munoff. A heritage is disappearing. Shall we walk around saying, "Povere me" (Poor me)?

"Certamente non!" Here's a call to arms to those of Italian descent tracing their roots to families who first settled in Fort Edward. Send a card or letter with your name, address, and phone to me, in care of *The Post-Star*, if you would be interested in sharing your memories for a book. Then we'll get together with Andy, Louisa, Mary, and others and get those memories and family histories on paper!

Are you ready? "Bene! E mille grazie!" Which means, roughly, "Good! And a thousand thanks."

"OVER MY SHOULDER" COLUMN FOR AUGUST 4, 1996
Recalling Loyalist stories

A cynic once wrote that histories are written by the winners. Another way of looking at it may be to say that those who picked the "wrong team" are often ignored.

Our area's relationship to the history of modern day Canada is a case in point.

For a long time, I've been fascinated by those colonists who picked the "wrong team" in the American Revolution: those who sided with King George III. They called themselves "Loyalists." Rebellious colonists called them "Tories" (among the more printable things). As the revolution raged, most had their lands and homes seized by government edict and these Loyalists fled, many to Canada, especially Ontario, where they became a powerful force in that nation's history, even helping to shape its accent. George III created a special order for them, knighting them for their loyalty as "United Empire Loyalists."

We all know the role our region played in the Revolution. Not many of us know about the Loyalists from this area who fought "the Rebels" as Loyalists called the folks we call "Patriots." There were many. Their stories have been either lost to us, or if remembered, not told because, simply, they were the losers! The "winners" and their history is what have dominated American history textbooks since the peace treaty of 1783.

Sometimes the losers were even incorporated into the winner's story. This happened as early as 1777 with the story of Jane McCrea. Jane was a young woman engaged to a Loyalist named David Jones, serving in the army of the British General John Burgoyne. In July of 1777, David sent Native American scouts to fetch Jane at the home of a friend in Fort Edward and safely bring her to him. According to Eileen Hannay, the Education Coordinator at the Old Fort House Museum, where artifacts from Jane are to be found, another set of Burgoyne's scouts came upon Jane and her party and an argument broke out over who should have the honor of escorting her to the British lines. Jane was accidentally shot dead during the argument. For whatever reason, she was scalped and when her scalp was brought back into camp, poor David had a nervous breakdown.

And throughout the countryside all hell broke loose. At the beginning of the campaign, Burgoyne had announced he would spare the Rebels' farms and homes if they cooperated. If not, he said he would let loose the "Indians" and all the "devastation, famine and every concomitant horror" that these native peoples could think of. That horrified colonists. Jane's accidental death was proof to them that Burgoyne had no hold over the Indians. The Colonists used her death as propaganda, first describing Jane's death as a "murder" then as a "massacre," a word meant to describe the murder of a group of people. With every retelling, the way in which she died became more and more gory. Her death was a real factor in Burgoyne's defeat at Saratoga, as thousands of previously neutral colonists joined the battle against Burgoyne solely on the strength of the "Massacre of Jane McCrea." The irony is that she was a Loyalist.

David later fled to Ontario, Canada with the others from his family, who all became part of the founders of modern day Canada. David died unmarried.

The Jessup brothers, Edward and Ebenezer, have also been forgotten. At one point from their homes in and around today's Lake Luzerne, they owned about one-third of the Adirondacks. They fought alongside Burgoyne and after his defeat, fled to Canada, where they were later knighted as "United Empire Loyalists." Their lands here were seized and homes plundered and burned.

The Jessups later commanded their own troops of Loyalists during the Revolution and Major Ebenezer Jessup joined with a British Major [*Christopher*] Carleton in the infamous 1780 "Burning," about which I'll tell you more, along with other Loyalist stories, in next week's column.

Stay tuned!

"OVER MY SHOULDER" COLUMN FOR AUGUST 11, 1996
More Loyalist stories

L ast week's column talked about people in our area who fought FOR the King in the American Revolution. They called themselves "Loyalists," while those who fought against them called them "Tories."

Historian A.W. Holden wrote that the founding families of many local towns remained loyal to the King, including "the Bradshaw, Moss, Baker and High families of Kingsbury; the Bitleys, Sherwoods and Durkees of Fort Edward; and the Paynes, Parkes and McCreas" (the family of Jane McCrea) in what are now Moreau, Wilton, and Northumberland townships in Saratoga County.

By and large these Loyalists suffered for their choice, many fleeing to Canada and having their lands confiscated. How deeply Loyalist they were, coupled with their neighbors' good will, made all the difference in their lives.

Take the family of Daniel Jones. His brother, David, who had been engaged to Jane McCrea, served under Burgoyne and another brother in Jessup's battalion in Burgoyne's army. Daniel had been a founding settler of Kingsbury and then moved to Queensbury, where he married Abraham Wing's daughter, Deborah. After the Revolution began, the whole Jones family fled to Canada. Their property was seized. Daniel's home was burned in [*Major Christopher*] Carleton's raid in 1780 and Deborah died in childbirth in Montreal in 1782. After that, Daniel moved on to Brockville, Ontario, where the crown awarded him with lands for his service.

After the war, he returned in an attempt to regain his property but was literally driven away. His son came in 1830 but was also driven away. Later the son sued for compensation but lost on a legal technicality and returned empty-handed to Canada.

Not all Loyalists were forgotten. Whitehall remembers its Loyalist founder, Philip Skene, whose name lives on in the rescue squad and beautiful Skene Manor. Skene and his son Andrew fought, and surrendered, with Burgoyne at Saratoga. His lands were confiscated, and it is said he had his own house burned to keep it from being seized. He died of old age in England. My understanding is that his son went to Ontario, for I have met a Mr. David Skene-Melvin of Toronto, who is his descendant.

To my knowledge, the only home of any Loyalist left in the region is the Old

Fort House Museum. Patt Smyth would be among those forgotten Loyalists if it weren't for his beautiful home, framed in 1772 with timbers taken from abandoned Fort Edward. (You can actually see them when you visit the museum.) He was a big-wig in the newly formed Charlotte County and his home served as a courthouse. Like many Loyalists, he had started out on the Patriot side. By 1777 he had changed allegiance and was arrested by Benedict Arnold. He eventually settled with his family in Sorel, Ontario.

When the British Major Carleton swept through this area burning everything in 1780, curiously, Smyth's House survived. At first, I thought, the house was spared because it belonged to Patt Smyth, a Loyalist. But other Loyalist homes were burned in Carleton's raid, so that is not necessarily true. In fact, as it was owned by George Washington's surgeon, it should have been burned. It's a puzzle.

After the Old Fort House reopened this July, I wandered through Smyth's elegant home. It must have been among the best in the area, its broad hallway and large rooms providing not just for a courthouse, but a person of influence. I wondered what Smyth's lot would have been had the Revolution failed. Perhaps his home might still be a museum today and Smyth would be a hero. Instead, history has until recently remembered it more for its Revolutionary role as headquarters for the British General Burgoyne as well as the American Generals Schuyler, Gates and Arnold.

While it is that to me, too, it also stands as a poignant reminder of those who chose the other side and whose allegiance to a King helped build a nation called Canada.

"OVER MY SHOULDER" COLUMN FOR AUGUST 18, 1996
Fair history

Among the largest county fairs in the state is the Washington County Fair, which starts tomorrow. What we today call the Washington County Fair is the legitimate heir of several fairs, all of which I'm going to try to describe to you in this column, with thanks to JoAnn Booth of Easton and to the writings of the late Joan Patton, historian and *Post-Star* columnist.

The first county fair was a "Farmer's Holiday" held between 1822 and 1826 by the first county agricultural society. These were held annually until the society died of apathy in 1826.

In 1841, a second society formed and its first fair in Greenwich, rotating yearly among towns until 1860. The Civil War cancelled it in 1861 and 1862. Then it ran on a ten-year contract in Salem. The fair, already booming, boomed more. By 1872, it had 3,000 visitors.

In 1872, the fair, lured by the villages of Fort Edward and Sandy Hill donation of $2,500 and 25 acres of land, moved to the Town of Fort Edward, where today the Washington County Municipal Center and General Electric stand.

"The Washington County Fair" ran at that site until 1933. In its heyday, it attracted tens of thousands of visitors by rail and train. This was the first of three fairs that would be the ancestors of the present Washington County Fair.

The second, a direct and continuing ancestor of the present county fair, was the Cambridge Valley Fair. From 1883 to 1889, the Farmers and Mechanics Agricultural Society held a fair at Lake Lauderdale, north of Cambridge. That was succeeded by the Cambridge Valley Agricultural Society and Stockbreeders Association, which created the Cambridge Valley Fair in Cambridge in 1890. In its heyday, like the Washington County Fair, it attracted 30,000 to 40,000 people by wagon, train, and trolley car. Like the Fort Edward fair, it too had livestock and agricultural displays and prizes, domestic manufactures and all things related to the county's greatest industry, and it had its share of pure entertainment: horse, pony and dog races, circus acts, magic shows. There were "wild west shows," and top vaudeville acts such as the renowned African American "Alabama Troubadours," who appeared in 1903, and dirigible flights in 1907. It's "fair" to say both fairs had it all.

The heydays of both lasted through to the late Twenties. In the 1930s the car, movies, radio, and the Great Depression brought about a decrease in attendance. The Cambridge Valley Fair closed in 1941 and resumed in 1947 in Greenwich by the intersection of Routes 29 and 40.

The third fair that comes into the mix is the Washington County Junior Fair, organized in 1945 by youth-oriented organizations, such as the 4-H, FFA and juvenile grange. Until 1953, it was held in Fort Edward at the old Washington County Fairgrounds site. In 1954, it joined the Cambridge Valley Fair and in that same year the board of the Junior Fair raised $6,700 to purchase the stock and charter for the Cambridge Valley Agricultural Society. The Society still existed separately, its trustees conducting the entire fair.

In 1960, the present fair site on Route 29 in Easton was purchased, basic buildings and exhibiting sites established and the whole site was called "The Washington County Fairgrounds." Building was feverish. In 1962, the Junior Domestic Building went up, followed in 1963 by the Pony Racetrack, Pony pull area, and Horse Show Ring. From 1964 to `66 the milking parlor and three large cattle barns were erected. In 1967, the original 25 acres were expanded to 68 acres. In the years to follow, 25 more buildings and other improvements too numerous to list were made.

Until May 13, 1992, the whole thing was technically run as the "Washington County Junior Fair and the Cambridge Valley Fair." On that date, the two organizations merged into the "Washington County Fair, Inc."

See you at the tractor pull!

"OVER MY SHOULDER" COLUMN FOR SEPTEMBER 8, 1996
The rich history of the canal system

There is a human-made stretch of water that is possibly one of the least appreciated resources the State of New York owns. I refer of course to the New York State Canal system.

It was with mixed emotions that I read of the state's scaling back on the $145 million canal improvement program: sadness that it was scaled back, delight that it was spared at all. There's real economic potential in that stretch of watery history but, in my opinion, because it's not a highway or a super-computer it's getting short-changed.

Over the next couple of columns, I'd like to share some history and personal reminiscences about our canals, and some facts about what other areas, and nations, have done with their "channelized aqueous resources."

Grab a cup of coffee and we'll barge through a bit of canal history. The canal is a vertebra in the spine of New York State history. My provinciality shows when I think of "the canal," because to me it means the Barge Canal, stretching between Whitehall and Waterford. Originally, it began as the "Champlain Canal," connecting Lake Champlain at Whitehall to the Hudson at Fort Edward. Later it was extended to Waterford to link it to the Erie Canal.

According to an 1854 state report on the canals, in 1768 Provincial Governor Moore first suggested that a canal circumventing the Mohawk River's rapids would be advisable. But the concept of creating a whole trade route was first put forth as early as 1775 by Revolutionary War hero General Philip Schuyler. Schuyler, who owned a summer home in Schuylerville (then Saratoga) had already begun plans for a Hudson-to-Lake Champlain canal, but the Revolution sidetracked his dream.

After war's end, Governor George Clinton pushed the idea and, again according to that report, in 1791 surveys and estimates for canals connecting the Mohawk to Lake Ontario and the Hudson to Lake Champlain were used. The reports states that canals and locks were built at Little Falls and German Flats to the west, and at "Wood Creek," by which I am assuming at Whitehall. What happened to those I don't know.

Gouverneur Morris is credited with being the first to propose a canal to link the Hudson with Lake Erie. That was in 1800 and by 1808 engineer James Geddes was designing it. After planning for both the Champlain and the Erie Canals was halted by the War of 1812, Governor George Clinton's nephew, Governor DeWitt Clinton, passed legislation in 1817 to fund them. The Champlain opened in 1823. The Erie, started in 1820, opened in 1825. New York State boomed!

The Champlain Canal profoundly affected from Waterford to the Canadian border and deep into the Adirondacks, to North Creek, Schroon Lake, Hadley, and Luzerne. Certain towns along the path of the "canawl" boomed:

Schuylerville, Fort Edward, Sandy Hill and Whitehall. It also saved some, like Glens Falls, from extinction. By around 1820, the poor hamlet was drying up. Local forests had been decimated and lumber mills were failing. Then a branch was dug to connect Glens Falls to the Champlain Canal at Hudson Falls and suddenly lumber from the southeastern Adirondacks is being shipped down to Glens Falls via log drives on the Hudson, milled in Glens Falls and shipped to Manhattan via the canal. Boom times began.

Prior to the Canal, it was similar to today, with trade and wealth centered along the major roads. The post road from Troy to Whitehall (today's Route 40) is a good example. After the canal was built, commerce shifted westward to the canal. Industry grew along it. It was the Northway of its day. Towns along it generally boomed and it touched every life.

I'll end off here. But hold that thought, and that coffee, and meet me here next week for a completion of the history and some opinion about today's news concerning the canals.

"OVER MY SHOULDER" COLUMN FOR SEPTEMBER 15, 1996.
Canals deserve better

Last week I wrote about our canals and the revision to the state's canal revitalization plans. With the Champlain Canal's completion in 1823, the next three decades saw towns from Waterford to Rouses Point and west to the mid-Adirondacks boom.

Schroon Lake's logs went to Manhattan as lumber via Glens Falls sawmills and the Feeder Canal. Crown Point's iron ore went to Troy to make Civil War cannons. Glens Falls shipped lime, Fort Edward stoneware, Sandy Hill lumber. Farms throughout the area sent vegetables, wool, farm animals, dairy and other products south. Trappers sent furs and hides.

Towns like Whitehall became rich inland ports, bringing back fine finished products on canal boats to fill elegant homes built by rich merchants. Today in Waterford, Mechanicville, Schuylerville, Fort Miller, Fort Edward, Hudson Falls, Fort Ann, and Whitehall you can see vestiges of pre-Civil War canal wealth and power: beautiful Greek Revival and Italianate homes, brick factory buildings, and lovely storefronts with cast iron decorative moldings.

Fort Edward demonstrates the canal's importance to the state. Where lower Broadway crosses over Little Wood Creek, there is an aqueduct that carried the canal itself OVER Wood Creek, an expensive engineering feat and the only one remaining from the Champlain Canal, according to historian Paul McCarty.[xxxv]

Even after the railroads post-Civil War rise to power, you'll see on a late 19th century map of Fort Edward feeder canals connecting the major factories with the main canal, prompted, I'm sure, by the state's removing all tolls in 1882. By then the canal had paid for its initial construction and all subsequent expansions! From Fort Edward the Hilfingers shipped their pottery on the canal and other manufacturers shipped lumber, paper, and other products. And people came to Fort Edward on the canal. Many Irish names in the phone book trace their ancestry to canal people.

In 1903, at an eventual cost of 107 million dollars (equal to a half billion today), the whole state canal system was expanded and rerouted. It was called "The Barge Canal," because it was decided to widen it enough for barges, but not for sea going ships. The Champlain Division was opened in 1917. Wider, deeper, and with mechanized locks, the canal allowed more freight to be hauled more swiftly and cheaply. Huge barges hauled grain, lumber, and coal, then fuel oil. And, importantly, pleasure traffic grew.

I grew up with the canal. As a child in Fort Edward, I sat on the "key wall" – the quay wall – at Fort Edward's yacht basin and drooled over the yachts, some sleek and narrow boats, some huge floating hotels with galleys, suites, telephones, and TV. Across the river Socony barges offloaded oil at the Mobil tank farm on Roger's Island. Today, the tank farm is gone. But the pleasure craft are larger and more numerous.

The transfer of the 524-mile-long Barge Canal system to the Thruway Authority in the 1980s saved it, but now I'm not sure for what. The 15-year, $145 million canal revitalization plan proposed in 1994 has been decimated, and according to the Thruway Authority's nine-page release, only $32.3 million will be spent over five years to improve harbors, service ports and locks, and to create a trail system along the Erie Division.

It's less – we spend more on pothole repairs in this state than this project does on canals. It's far less for us: I found only ONE reference to our Champlain Division: funding for Whitehall's harbor in the year 2001. Great! But where are the other projects? And no trail system for here?

In England, government and private groups similar to our own Feeder Canal Alliance have rejuvenated canals that now have pleasure craft pumping millions into the economy.

Why not here? Why can't we do the same for our canals, the backbone of our state's history?

Can anybody tell me?

"OVER MY SHOULDER" COLUMN FOR NOVEMBER 10, 1996
'Old days' not exactly golden for schools

Since the beginning of the Republic people have carped about the education of children.

Recently I've read some wondrous twaddle about some new initiatives that would, in some ways, return us to those halcyon times of "education in the old days," in this case the "old days" being those in the times from the 1820s to the 1870s. The authors of the new initiatives look back fondly to the days when children sat clustered around the schoolhouse woodstove with their McGuffey's reader, soaking up English, History, Greek, Latin, Mathematics, Science, and the rules of civilized behavior from one omniscient teacher. The children helped teach each other and all grew up to be community leaders.

This is a vision spawned by too many viewings of the movie version of "Little Women." The reality of that time was that even by the late 1830s the majority of people had identified the educational system for what it was: pitiful. Teaching children by a hodgepodge system of private schools and small public schools, the latter at the mercy of the local population, had left whole segments of society uneducated, literally untouched by schools or any means of learning even the fundamentals of reading and writing.

Local school districts controlled public schools' funding and curriculum and sought to get the most for least. Teachers, hired at the lowest possible salary, taught a few subjects to the eldest children who in turn taught the younger – trickle down education for those few who made it to school. Many kids on farms, in factories and on canal boats never saw a book – anywhere. Oh, and those attending school learned fewer subjects than I mentioned before.

In 1849 New York State passed public education laws, opposed almost to the point of street battles. In 1867 public education was made available for all children and radical change occurred. According to "A Short History of New York State": "from 1869 to 1917 public school enrollment increased from 998,664 to 1,626,051, the number of public school teachers from 17,140 to 51,036, and annual expenditures for public schools from $11,312,325 to $76,408,430."

Our current system of kindergarten through high school emerged and matured in this period, replacing the previous one that had existed since colonial times. The old system had broken down and a new one had taken its place. The state's role grew, as it mandated laws regarding who had to go to school (everyone) and until what age, and laying out rules governing school curriculum, teachers' accreditation, building design, and other issues. It was a huge change.

But it wasn't a total change, for it continued one fundamental aspect right out of the 1700s: how the schools were funded – by local property taxes. From colonial times to the late 1800's, a land tax was one of the few sources of revenue for government, because real wealth was in land. Land taxes were the domain of local governments. The state reasoned that, if its mandates were fulfilled, then let the local governments provide the school funding as they had since the 1700s. While in our century state funding through bond acts and yearly school aid has grown, it is still local property taxes that are the basis for school funding.

The problem is, in my opinion, that this legacy from the 1700s doesn't work anymore. Property taxes then were on the primary source of wealth in America, land. Today, wealth is different: you can have millions in stocks and bonds and not own an acre. Conversely, you can own huge tracts of land and be "land poor." Look at farmers.

Today, state government functions as it did a century ago, mandating changes to local schools, usually with no accompanying funds – causing property taxes to skyrocket and causing serious local financial problems. Viewed historically, while education is in the computer age, funding it is still in the 1700s.

Everything old isn't necessarily good.

"OVER MY SHOULDER" COLUMN FOR NOVEMBER 24, 1996
Methodism founder's ties to area

NOTE: In this column, focusing on Philip Embury, Founder of Methodism in the United States, I did not know at the time of writing how his story would impact modern day Canada.

The other day, a friend of mine showed me two engravings that showed me that there is a never-ending supply of surprises in local history – and that local history can sometimes be international history.

The first engraving was of a drawing by a G. G. Saxe done somewhere in the late 1830s. The image, which looks for all the world like a print by the English artist William Henry Bartlett, shows a graveyard and a house. This information is also on the engraving: "Grave of Philip Embury, Ash Grove, New York. Engraved expressly for the Ladies' Repository." The second print, published in 1888, showed the same site, but also had additional images incorporated in it, including a portrait of Embury and his cousin.

The second engraving was confusing to me, because it identified Embury as being "the founder of Methodism." I thought John Wesley was the founder of Methodism. Secondly, if Embury had been at "Ash Grove," that meant he lived in Washington County. The Founder of Methodism was buried in Washington County, New York?

I made a dash for several books, including the 1878 history of Washington County and *From Circuit Rider to Episcopacy*, William Larowe's 1970 history on the Troy Conference of the Methodist Church. Philip Embury was indeed the founder of Methodism – in America. Let me tell you his story and his connection to our area.

Embury was born in Ireland around 1728 and was converted by John Wesley's preaching, which was a powerful oratory that had tremendous appeal to working people in the British Isles, especially in Ireland. Embury immigrated to America in 1760, settling in New York City. There his cousin, Barbara Heck, who is called "the mother of American Methodism," encouraged Philip to preach and he began doing so in 1766. He organized the first Methodist Church in America in New York in a shop designed for rigging sails. In 1768 he built Wesley Chapel. The first of thousands of Methodist "societies," as they were called then, and churches established outside of England had their beginning with Philip Embury's New York society.

Now, how did he come to be in Washington County? Well, around 1770 Embury, his cousin Barbara Heck, and some friends had moved to the Camden Valley in the Town of Salem in southern Washington County. He met an old friend named Thomas Ashton, who was also from Ireland. Ashton had settled a little hamlet that had been named Ash Grove, for the grove of ash trees that they found there and probably for Ashton's last name. That "Ash Grove" is today called Ashgrove, located in the Town of White Creek a couple of miles East of the Village of Cambridge.

Embury founded the second Methodist society in America in Ashgrove and for the next three years, he preached and set up other Wesleyan societies. Embury died at his Camden Valley farm in August of 1773 and was buried in the cemetery at Ashgrove. Somewhat later, I don't know when, his body was moved and reburied in the cemetery in Cambridge. I do not know what became of Barbara Heck. [See column below: *Reliving our local history.*]

Methodism itself spread rapidly and the Methodist Church became one of the 19th century's most powerful forces for social change, encouraging public education, the abolition of slavery, equal rights for women and labor unions, among other things.

Today, the Methodist Church claims about 10 million people in the United States and 38 million adherents worldwide. I find it fascinating that the person responsible for Methodism becoming an international religion had lived his last days in southern Washington County. As the Towns of Salem, White Creek and Cambridge and the Village of Cambridge review their rich histories, they can all lay a legitimate claim to the proud heritage of Philip Embury, Founder of Methodism in the United States.

"OVER MY SHOULDER" COLUMN FOR DECEMBER 1, 1996
Can you place a name?

It's impossible to write about the history of this region without becoming mesmerized by the place names. The fame of some, such as Ticonderoga or Saratoga, for example, and the obscurity of others. Why were some names chosen and why were some changed? And why did some names remain the same?

There are those names which baffle historians. The Town of Bolton on Lake George is a good example. No one knows exactly why the first settlers chose the name in 1799. Hague on Lake George is another. Nice sounding name, but why "Hague"? It had been called "Rochester" until 1808. And no one knows why it was called Rochester, either.

Sometimes we assume the wrong reason for a place's name. For example, Pumpkin Hook in Lower Washington County is not a place where they used to hook pumpkins. That name is a corruption of the Native American "Pompa nuck," the name of a Connecticut tribe of Native Americans who had settled there. Or consider Lake Luzerne. It was not named because someone thought the area was as lovely as Lucerne, Switzerland. It was named to honor the Chevalier de la Luzerne, a nobleman France had sent to aid the US during the Revolution. If we had lost the Revolution, that area would have probably been called "Jessupville" after the founding Jessup brothers who were Tories. As it was, the Jessups are not forgotten. There is still Jessups Landing.

That forgiving attitude, by the way, is prevalent in our place names. After the Revolution there was an understandable tendency to name things for American heroes, such as the way that what was originally Saratoga was renamed Schuylerville in honor of General Schuyler. There was also a tendency to ditch names associated with Tories and things British. Skenesborough, named for Tory Philip Skene, became Whitehall, although history books neglect to tell why "Whitehall" was chosen. As it is, Whitehallers have been naming so much else in honor of Skene that I guess he's been forgiven. The Colonial "Charlotte County," named after King George the Third's wife, was renamed "Washington County" and I don't need to explain THAT name.

However, many names remained the same after the Revolution. King George II lives on in Lake George. King George III and wife Charlotte are very much alive and well, thank you, in the neighboring towns of Kingsbury and Queensbury. George III's brother Edward survives in Fort Edward. Queen Anne lives on in Fort Ann, which was originally called "Westfield." The name "Fort Ann" was not adopted until many years after the Revolution! Crown Point took its name from a nearby British fort, as did Fort Miller.

The Napoleonic era had its effect upon our place names. The Town of Moreau was named for Marshal Moreau who found it expeditious for his health to spend some time away from France around 1806 and visited the town. I can't tell you why the townsfolk were so enamored of him to name the place for him, but maybe someone can. I think Dresden was named after that Napoleonic battle, but no history confirms my guess.

Sometimes a name change was made, but vigorously opposed by some of its residents. After Sandy Hill became Hudson Falls in 1910, an attorney named Ingallsbe was so infuriated that on his letterhead's address, beneath the words "Hudson Falls" he had inscribed "formerly Sandy Hill" and gave the date when it changed.

Native American names, usually corruptions of them, survive in "Schroon" Lake, Ticonderoga, Saratoga, and Horicon among others. They are enshrined in American history.

I'm almost out of room and have barely touched this topic. Let me know if you have any humorous or unusual stories surrounding the name of your town. The origins of some place names are a real puzzle.

For example, what about the origin of the name "Paradox Lake"? I just don't know. It's a "mystery" to me.

"OVER MY SHOULDER" COLUMN FOR DECEMBER 8, 1996
Reliving our local history

A couple of weeks ago I had written about Philip Embury, "the Founder of Methodism in America." The response has been quite incredible.
First a bit of background for those who did not see the column. Philip Embury had been born in Ireland and was later converted to Methodism by John Wesley's preaching in England. Embury arrived in New York City 1760 and, encouraged by his cousin, Barbara Heck, began to preach in 1766. He organized the first Methodist "class," that is the first society, outside of England in New York. Under him the first Methodist church building was constructed.

In 1770, Embury migrated with Heck to the Camden Valley in Washington County where he established the second Methodist society in the country at Ashgrove, in the Town of White Creek. Embury died in 1773, three years shy of the Revolution.

According to my histories, no physical church building was constructed at Ashgrove during Embury's lifetime.

Regarding the topic of a church, my first phone call on the article came from Kathy Bain, who is a member of the West Hebron United Methodist Church. Kathy told me that the first building that her church occupied was moved to West Hebron from Ashgrove! The first church edifice built at Ashgrove was completed in 1789, according to the 1878 History of Washington County.[xxxvi] That stood there until 1832, when it was physically moved to Sandgate, Vermont. At the time the county history was written, the church had been converted to a home. Do any of you know if the building is still standing? Write me care of *The Post-Star* and let me know.

A second church was built at Ashgrove, but burned in 1835 "by an insane man," according to the county history. At that point, it was decided to rebuild the church in the Village of Cambridge, and so a new Methodist Church was completed there in 1837. However, the county history relates that a "chapel" was built at Ashgrove. This was later moved to West Hebron in 1859, where the "first class of the Methodist Episcopal Church was organized" in that year. That building served as the church until 1874, when a new structure was built.

The old church still stands today as a grange hall, owned by West Hebron United Methodist Church. The church is now looking for funding to restore the grange hall and I wish them well in saving and restoring that historic building.

Another call came. This time from Harold Craig, who said that he was related to Barbara Heck[xxxvii] through his mother's family. Heck, who is called "the mother of American Methodism," had to flee to Canada, because she was a supporter of the Crown. Certainly, between Embury's death in 1773 and then the political division that subsequently resulted in the Revolution, the building of any church structure in Ashgrove would have stalled. Things were in chaos until well after the Revolution's end in 1783, really until the late 1780s.

Mr. Craig recommended my reading *Bench and Bar*, a history by Fort Edward Historian William Hill if I wanted some good information on Barbara Heck and he said that Heck was buried in Prescott, Ontario. That is a lovely village that sits on the Canadian side of the St. Lawrence River, not too far from Ogdensburg, New York.

A third call came. This from my friend Rhoda Henry Clearwater, who lives in the Embury Apartments in Saratoga Springs. Did I know, she wondered, from where her apartment building got its name? Yes, Philip Embury. The apartment complex was built by the Troy Conference of the United Methodist Church, which named it in Embury's honor.

I received other calls as well, including one from William Richards, and I thank everyone for their interest, for teaching me a bit more about local history, and for showing me that Philip Embury, the "Founder of Methodism in America," is certainly not forgotten.

"OVER MY SHOULDER" COLUMN FOR JANUARY 5, 1997
A place by any other name...

The paradox about Paradox Lake is solved.

Thanks go to William Lee Richards, Helen Cackener, and Bruce Cole, who, in that order, called in response to a previous column regarding place names. I mentioned Paradox Lake, a beautiful lake, by the way, if you've never seen it, that had a mysterious name, I thought.

The lake is well named, according to my sources. The reason it is called "Paradox Lake" is that the stream of water that flows from Paradox Lake into the Schroon River will flood in high water seasons, causing it to reverse itself and flow backwards into Paradox Lake!

Speaking of Schroon Lake, Bill mentioned to me that he thought the name derived from a Madame Scarron. I had attributed it to Iroquois origins. Bruce Cole said that Smith's 1885 *History of Essex County*[xxxviii] relates the legend that the lake was visited by the French in their expeditions. They named it "Scarron" in honor of the widow Scarron, "the celebrated Madame de Maintenon of the reign of Louis XIV." Smith said that there was also a claim that the name was of "Indian origin, signifying a child or daughter of the mountain."

After many scandalous affairs, Louis XIV, the Sun King of France, secretly married Madame de Maintenon in 1683. She consoled the Sun King through his military defeats and the deaths of most of his heirs. While the sensational aspects of the Madame de Maintenon story could make having her name associated with the lake appealing, it is nonetheless attributed to legend, as is the Indian origin of the word. Anybody in the Schroon Lake area want to help me here?

Many other people volunteered names that they thought I should include, including odd names for roads. Donna English of Easton, in southern Washington County, said there is a Fly Summit Road, just south of Willard

Mountain. This has nothing to do any insect problems down there. The "Fly" derives from a corruption of the Dutch "vlaie" (pronounced "Vly" or "Fly"), meaning a swampy area. (There will be an essay test on this later.)

Willard itself takes its name from a Mr. Willard, who was perched on that mountain in 1777 and watched General Burgoyne's troop movements through his spyglass. Willard helped with Burgoyne's defeat by keeping tabs on the General, who sent troops foraging through Easton. Still, Easton let bygones be bygones. They named Colonel Baume Road after one of Burgoyne's officers. A forgiving people those Eastonites.

Oh, and about Easton? Somebody asked where that name came from. It was the easternmost town in the original 1684 Saratoga Land Patent. (You are taking notes, right?)

Now, from insects in Easton, we move upcounty to deal with names relating to swine. In addition to his other information, Bruce Cole also told me that a Teddy Akary of Glens Falls had told him of a place named "Pig's Ear," that was located on Route 4 just south of its junction with Route 22 near Comstock. That's a new one on me! It's not listed on any map I have.

And speaking of pigs, have you ever heard of "Hogtown?" Like Pig's Ear, Hogtown was in the town of Fort Ann. The name survives in Hogtown Road. I had heard that the name derived from the early settlers raising hogs to kill off the snakes on the mountain. Bruce heard that it came from the long winter of 1816, during which the snows continued almost unabated right through the spring and summer. The settlers set their hogs free to forage for themselves, as there was no food for them.

As it was with the last column on names, there are too many names and too little space. We'll continue in a future column. But, I can't leave without a question: what is the truth behind the naming of Truthville, located in Granville?

There'll be an open-book test next month.

"OVER MY SHOULDER" COLUMN FOR JANUARY 12, 1997
Signs of history

Perhaps you saw the article in a recent issue of *The Post-Star* about the firm planning to build a new CVS pharmacy on what was Doyle's Garden Center at the southeast corner of Bay and Quaker Road. Happily, the firm has halted things until an archeological review can be done.

Many don't realize that Quaker Road is named for the Quakers who founded Queensbury in 1762 and many more are unaware that right next to what was Doyle's sits the original Quaker burial ground, containing, among others, the remains of Abraham Wing, considered to the Founding Father of both Queensbury and Glens Falls. It's a very healthy sign that the company is aware of the graveyard and will make provisions for it. Somewhere around where they will be digging was also the first Quaker Meeting House and school in

Queensbury. For the sake of our heritage, a warm thanks to that company.

I have to confess, though, that seeing the article on the graveyard has at last given me the opportunity to "discuss something" (that's polite talk for "nit-pick") about the signs you see as you drive into Queensbury. You know, the ones that say that the town was "settled in 1763."

What drives me crazy is that the signs don't say just "Founded in 1762."

You see, this year marks the 235th anniversary of Wing's Quaker group of families receiving the patent (a land grant) from George III. So, 1762 is the founding date. Sure, if you're nit-picking, the Quakers didn't come up the first year, but waited until 1763. According to Holden's history of Queensbury, Abraham Wing built his sawmill that year on the site of today's Finch Pruyn & Co. in Glens Falls.

But, getting back this issue of "settling" the land, you could get even more nit-picky and say that a certain Jeffrey Cowper was the first settler in what was officially the town in 1762. (The Queensbury land patent was issued in May of 1762.)

Cowper, a nephew of Lord Jeffrey Amherst, actually came before the Quakers. He was not even a part of the original petitioners for the patent. But, he was living here when it became a patent. His uncle, definitely a "big wig" in the days when wearing a big wig meant something, said the nephew could live in the blockhouse that stood on Halfway Brook, about where the Route 9 Price Chopper parking lot is today.

So, technically, the first settler of European descent living in the newly formed town of Queensbury was Cowper, who a few years later held the post of Assessor. Louis Hyde says in his history of Glens Falls[xxxix] that perhaps Cowper was "unsatisfactory" in his job, because a few years later his name disappears from the town records.

Hyde missed the point completely! Then, as now, the poor Assessor had what must be the crummiest job in town politics: the Assessor. Can't you see it? Jeffrey comes up to someone's door and shouts in, "Hey Caleb. Your new pigsty will up your tax assessment about 70 pence, old friend. Sorry about that," he says as he runs off, Caleb's dogs chasing him down the lane.

Well, while I'm harping on the topic of signs, it seems like the welcome signs could also say who founded Queensbury. I know, you don't want a history book, but just a little something, perhaps?

And another thing is, couldn't the City of Glens Falls tie in with that and indicate that the same Quaker people who founded Queensbury also founded Glens Falls?

There. I think I got that off my chest. Well, wait. Couldn't there be a sign on the northeast corner of Warren and Ridge Street to indicate the spot where Abraham Wing had his famous tavern that Ben Franklin and the Carroll Brothers stayed at?

I could think of more, but I think I'd better sign off before someone tries to sign me out.

"OVER MY SHOULDER" COLUMN FOR JANUARY 19, 1997
Happy Birthday K of C

Although I'm late in acknowledging it, nonetheless I want to wish a happy 100th anniversary to the Glens Falls Council 194 of the Knights of Columbus.

On December 13, 1896, the Glens Falls "K of C" was formed. Eighty-four men established the Glens Falls K of C. Of them, C. W. Minihan was elected as the Grand Knight, the organization's leader. It immediately became the center of the Roman Catholic community, swollen with the heavy influx of Irish immigration. In subsequent years, many other nationalities would be added.

The Knights performed an important social function. After the Civil War, social and religious fraternal organizations – "men's clubs" – blossomed. Often, membership was not allowed to Roman Catholics, either because of an organization's own restrictions or because the Roman Catholic Church had banned its members from joining a particular organization.

The Knights provided a place for Roman Catholic men to socialize and to have recreational activities, such as baseball and basketball. For the first 25 years, the K of C called the Wellington House, opposite City Park, its home. However, by the late teens, increasing enrollment demanded that a new permanent structure be created and on September 10, 1922 the cornerstone was laid for the first, permanent home of Council 194.

The building was an imposing Neo-Colonial red brick structure on 68 Warren Street, at the corner of Center Street. Today it is the headquarters for Genpak, Inc. The Warren Street site was chosen for its central location, which tells us a lot about Glens Falls in those days. It was near St. Mary's Church and school and was within walking distance for the majority of its members. In 1922, cars weren't as plentiful as today (a blessing in disguise?) and many members would either walk or take a trolley to the K of C.

The new facility had everything. There was a combination gymnasium and auditorium, that seated 1,200 and had a portable stage. This was much like the schools of that era. In addition to office and meeting space, there was a barber shop and lounge. There were even bowling lanes! Basketball tournaments became a major part of the K of C.

Now, I could recite dry facts and figures, but let the words of my friend Tom Wade, whose Center Street home is near to the old K of C building, give you the soul of the K of C: "It was a beacon for young children," he said. Tom, who grew up on Second Street, recalled semi-pro basketball leagues that played there. He'd go with his father to watch them, as well as the amateur and semi-pro fighters, such as "Sailor" Barron or "Honey Boy" Hughes.

Tom told me of the boys' basketball league that was to count among its participants so many of today's community leaders. He also said that, because of its size, the K of C gym was used many times for St. Mary's games. "That whole building would rock when Glens Falls High School and St. Mary's played," he said with a laugh. He recalled, too, the cooking schools and other kinds of classes for men and women. In short, "the beacon" was a family center.

So many things led to the end of the K of C being on Warren Street: the car, people moving to the new homes in the suburbs of Glens Falls. The change could be seen as early as 1962, when, after a disastrous fire, it was decided not to replace the bowling lanes. The building did not have the same level of use anymore. By 1979, it was being sold to Genpak.

But we must remember that the Knights are an organization, not a building. And a new home was built on Route 9 in Queensbury, where today the Glens Falls Council 194 of the Knights of Columbus looks forward to another one hundred years.

May they be joyous!

"OVER MY SHOULDER" COLUMN FOR FEBRUARY 23, 1997
History in walls of stone

The history of the important 19th century African American minister, George S. Brown, is a book waiting to be written.

I am indebted for today's column to Judge John Austin and to William LaRowe's book, *From Circuit Rider to Episcopacy.*[xl] George S. Brown was born July 25, 1801 in Newport, Rhode Island. In 1827, he came to the Town of Kingsbury as an entertainer, playing the clarinet, bagpipe, and other reed instruments. He also arrived as a drunk.

Brown stayed on the Kingsbury farm of Samuel Cole and was won over to the Baptist faith, and sobriety, by Rebecca Shay, Anne Guye, and other Baptists. He became a powerful preacher, as he turned his natural talents toward the ministry, drawing overflow crowds to his evangelistic services up on Vaughn Road. Now, at this time Methodists were an incredible force to reckoned with and were converting people by the tens of thousands. They were disliked, even loathed, by many for they reached to embrace society's poorest and most shunned.

Brown kept a journal which was in the possession of the George Webster family at the time LaRowe wrote his history in 1970. What has become of that journal I don't know. In it, Brown wrote that he met the evangelist Methodist minister William Ryder, who won Brown over to Methodism 1828. In 1829, Brown moved a few miles west to Sanford's Ridge in Queensbury to live and work on the farm of Gould Sanford, a Quaker. In his journal, Brown had related that he was the Superintendent of the Sabbath School at Sanford's Ridge.

He also had become a stone mason and built beautiful and durable stone walls in Chestnut Ridge and Harrisena that stand to this day. He built stone homes, as well. One, according to LaRowe, built at the corner of Geer and Hicks Road, had secret rooms to hide runaway slaves. And LaRowe states that Brown constructed stone markers, used by the Underground Railway to guide runaways to Canada.

Of course, as an African American, Brown's opposition to slavery would be understandable. But additionally, he had embraced a faith that openly espoused the abolition of slavery and he worked to maintain the Underground Railroad. Brown had become an activist. His next major move was to Liberia, the west African nation established in 1820 to "repatriate" freed American slaves to Africa. According to an article in a February 1886 issue of the *Glens Falls Messenger*, Brown first went to Liberia in 1836 to teach. He stayed two years, then returned to be ordained. He again went to Liberia, returning a second time to raise funds. He also married.

Brown's third and last trip was in 1841. He stayed two years. Tragically, during this time his wife died in Queensbury. He never remarried. Back in Queensbury, Brown lived on Daniel Wing's farm. His reputation as a stone mason had grown so that, around 1851, Abraham Wing II paid Brown to go to Michigan to build a stone wall around the entirety of Wing's daughter's new farm. (What a wedding present!) That wall stands today, a part of a museum on the National Register of Historic Places.

Brown died in April 23, 1886 on Third Street in Glens Falls. His burial was attended by a veritable who's who in Glens Falls, including the Rev. R. M. Little, a Methodist minister who was also a founder of the Glens Falls Insurance Company. Brown was laid to rest in the Gould Sanford lot of the Friends Cemetery.

Judge Austin points out that few if any of the walls Brown built in Kingsbury and Queensbury are accurately identified as being his. Work, Judge Austin said, should be done to identify and record them all.

I agree totally, for those walls, along with the homes, would provide marvelous monuments to an African American man who fought for those values most cherished by every human being: freedom and dignity.

"OVER MY SHOULDER" COLUMN FOR MARCH 2, 1997
Birth of a pinball wizard

When we were kids, Guido Del Signore's Broadway record shop in Fort Edward was our source of rock'n'roll. He'd sell us the newest 45 of Chuck Berry or Elvis and in our limited, childlike way, we'd think that was all Mr. Del Signore did.

We would learn later, to our intense astonishment, that from Northern New York State through to the Maine coast, Guido Del Signore was one of the kings of the jukebox vendors. In fact, jukeboxes were one of many coin operated machines Guido had taken up after he had started his first major career: pinball machines.

I've had the privilege of visiting with Guido recently, coming to know him again and to appreciate a man who is as much historian as pinball wizard. He was born in Fort Edward in January 1910, but his memories of 70 years ago are as vital as those of 20 years ago. Like every person who has "conquered age," Guido is incredibly active. Let me tell you a bit about him – and remember, what you will be reading is a fraction of his fascinating life.

He was one of four boys born to Italian immigrants. The Del Signores (in Italian, pronounced Del-seehn-yore-ay) had an ice cream parlor in Fort Edward. (I smiled when I heard this. Guido and I share a similar childhood of making sundaes and ice cream sodas, as I grew up in a drugstore with a soda fountain.) Their first was in the Harris Block, which they owned, on the corner of Broadway and East Street. It burned in 1928 and was replaced by a new building across the street.

His memories of his early life are phenomenal. He remembers vividly his mother taking him to the Empire Theater in Glens Falls to see the first run of a new movie called "Birth of Nation" in 1915. He also remembers his brush with death in 1917, when ice skating with his classmates on the Barge Canal, where nearby crews were sawing blocks of ice. He was on the end of "the whip" and fell in. He remained under for thirty minutes! His rescuers retrieved his "body," and thinking him dead, covered all of him with a blanket. When Dr. Silas Banker arrived, he diagnosed otherwise and had two strong men turn Guido over and pump the water from him. The astonished crowd watched as the little boy revived. Although Guido would experience severe equilibrium troubles thereafter, otherwise he was fine. Fate had other things waiting for this little boy.

Around 1924, Guido convinced his father to allow him to buy two "trade stimulators," small machines in which a customer put a penny and, with luck, got a free cigar.

They cost $8.50 apiece. Guido put them on the counter. In TWO DAYS they paid for themselves. Guido bought five more; the career began. Now the penny machines of that era were simple things by contrast with today. From the early 1930s on, true pinball machines and other complex play machines would be invented. In 1927, a family friend, a state trooper, convinced several stores throughout the Hudson Falls area to rent ten machines from Guido. By 1928, this high school boy had a territory that covered the Tri-counties.

He bought scales, strength-testers, punch-games, whatever a person could put a penny into. In 1928, a man whom his family had befriended gave Guido free use of his building on Canada Street in Lake George Village, where the post office is today. Guido said Lake George was "so boring" in 1928 that cars squashing bugs on Canada Street was the sole excitement. He called his first arcade "Playland" and it must have been the right thing at the right time, because by the late-1930s, Guido had 17 of them, stretching from Lake Placid to Kennebunkport!

Next week, the birth of pinball and the rise of the Del Signore fame.

"OVER MY SHOULDER" COLUMN FOR MARCH 9, 1997
Continued story of the king of coin machines

We continue our story of Guido Del Signore. In 1924, the 14-year-old Fort Edward native borrowed $17.00 from his father to buy his first two coin machines. In two days, the machines had paid for themselves. Guido bought five more and within four years had a business that included his first "Playland" arcade in Lake George Village and a territory that went into Vermont.

While in high school, Guido depended upon friends who drove to help him service his machines. He must have exasperated his teachers, who I'm sure never had a student writing English composition while operating an enormous business!

Ironically, his business saved his family. In 1928, fire destroyed the family-owned Harris Block and their store within it. The family would have been ruined, but for Guido's business. Sadly, Guido had to quit school, but he never looked back. Instead, he bought his own car, hired extra help, and began his expansion to the Maine coast.

It was the era of flappers, bootleg liquor, and Rudy Vallee. Guido tells a wonderful story of supplying a party of Dartmouth students with liquor he smuggled past the police in the hollow backs of his coin machines.

Just as Guido helped his own family, including a brother going to college, he inadvertently did the same in many New England towns during the Depression. Guido said, "I'd go into these mill towns, like Androscoggin, where the woolen mills had shut down and a thousand people were laid off. I'd go into a small grocery store and put a machine in. I'd say, `Try this.' Later, the family would tell me, `If it hadn't been for your machine, we couldn't have made it.' The machine paid the rent."

Don't speak badly of Franklin Delano Roosevelt to Guido. "I saw it. I saw the Depression and what it did." For Guido, Roosevelt saved the country.

Besides the Depression, the thirties also saw the invention of the pinball machine, which of course Guido bought and installed alongside the shuffle boards, punch cards, and dozens of other coin machines that filled his expanding, thriving territory. There's a wonderful 1933 photo of Guido and his Ford Roadster, showing this wording painted over the cover of the spare tire on the back: "Del Signore. Fort Edward, New York. Coin Machine Jobbers. Dial 5-5801."

And right up on the back seat are two slot machines. Guido said that "slots" were a way of life. He had "between 300 and 400 in New York and Vermont." Things were tough, and he even had "protection" for himself and his machines. By the early `forties, slots were on the way out, as stricter law enforcement made them too risky.

In the early thirties he bought an enormous barn in Rutland, which served as the center for his New England business. By the late 1930s he would have 18 Playlands in New York, Vermont; New Hampshire and Maine.

When World War II erupted, Guido promptly got rid of most of his businesses and went to enlist. "I should've waited," he said, referring to the fact that four separate times, Uncle Sam turned him down because of his equilibrium problem. Taking what little business he had left, Guido started up again.

"Jukeboxes, the ones that played those old 78s, had come in around 1936," Guido said. He bought them, too, reselling them to businesses, and to individuals who wanted a jukebox at home. From the mid-forties until retirement in 1969, Guido DelSignore, the pioneer of coin machine operators from Northern New York to the coast of Maine became "The King." His name was everywhere one saw a Wurlitzer jukebox or the Gottlieb or Bally pinball machines, the kind Tommy, the Who's "Pinball Wizard" plays.

And what has this king been doing in his retirement? Why, collecting and restoring old coin operated machines. What else?

Congratulations, happy birthday and happy collecting to Guido Del Signore!

"OVER MY SHOULDER" COLUMN FOR MARCH 30, 1997
A girl's life on the canal

Recently, I received some wonderful letters from Cora Archambault of Whitehall.

She began by writing, "There were many families on canal boats when I was a child," and I was hooked, reading the history of her life on a canal boat with her parents, two sisters and a brother during the first two decades of this century. Cora has given me permission to share her vibrant memories with you.

A bit of background. Cora Archambault was born in 1905 – presumably in Whitehall, although she did not say. Frankly, given the way the family traveled, it could have been anywhere from Montreal to New York City or from Whitehall to Buffalo! Cora's childhood would have taken place during most of the 1903-1917 construction of the present-day New York State Barge Canal, during which the whole state canal system was expanded and rerouted. So, actually, Cora began her canal career on the original Champlain Canal.

You have to imagine the boats: long, narrow, and not very deep as they would have been designed for shallow canals; room enough for a family of six to live (with galley, sleeping areas, etc.); and room for loads of lumber, iron ore, grain, whatever. Boats were drawn along the canals by teams of mules. Cora's mother would make a lunch onboard for the mule drivers and "wrap it in a newspaper. My father would toss it to the driver."

Canal life meant traveling! Listen to Cora: "We used to go to Three Rivers in Canada for a load of pulpwood and bring it to the paper mill in Ticonderoga." Or: "Besides coal, which we loaded in the coal chute at Whitehall for Canada, we went real often to Port Henry for iron ore. I remember how dirty and uninteresting the docks were there to us kids." Or: "We went to Northumberland for a load of ice once...It was like sleeping in an ice box." Or: "I remember the second time we went to Buffalo. This time for a load of grain," which turned out to be full of insects! Cora Archambault saw more of New York State as a child than the average adult ever will.

Travel brought reality abruptly into canal life: "One time...in Montreal, we were tied up below a big old waterfront warehouse that had a lot of knotholes in the siding...An excursion boat had something tragic happen with a great loss of life." The bodies were placed on tables in that adjacent warehouse and Cora's sister was found gaping at them through the knotholes.

Montreal sounded like a truly tough port. Cora said that her father had purchased a new boat. The family sailed to Montreal with the old boat filled with a load of sand and the new boat empty to take on a load of lumber. At Montreal, a lock gate broke, sweeping a large ship past their two boats and throwing a huge wake. "My mother worried about the old boat, so she sent my oldest sister to the bow to see if the boat was taking in water." It was sinking! Cora's mother "got us children onto the good boat" and went back for her new sewing machine. "I'll never know how she got that heavy machine up the stairs through the companionway and onto the other boat."

The drama did not end there. Cora's mother cut the new boat loose from the sinking old boat, which was tied to the dock. The new boat was floating free in the rushing water and her mother called "to several Frenchmen on the dock...to take a line, but they didn't respond." Her mother spoke again, this time "in French, which she spoke fluently...Still, none of them moved to help"! Fortunately, Cora's father arrived at just that moment. He jumped in the water and brought the boat to safety.

Next week: Cora's canal boat perspective of New York City!

"OVER MY SHOULDER" COLUMN FOR APRIL 6, 1997
More tales from a canal girl

Cora Archambault of Whitehall has been writing me of her family's life on a canal boat in the first two decades of the 20th century. As we ended last week's column, we were about to discover what New York City looked like to a young canal boat girl around the time of World War I.

Cora writes: "New York City certainly looked different at night, especially as seen from the top of the cabin of a canal boat out in the middle of a harbor." The children would beg to be allowed to stay up, no matter what the hour. If they arrived at day, "when we reached the harbor all was bedlam, with water traffic going in all directions. It was like Grand Central Station on water. Tug boats pushing scows, railroad cars on large flatboats being pushed, ferry boats and every other kind of boat you can think of going somewhere with whistles blowing and bells clanging. The noise was deafening. I expected to see boats crashing into one another, but they didn't."

However, if arriving at night, "the harbor was quiet, as most water traffic was tied up for the night. The whole New York skyline would be lit up with...lights flashing on and off. We especially liked the one with the hand pouring beer into a mug, then going off and flashing on again pouring the beer." She remembers "the little dog, with his head cocked on one side, listening to `his master's voice.'"

Life wasn't all business in New York: "When time permitted, my parents took us to Coney Island. That was a real treat for us kids. The amusement park with its rides, so much to see and so many people. I remember the man at the hot dog stand yelling through his horn, `Come and get your Coney Island chicken.' In fact, at Coney Island I ate my first hot dog."

They tied up at Pier 6, "within walking distance of the Battery Park where the Aquarium was located." The fish, the seals and sea horses were a fascination, as were the other sights, sounds, tastes and smells: "bums...eating raw hamburger sandwiches with slices of onion;" horse drawn wagons on the piers, doing all the work trucks would today; ice cream sandwiches sold for a nickel; "and, of course, there was always the organ grinder man with the little monkey."

Life on the water meant vigilance: "There was one summer when my four-year-old sister almost drowned." Cora was six and the family had taken a load of hay to Sorel, Quebec. The boat was tied to a large boom in the river and the family had to walk along ladders to get to shore. Cora writes that when her sister fell in, her mother "jumped in the water, although she couldn't swim...I remember clutching my mother's arm and holding it, so she wouldn't go down." The screaming of Cora's older sister awakened her father, who saved mother and child.

Schooling? "About the later part of April our parents would take us out of school as our father wanted us with him. We felt very smug and looked with pity at the other kids who had to stay in school while we were free. But come fall it was a different story as we returned to school in October. We didn't feel smug then, but dumb and stupid as we were so far behind in class subjects." She says it was no wonder so many canal children dropped out of school.

"But my sister and I were avid readers. We read everything we could get our hands on," including her brother's Horatio Alger novels.

I am so sorry to have end here. It's certainly obvious that Cora's education nurtured her wonderful writing skills that have provided us with an excellent history of a bygone era. Thank you, Cora. And please keep writing!

"OVER MY SHOULDER" COLUMN FOR APRIL 20, 1997
Recalling the roots of ADK

The concept of "The Adirondacks" hit me upon my moving to Ticonderoga. Before that, my notion of "The Adirondacks" had been confined to the southern Lake George area. However, living in Ti necessitated really traveling around the Adirondacks. It was nothing to go 50 miles to attend a track meet or see a movie.

I learned that there were many people passionate about the Adirondacks, including those far away, such as my uncle Jim Kalbaugh from Binghamton. Jim was a "46-er," that is, someone who had climbed the 46 high peaks of the Adirondacks.

However, my true "Adirondacks education" started in 1975 in Glens Falls, where I met so many people involved with an organization having an intense – might I even say evangelical? – interest in the Adirondacks: The Adirondack Mountain Club. My first experience with the club was through Grant Cole, who had been chosen to be the club's first Executive Director. A most fortunate choice, I'd say, as Grant, born and raised in the Adirondacks, exemplifies the best of what the Adirondacks can produce.

Well, it's twenty-two years later and I'm still learning. And among the things I recently learned is that the Adirondack Mountain Club, "the ADK," is celebrating its 75th anniversary. So, I thought I'd share a bit of the club's early history with you. You can find a more complete history in the special issue of the club's magazine "Adirondac" or in "With the Wilderness at Heart" by ADK historian Bruce Wadsworth.

To me, a wonderful irony is that the club began with a meeting held in the center of Manhattan! The first meeting was comprised of 64 men and women who gathered in the Abercrombie and Fitch Building on Madison Avenue and 45th street in New York City. It was April 3, 1922 and, for a further enjoyable bit of irony, it was in the "Log Cabin Room." Isn't that great?

The minutes record that the first chair, Meade Dobson, introduced a Mr. Howard who proposed that the club's name be "'The Adirondack Mountain Club, which shall be abbreviated ADK.M.C.'" It was to be an organization for the improvement and preservation of the Adirondacks. Similar to the already established Appalachian Mountain Club, which was referred to as the AMC, The Adirondack Mountain Club would also be referred to as the "ADK.M.C."

True to the majority of meetings containing more than one person, a spirited discussion arose. In short, the mud hit the fan. Some thought the word "club" was too lightweight and that the word "association" should be used. But others noted that there were already other mountain "clubs," such as the Appalachian Mountain Club or the Green Mountain Club. To them, the words "mountain club" said it all. Others felt the proposed name actually infringed upon the Appalachian Mountain Club.

Some suggested dropping "Mountain," but there already had been an "Adirondack Club" (the "Philosophers Club" founded before the Civil War by Ralph Waldo Emerson, John Holmes, Louis Agassiz, and others). So, that was out for some, but not for others, who rightfully claimed the club was, after all, defunct.

Then, how about that shortened "ADK.M.C"? Well, some proposed that the term "Adirondackers" be used instead. Nobody had an immediate beef with that. Note the word "immediate." Finally, after two hours of intense discussion, the group agreed upon this name: "The Adirondack Mountain Club."

However, the last shot had not been fired. An amendment to the proposed constitution was later made, changing the designation "Adirondackers" to "ADK."

The roots of the ADK go back into the conservation movement of the 19th century, drawing upon conservationists such as John Muir, philosophers such as Ralph Waldo Emerson, and artists such as Winslow Homer and Seneca Ray Stoddard, for inspiration and direction, and ultimately leading to the first meeting in 1922. Next week we'll look at the "high peaks" of what the ADK has accomplished in 75 years.

"OVER MY SHOULDER" COLUMN FOR APRIL 27, 1997
More about the ADK

We continue our happy 75th birthday wish to the Adirondack Mountain Club, the "ADK," headquartered in Glens Falls. Began informally in 1916 as "The Adirondack Mountain Club" and formally incorporated on April 3, 1922, the early ADK worked to involve everyone from the most ardent conservationist to the weekend hiker to the maker of forest industry products. I was delighted to note that one of the founding members of the ADK was a Glens Fallsian, Maurice Hoopes, then president of Finch Pruyn.

I was also pleased to see among its founding members a good number of women, such as Virginia Gildersleeve, the Dean of Barnard College and Jane Deeter Rippin, director of the Girl Scouts. In the ADK's recent history issue of "Adirondac," authors Karen Eagan and Linda Laing wrote that "probably the last documented example of overt preferential treatment" of woman in the ADK occurred in 1924. That was when the men designed the separate bunks rooms at the Adirondack Loj so that the women could view the lake. The men viewed the outbuildings.

The first ADK act was constructing "The Long Trail," now the Northville-Placid Trail in 1922. However, the Club evolved quickly from an organization created for teaching people how to be in the Forest Preserve without destroying it or themselves. In 1923, it stepped into the political arena by opposing a constitutional amendment that would have opened the Forest Preserve to construction of hydro dams. ("Dam wrong," I think someone said.)

The ADK actually oversees the Adirondacks and the Catskills, as both were included in the 1886 constitutional amendment creating the Forest Preserve. As that amendment has always been a lightning rod, it was understandable that the ADK's fourth president, Pirie MacDonald, emphasized protecting the Preserve. In 1928 the Club produced its first conservation policy.

Of course, there were many "nonpolitical" things to be done. After all, hikers have to stay somewhere. In addition to lean-to's, lodges were built, its first being Johns Brook Lodge in 1925. In 1932, during the Winter Olympics at Lake Placid, it leased the Adirondak Loj from the Lake Placid Club (which it purchased in 1958).

And hikers have to know where they're going. So, in 1934, the Club produced its first guidebook, and the first of the Club's many publications.

Coordinating with other organizations was important, too, and the Club initiated its first Trails Conference of over 100 organizations in 1935, followed by a statewide ski club conference in 1936, even organizing its own ski team in 1939. Busy people!

With World War II's end in 1945, the ADK stepped up the "battle for the Preserve," giving strong support to the state constitution's "forever wild" portions of the Forest Preserve, as well as for purchase of more land for the preserve. In 1945, it also successfully fought dams being placed on the Moose River.

It lost some battles, including that against the Northway's construction in 1960, but did exert enough pressure to save the Pharaoh Lake region, which later became a "Wilderness Area." It successfully fought for the Adirondack Park Agency's creation in 1972, a year after Grant Cole became the Club's first full-time Executive Director. In 1973, the Club established its first permanent headquarters in Glens Falls. Membership was soaring and by 1984 would reach 10,000 people – and by 1994, 20,000!

Pressure to develop the Adirondacks has grown exponentially since the Forest Preserve's inception in 1886, and in recent times the Club has backed various bond acts for land purchase for the Preserve. And the `80s and `90s have also seen it fighting such ecological time bombs as acid rain.

Whether through the ADK's hiking trails, lodges or lean-to's, its education, publications, or legislation – or its campaign of "If you can carry it in, you can carry it out" – the Conservation Movement is being propelled into the 21st century by the Adirondack Mountain Club. Happy Birthday, ADK!

"OVER MY SHOULDER" COLUMN FOR MAY 18, 1997
A salute to the Hudson Falls BPW

On the 40th anniversary of the Hudson Falls Business and Professional Women's Club – the BPW – let's pause to look at a bit of the club's early history. My mother was a member of "The Beep" (as she used to call the BPW) in Ticonderoga. As a medical secretary, she benefited tremendously from this national organization, which had been founded in 1919 "to elevate the standards and promote the interests of business and professional women."

On February 27, 1957, an organizational meeting was held by BPW District 4 Director Dorothy Meehan, also a past president of the Glens Falls BPW, in the

Hudson Falls Methodist church. Mabel Gratton was temporary chair and Dorothy Malan temporary secretary. Ellen Pattee, Barbara Goebel, and Jean Graziano formed the nominating committee.

The group voted to have the first meeting of the Hudson Falls BPW be a dinner meeting at 6:00 p.m. on March 13th at the old Kingsbury Hotel, which stood on Main Street. It must have been quite an assembly, because 25 new members were there in addition to 11 members from the Glens Falls BPW, which has since disbanded.

That night the charter was signed, dues were collected (of course), and these officers were installed: Mabel Gratton, president; Margaret Leombruno, 1st vice president; Ann Weiselberg, 2nd vice president; Dorothy Malan, secretary; and Mary Cormie, treasurer.

The first year was a dynamic one. The theme for the 1957-58 year was "support opportunities for qualified women in the field of education." A joint meeting of area BPW's, schools and other organizations was held with the main speaker being Rose F. Fox of Adult Education of New York State.

A scholarship program was initiated after Hudson Falls Central School Principal, Bernard LaBour, spoke on the various scholarships already available. The new BPW held raffles, rummage sales, and fashion shows to support the scholarship fund. And they made time to work on behalf of the American Cancer Society.

In 1959, Ann Weiselberg took over as president. Talks on the public health field, real estate, and education show the club's interests in diverse employment for women.

Meetings were being held in the members' homes in those early days. Under Ann Weiselberg, the club's first Christmas meeting was held at the El Roto Restaurant, which was on River Street in Hudson Falls.

During the presidency of Iona McCoy in 1962-63, the meetings came to be regularly held at the El Roto, owned by Sally and George Brooks. Sally was a BPW member and at 8:00 p.m. after the restaurant had closed for the day, she'd reopen so that the BPW could hold its monthly meetings.

At that time, the club faced its first crisis. Membership had dropped to 10 members and the national BPW considered revoking the club's charter. President McCoy and the other nine members, rallied. Dubbed "The Traveling Ten," for attending every district, state, and legislative conference, they recruited 15 more members. Today it stands at 43.

Under president McCoy, the first "Woman of the Year" award ceremony was held honoring an outstanding woman in the community, not necessarily a BPW member. For the record, it was in Sally Brooks' apartment over the El Roto. Iona McCoy was rightfully honored "Woman of the Year" in 1975.

Now in its 40th year, the Hudson Falls BPW thrives. My sincere thanks BPW members Barb Shivka and Agnes Lawrence for their guidance in my assembling this column. As my mother would have said, "Keep up the good work, Beeps!"

"OVER MY SHOULDER" COLUMN FOR JUNE 22, 1997
And now, a bit about Thurman

If you live in the Town of Thurman, you know that at one time Thurman
included almost all of today's Warren County and that, as a town,
"Thurman" disappeared for about forty years.

First, for those living in places distant from it, Thurman is in western Warren
County, bounded by the Town of Johnsburg on the north and the Town of Stony
Creek to the south. It is a rugged and beautiful area.

In fairness, Queensbury holds the record for having embraced the greatest
amount of Warren County at one point in its history. When founded in 1762,
Queensbury was actually a little smaller than today. But in 1786, the state
Legislature extended Queensbury to include what is today the Towns of
Queensbury and Luzerne and part of the Town of Lake George. At that point
they were all a part of Washington County.

Queensbury must have of lobbied the state hard, because in March of 1788,
another legislative act expanded Queensbury's boundaries to include all of
present-day Warren County.

That lasted all of four years and along came John Thurman. Actually, John had
arrived in 1778, when he secured by land patent all of what would be later the
present-day Towns of Bolton, Chester, Johnsburg, Stony Creek, Warrensburg,
and a part of Lake George.

In 1783 John sent his nephew, Richardson Thurman, to act as his land agent.
Settling at the fork of the Schroon and Hudson Rivers, Richardson bought
thousands of acres for Uncle John. Though not in any histories I've read, it is
easy to infer that Uncle John already held sway in the state Legislature. For
example, Brown's *History of Warren County* tells us that in 1783 Governor Clinton
named Richardson Thurman the Major-Commandant of the Totten and
Crossfield Battalion. But the more telling evidence is that in 1792, Queensbury
was divided up into two towns, Fairfield (later Luzerne) and Thurman – with
Thurman now the largest town! And John wasn't even living there. The three
towns comprised the exact area that, in 1813, would be set off from Washington
County and called "Warren County."

In 1773, before Richardson ever arrived, there had been settlers in the future
Town of Thurman. James Cameron, of the Blair-Athol area of northern Scotland,
settled along the river. As you'll see, his family would see part of that Scottish
name, "Athol," grace a future town – at the expense of Thurman's name.

Born in New York City, John Thurman moved to his new lands in 1789.
Smith's "History of Warren County"[xli] states that Thurman settled about a mile
south of Johnsburg Corners and called the place "Elm Hill." Within a few years
he established the first saw mill, grist mill and, to use an old phrase, "gin mill."
Thurman erected a general store along with a distillery for all the rye being grown.
Smith writes, "It is said that most of the whiskey made was used in the town."

Possibly as early as 1795, Thurman built the first woolen mill, which he changed to a cotton factory. In 1797 he created a calico printing works, said to be the first in America. Around 1800 he built a potash factory, and all thrived until 1809 when Thurman was gored to death by a bull. All but his saw mill and grist mill closed forever immediately after his death.

Towns started to be created from the Town of Thurman as early as 1799: Bolton and Chester (1799); Johnsburg (1805); Hague (1807); and Lake George (1810). When Warrensburg and Athol were created in 1813, Thurman's name disappeared!

In 1838, Horicon was created from Bolton and Hague. Finally, in April 1853, the Town of Athol was divided into Thurman and Stony Creek. Thurman was back, but Athol disappeared as a town name!

My only question is, which founding anniversary date does Thurman celebrate – 1792 or 1853?

Heck, if it meant having two parties, I'd celebrate both.

"OVER MY SHOULDER" COLUMN FOR JUNE 29, 1997
The story of a dry cleaning family

This week's column salutes the anniversary of a local business that has achieved an astounding record for longevity and service – Feigenbaum's Cleaners and Furriers.

Eighty years is an incredible amount of time for one business to exist. Looked at historically, Feigenbaum's started just after America's entry into WW I. "Feigenbaum's" and "dry cleaning" have been synonymous for so long in Glens Falls – since 1917– that it is difficult to believe that 80 years ago it was pure chance that placed the Feigenbaum family in Glens Falls.

The man who began it all, Herman Feigenbaum, had come from a small town outside of Lvov in the Ukraine, according to Todd Feigenbaum, Herman's grandson and current co-partner in the business. Sent to England to apprentice to be a tailor with an uncle, Herman realized times were not good in Eastern Europe. World War I was looming, and Herman decided to go to New York City, where as Todd says, "he worked in one of the infamous sweat shops on the Lower East Side." Two other brothers joined him in New York, where Herman also met his wife, Jennie.

Several years later, in 1917, Herman and Jennie decided to relocate. But where to? According to Todd, in May of 1917, Herman saw that a tailor shop was for sale in Whitehall. He and Jennie, who was pregnant at the time with their second son, Louis, "boarded a train with their three children and the sewing machine," Todd said.

On the way, they stopped over with a friend who was a tailor in Glens Falls and decided to stay. Todd says there are two conflicting family stories about how it is they came to stay. One is that Todd's "Aunt Annie," who was a little girl at the time, "complained about getting back on the train." The other is that Todd's "grandmother was not feeling well because of her pregnancy." Whichever is true, and Todd thinks both are, he said, "They asked if there were room in Glens Falls for another Jewish tailor" and the family friend said there was business enough for them both. The Feigenbaums remained for good.

Herman first established himself as a tailor in Glens Falls, but within the year he expanded his business to include the laundering and dry cleaning of clothing, becoming the very first dry cleaning establishment to be opened in Glens Falls. Before that, people in this area had to send their clothes to Albany to be dry cleaned.

For a few years, the family lived and worked in a home on Bay Street, and then moved to 3 Fulton Street, where they, again, lived and worked. As Todd told me, the entire family, adults and children, participated. The cleaning and spotting was done in a side room, the freshly cleaned laundry hung to dry on the line, and the packages of clean clothing given to the customers in the front room.

The Feigenbaums were innovative. Being the first to offer dry cleaning wasn't enough – they began to deliver to their customers' homes. In the 1920s they even got a delivery truck for their laundry, the first in the area. Of course, not everybody in the family was old enough to drive. When Todd's father, Louis, was a boy he made deliveries on his bike.

Around 1946, Herman Feigenbaum moved the dry cleaning operations into the main plant at 89½ Bay Street. The large building had been, at various times before the Feigenbaum's, a silk-making plant and then later a stable for boarding horses.

The war was over and so was the Great Depression. Prosperity resumed after nearly two decades. A new generation of Feigenbaum's had come to maturity and were ready to take over the family business.

In next week's column, we'll conclude our story of the Feigenbaums.

"OVER MY SHOULDER" COLUMN FOR JULY 6, 1997
A family story of America

In last week's column, we were recognizing the 80th anniversary of Feigenbaum's Cleaners and Furriers.

To recap the earlier years, Herman and Jennie Feigenbaum had been on their way from New York City to purchase a tailor shop in Whitehall in May of 1917. Todd Feigenbaum, their grandson, and a current co-partner of Feigenbaum's, said the couple, who were expecting their next child at the time, stopped over with a friend who was a tailor in Glens Falls. Assured by the friend that there was business enough to support both tailors, the Feigenbaum's stayed and the next year had started their laundering and dry cleaning business.

Shortly after World War II, Herman and Jennie's two sons, William and Louis, joined their father in the dry cleaning business. Around 1946, Herman

Feigenbaum had moved the dry cleaning operations into the main plant at 89½ Bay Street, a large barn that had previously been, at different times, a silk-making plant and a stable for boarding horses.

Now the barn was expanded, with rooms being added. About 1950, a further expansion provided the current service area for customers, with the rotating racks and a business office. Its style is classically post-World War II. The postwar era saw prosperity return to our area and it saw more and more people discover Feigenbaum's. The postwar era also introduced synthetic fabrics on an unprecedented scale. Dry-cleaning became more complex. As Todd Feigenbaum noted, his father Louis became a walking library of knowledge on cleaning formulas, a knowledge that he passed along to the employees that he trained. Feigenbaum's also began cleaning and storing furs and installed one of the largest refrigerated vaults between Albany and Montreal.

Herman Feigenbaum died in 1957, forty years after he had come to Glens Falls. However, he had lived long enough to see the expansion of his business lead to an ever-widening clientele. His wife, Jennie, lived until 1969.

In 1977, William Feigenbaum retired from the family business, leaving his brother Louis and his family to maintain the business. All of Louis' children had worked in the family business but had later left to pursue different careers. By the mid-1980s, it looked as if the Feigenbaum tradition would end with Louis. However, in 1986, his son, Todd, came back to Glens Falls. He took ownership of the family business that year. Sadly, Louis died not too long after Todd's return. I had the very good fortune of knowing Louis Feigenbaum, a gentleman in every sense of the word.

The third generation of Feigenbaums continued the family's innovative spirit. Todd began using newer cleaning solvents and computerized the whole system. He also expanded the firm. In October of 1986 Feigenbaum's introduced the first drive-through dry cleaning outlet in the area on Bay Road. That operation has since moved to Quaker Plaza on Quaker Road. Then, in 1992, the firm opened a store in Saratoga. Todd's wife had been working with him until 1992, but with their family growing, she made the decision to devote more time for the family. The sheer size of the business demanded more people being involved and so, in 1992, the Feigenbaums went into partnership with Bonnie Smith.

History continues to be made by Feigenbaum's. This fall, in the year of their eightieth anniversary, the firm will be opening a fourth store in the Berry Mill Place on Western Avenue in Queensbury.

I have always liked the Feigenbaum Family's story. On this July 4th weekend, it is appropriate, as it typifies the immigrant story of America and the concept – now considered old-fashioned by some – of America as the "Melting Pot." For those of us with diverse family backgrounds that combined, or literally "melted," into this generation, there is nothing outdated about that concept.

To Feigenbaum's Cleaners and Furriers and to the Feigenbaum family itself, a very happy 80th anniversary – and many more to come.

"OVER MY SHOULDER" COLUMN FOR JULY 13, 1997
Summer in Lake George

NOTE: *The Glens Falls Times* was the sister newspaper of *The Post-Star* for many years. A. B. Colvin started it as *The Glens Falls Daily Times* in 1879 as Glens Falls' first daily.

I t's summer and a news clipping received from my friend, Wilbur Simpson, is a perfect way to introduce this summer's season on Lake George.

The clipping is from *The Glens Falls Times* of March 26, 1936. The article's author, L. (Louise) Cheritree Hubbell, condensed news stories from the 1880 and 1881 issues of the *Lake George Mirror*, a four-page weekly, founded in 1880 by Alfred and T. J. Merrick. In 1905, the "Mirror" was sold to the Arthur Knight family.

Hubbell wrote with a knowledge that stemmed from her and her readers' chronological proximity to the period, and with their being very familiar with many of the people described in those early issues of the "Mirror." It's as if I were writing an article based upon issues of the "Mirror" 55 years ago. Though I wasn't alive then, I certainly would know so many of the people and places described.

With Hubbell's article, many times I could fill in the gaps, as I knew the people being described in her commentary. Other times, I was left with questions.

An example of the latter concerns "the first murder case to be tried in the Warren County court," that of George Willett for the murder John B. Pair in 1880. One of the prosecuting attorneys was a "Lawyer Cheritree." A relative of the author? Does anyone reading this know? By the way, Hubbell wrote that "Willett was defended by Charles Hughes and acquitted." In 1936, Charles Evans Hughes was Chief Justice of the Supreme Court, so everyone knew his name. [*See correction in next column.*]

Here's an example of my being able to fill in the gaps. Hubbell wrote that "S. R. Stoddard chartered the Owl to take `triangulations' of the lake for a new and more perfect map to accompany his guidebook." What wasn't in there was that this was the start of a long run of Stoddard's "Map of Lake George" which, like his Lake George guidebook series, was so famous and so popular. By 1936, Stoddard was 19 years gone and on his way to being forgotten.

Here's another "gap filler": earlier in her story, Hubbell had written that "during the season of 1880, Cornell defeated Columbia in rowing races at Lake George. A canoe association was formed...called a cruising brotherhood...for the sole purpose of testing canoes. The Sisters or Canoe Islands near Diamond Point were allotted by their owners...for camping sites for the contestants, who came from all over the United States and Canada to participate in the Canoe Congress held in 1881."

What Ms. Hubbell did not report is that this association was none other than the American Canoe Association and that Stoddard was appointed as its official photographer. An avid canoeist, Stoddard was an inventor as well and several serious canoe publications of that day, including one by the famed architect Calvert Vaux, had praised Stoddard's innovations. Vaux and Frederick Law Olmstead designed Central Park in Manhattan. In 1872, they also designed the landscaping for the Fort William Henry Hotel, owned and managed at that time by T. R. Roessle – who had hired Stoddard to photograph the hotel and grounds. Was this the beginning of a connection?

In the "Some Things Never Change Department," the 1880s issues of the *Mirror* talk about Lake George Village's famous "Stone Store," which had been built by Halsey Rogers in 1819. Hubbell, in 1936, assumes that readers know exactly which "Stone Store" the 1880 articles mean. She wrote, "The Welch Brothers had a hardware store in the Stone store, still used as a store," in 1936. In 1997, just as it was in 1819, 1880 and 1936, the Stone Store is "still used as a store" – "The Corner Stone," a gift shop owned by Karen Hanchett. Now there's tradition!

Out of space but not information. Join me next week for more about Cheritree Hubbell's article on Lake George.

"OVER MY SHOULDER" COLUMN FOR JULY 20, 1997
More news stories from lake's past

L ast week we were exploring Lake George via 1880 and 1881 news stories from the *Lake George Mirror*, condensed in a 1936 *The Glens Falls Times* article written by L. (Louise) Cheritree Hubbell.

Last week's article was giving the news behind the news, filling in very understandable gaps left by Hubbell, who, with her readers, was much more familiar with the people and places recounted in the *Mirror*, a weekly, published then only during the summer seasons.[xlii]

Speaking of gaps, in my own reporting last week on the first murder trial at the County Courthouse in Lake George, the famous "Willett Trial" of 1880, I neglected to mention several important facts. First, that courthouse is now the Lake George Historical Association's museum. You can stand in the courtroom where Willett was tried, and where other jurisprudence was dispensed until 1963, when the county seat was moved to Queensbury. The first courthouse was completed on the site around 1819. An 1843 fire destroyed it and the clerk's office and new buildings were erected in 1845. An expansion took place in 1869, and then another in 1878. Just in time for Willett's trial.

Also, a model of a church Willett built from match boxes and cigar boxes is now in the old jail cells in the museum. And shades of trials today, the imprisoned Willett was visited by 1,600 visitors and Willett's lawyer, Charles Hughes, got Willett acquitted on a legal technicality, not Willett's innocence! However, Fort Edward Town Historian R. Paul McCarty corrected a mistake I made in last week's article: the attorney was not the famed Charles Evans Hughes. Thanks, Paul!

Hubbell's article reported many firsts: "In the spring of 1880, Samuel Bates installed the first water system," for the village, "procuring the water from the present north reservoir." In 1881 (and Dr. David Starbuck over at Fort William Henry, please take note), while digging to lay the water pipes, the bodies of six soldiers were exhumed near the Catholic Church[xliii], the *Mirror* noted "after having lain 122 years, 8 months and 20 odd days in undisturbed repose." Note the Victorian avoidance of the word "dead."

Also, within this time period, but Hubbell does not specifically say when, "the first telephone and telegraph lines were strung to Bolton and to Warrensburg." In the early 1880s, those were of far less interest to Lake George than the coming of the train, for which the *Mirror* lobbied hard. It noted that 40 freight stages passed daily through the village and that 30 trains went through Fort Edward every day, 22 carrying freight and 8 with passengers.

The newspaper carried news of the assassination of President Garfield and the start of the rail connection from Glens Falls to Lake George in the fall of 1881. Ironically, the 1885 *History of Warren County* noted that because of the "diversion of commerce," Fort Edward "suffered materially from the opening of the road...while Glens Falls...benefited greatly."

The lake's tourist dollars were sincerely interesting to merchants in Glens Falls, such as the grocery business of Coolidge and Lee which also set up shop in the Village. The locals met the competition, however. "James G. Lockhart started a milk route that year," Hubbell wrote of 1880, going on to write that Lockhart soon expanded into selling fruit and vegetables, which he was still doing so in 1936 – 56 years later!

Louise Cheritree Hubbell had a dry sense of humor. Introducing the topic of politics, she wrote: "Politics of that day were about as scrambled as those of today." She also included, this "Mirror" commentary on the 60 people raising a barn at the Kirkpatrick farm: "Times have changed for the better. Some years ago, it took ten gallons of whiskey to raise a barn on this same farm, while this was put up with only five gallons of cider."

Wonder what that barn raising would take today?

"OVER MY SHOULDER" COLUMN FOR JULY 27, 1997.
A human face on the regiment

He told us he was a private in the Black Watch Regiment. The words, "The Black Watch," a part of his everyday speech, sent a thrill through me. We sat with him a few weeks ago beneath a tent at Fort Ticonderoga, where the forebears of his regiment had arrived by ship, directly from Scotland. However, he had just flown in from Hong Kong, still having to have felt the effects of jet lag but forgetting it in his excitement at his first time in America.

"What's your name?" I asked.

"M'na-mizz-DOO-ee," he replied.

"Dewey?" I asked.

"Ma namizz Doogie. DOOgie." Seeing my blank look, he slowed his brogue. "My name is Douglas, but ma friends call me DOOgie." His face burst into a contagious smile.

Private Douglas Maxwell, Doogie, is from the southern part of Scotland, "like the other lads," to whom he pointed, all seated around a table. Their faces had flashed around the world via television satellite from the historic ceremony that had returned Hong Kong to China. Now they were at Fort Ticonderoga for the annual "Military Tattoo."

Some of the "lads" played with the United Black Watch Pipe Band, such as Lance Corporal A. C. R. Lambert, while others, such as Lance Corporal A. Wilson, Private S. J. K. Paton, and Private Douglas Maxwell – Doogie – were a part of "The Black Watch Colour Party," the color guard.

As these young men laughed and joked, and shared their memories with us of the events that took place in Hong Kong, it occurred to me how similar they had to be to their counterparts in 1758 when the Highland Regiment, the "Black Watch," marched under the British General Abercromby against the French fort named "Carillon" (now Fort Ticonderoga).

I could see these same faces – young, Scottish, imbued with a sense of humor, and inquisitive about this "New World" – assembling at the southern end of Lake George on that July 5th of 1758. None of them knowing then that their inept General would lead the Black Watch and others to slaughter as the British moved to take Carillon.

On that day at what is now Lake George Village, Abercromby assembled 16,000 British regular and colonial troops, 10,000 of whom had marched up from Fort Edward, then sailed north in over 1,000 boats. They assaulted Carillon July 8, 1758. Of the 1,074 Black Watch men with them, 205 died and 297 were wounded, among the thousands of casualties at Ticonderoga. As Doogie and the others spoke, I pictured them marching into battle, line after orderly line, bagpipes and drums playing above the roar of cannon and musket, watching as their ranks were mowed down ahead of them, so many young men with homes and families an ocean away.

Ticonderoga would become one of the Black Watch's legends and one of their dead, Duncan Campbell of Inverness, Scotland, would become a legend within that legend. Campbell, later immortalized in Robert Louis Stevenson's poem "Ticonderoga," had unknowingly shielded his cousin's murderer. The murdered man's ghost warned Campbell he would die in a place called, "Ticonderoga," unknown to Campbell then. Years later, Campbell would learn the name, as his Black Regiment readied for the battle to take Ticonderoga from the French. He died in battle. He was later buried in Fort Edward and today lies in the Union

Cemetery there.

One of Campbell's descendants is today with the Regiment.

For all that, I must confess that, until now, my interest of the Black Watch has always been academic, even spurred as it was by having lived in Ticonderoga and Fort Edward, where the Black Watch legends are kept alive. But that changed a few weekends ago as this great Regiment took on, for me, a very human face, as I met a fine group of young men, among them a Private Douglas Maxwell of the Black Watch – who asked that I call him Doogie.

Postscript: The Black Watch Regiment band returned to the United States that Fall, in September of 1997, to play New Hampshire Highland Games at Loon Mountain in Lincoln, New Hampshire. I had the good fortune to be there and sought out the band. However, Private Douglas Maxwell was not with band. Instead, he had been promoted and was serving on the Queen's Guard at her summer home in Scotland, Balmoral Castle. Congratulations, Doogie!

"OVER MY SHOULDER" COLUMN FOR AUGUST 17, 1997
Cemetery's regiment mystery

Do you like mysteries? I have great one for you.

This mystery is courtesy of Janet Hanson, the Librarian of the Old Fort House Museum in Fort Edward. For many years, because of Archivist Mary Jane Ellis and Librarian Janet Hanson, the museum has been able to open every Wednesday, as well as by appointment, for researchers. Both are volunteers, and both are unsung heroes.

In the course of Janet's work, she came across a most unusual circumstance that centers around the 54th Massachusetts Regiment– the famed "Colored Regiment" – of the Civil War. If you have seen the movie "Glory" with Denzel Washington and Mathew Broderick, you know the story of Colonel Robert Gould Shaw of Boston, who organized the first regiment of African American soldiers. The regiment fought with distinction at their first engagement, Fort Wagner, South Carolina, in which so many troops, including Colonel Shaw, died. Today, in front of the Massachusetts Statehouse in Boston, you may see the famous Saint-Gaudens memorial to the 54th.

The bravery of the African American soldiers of the 54th Regiment at Fort Wagner, and in subsequent battles, was of absolutely paramount importance during the Civil War and in years to come. The reason was that the regiments' actions overcame two major assumptions by most white Northerners, assumptions based upon prejudice: the first that Blacks could not and would not fight; the second that freeing slaves was not a proper war aim. The 54th proved to the Army the ability, and willingness, of African Americans to fight, and to die, for their freedom. And it proved to the average Northerner that that freedom for African Americans was among the highest and most worthy of reasons for which to fight the war.

While their bravery overcame assumptions based upon prejudice, the prejudice itself lingered. It was not, to paraphrase Churchill, the end of that prejudice, but only the beginning of that end. Yet it was a beginning and a noble one. In the wall of unthinking bigotry and racial hatred that existed in white people of both the North and South, the 54th put a huge crack. Through that crack, the light of truth came through: that black people were fully capable of being excellent soldiers, which by logical extension meant they had to be fully capable as human beings, a notion unthinkable to many until that time.

There were staggering casualties among those of the 54th. Of the 1550 Union men lost, 252 were of the 54th. Others of the 54th were to die at subsequent battles at Richmond, Honey Hill, and Olustee. Yet there were those who managed to live.

And so, we come to our mystery. Janet Hanson writes that "In Union Cemetery (Fort Edward), in the section reserved for the Civil War veterans, there are two stones with the inscription `54th Reg't. Mass. Col'd. Vols.' Both stones reveal the surname `Jackson.'" In fact, Janet copied the stones inscriptions verbatim. One reads "Francis Jackson/ Col. 54 Reg't. Mass./Col'd. Vols./Died/June 18, 1886" and the other, "Elmer Jackson/Mass. Col. Vol./Died/ Oct." The date is illegible.

How, she wonders, did two African American veterans of the 54th come to be buried in Fort Edward's Union Cemetery? According to her research, there were 17 Jacksons in the 54th. Were these two related?

So little is known of these two men and yet, so much is said about them in those few abbreviated words "54th Reg. Mass." inscribed on their stones. For, as much as the Emancipation Proclamation of 1862 stated that black people were free, it took the sacrifice of 54th Massachusetts Regiment to prove that those black people would assume the responsibility that freedom mandates. And they did, gloriously and oh so bravely, with their willingness to fight and to die, as free people.

Would you please contact me if you have any information regarding this mystery?

"OVER MY SHOULDER" COLUMN FOR AUGUST 31, 1997
Despite some calls, mystery remains

Calls from people interested in Civil War history have been coming in regarding a mystery introduced in this column a few weeks ago.

The mystery began when Janet Hanson, Librarian of the Old Fort House Museum, had discovered that two veterans of the famed 54th Regiment of Massachusetts – a regiment made up almost entirely of African Americans – were buried in Fort Edward's Union Cemetery, in the section for Civil War veterans. However, nothing else was known about these two African American men except what precious little was on their tombstones, one of which reads

"Francis Jackson/ Col. 54 Reg't. Mass./Col'd. Vols./Died/June 18, 1886" and the other, "Elmer Jackson/Mass. Col. Vol./Died/ Oct.," with its date illegible.

I am indebted to Nancy Barette of South Bay, Rita Hofmann of Gansevoort, and Don Wickman of Rutland, Vermont, for having called with information that makes who these men were a bit clearer. However, the mystery of how they came to have lived in Fort Edward – or at least to have been buried in Union Cemetery – has NOT been solved.

I'll distill their findings. About the 54th itself, a misconception is that it recruited only ex-slaves, or that at least the majority were ex-slaves. Actually, most were freemen of all different professions, recruited from New England, New York, Pennsylvania, New Jersey and Ohio. The 54th was in a bidding war against other communities recruiting soldiers and would have had to pay significant bounties to any enlistee.

Regarding our two veterans, neither was among the original enlistees for the 54th. Francis Jackson was born was born in Rockingham, Massachusetts around 1840, possibly 1842. Coincidentally, he enlisted in Company I on December 13, 1863 in "Rockingham," but this time Rockingham, Vermont, where he lived. He was mustered out of service Aug. 20, 1865. He died June 18, 1886.

Elmer Jackson was apparently no relation to Francis, although that is not a proven fact. There are some discrepancies in my three callers' information. All agree that Elmer was from Troy, New York, and enlisted in Rockingham, Vermont in December of 1863. Nancy gives the date as December 13, Don as December 15. Don states he was in Company A, while Rita gives Company K. Elmer also mustered out August 20, 1865.

Additional, and happy, discoveries related to our mystery include the fact that there were more African American veterans from the area, demonstrated by Will Doolittle's recent article about a black Civil War veteran from Argyle. Both Nancy and Don spoke about a third veteran, Horris Jackson, who is buried in the South Glens Falls Cemetery.

Horris Jackson was a resident of Glens Falls who enlisted (I am assuming in Rockingham) on April 9, 1863 and served in Company G. He was mustered out after having been wounded at Olustee, Florida. Born in 1838, he died in 1905. It is not known if he were related to either Elmer or Francis.

But that's not all. Don also found two other veterans of the 54th who were Glens Falls residents who also enlisted (I am assuming in Rockingham) on April 9, 1863 and served in Company G. Charles Stanton was wounded in action at Fort Stanton and died in the Florence, South Carolina prison on February 25, 1865, amazing when one remembers that the Confederacy had ordered all Blacks in uniform to be executed upon capture! John H. Williams, age 19 upon enlistment, mustered out on August 20, 1865.

Still, we are left wondering how the two Jacksons came to rest in Fort Edward. Is there a clue in the call from a Mr. Howard Rogers regarding an African American named Jackson who lived in the Granville West Pawlet area in the mid-

1800s? The family was large, he notes, and spread out to several other communities.

As soon as I discover more, I'll continue this fascinating story. In the meantime, the mystery continues!

"OVER MY SHOULDER" COLUMN FOR SEPTEMBER 7, 1997
Story of a local tabloid

If ignorance is bliss, I am roaring with laughter.

Have you ever heard of a newspaper called *The Graphic* that was first published in Hudson Falls in September of 1949? If you did not, then you'll make me feel better – if only slightly – for not knowing about it myself. Recently Wilbur Simpson gave me several copies of various old newspapers, among which were seven issues of *The Graphic*

This weekly called itself "Hudson Falls' Picture Newspaper" and also referred to itself as *The Evening Graphic*. It was a photo-oriented tabloid, like the "New York Daily News," and as such was about half photographs, half text. Like the News, it sold for a nickel.

I do not know how long the paper continued and would like to have any and all issues to ensure that they are microfilmed. Wilbur gave me the following issues: Vol. I, numbers 1, 2, 3, 4, 8, 9 and 12.

Wilbur was a contributor to the first issue, doing a piece on a Training Cruise taken by the members of the U. S. Naval Reserve 3-67 of Glens Falls. Illustrated with four photographs "taken by the author," the article detailed a stint on the Great Lakes aboard the PC 1193. Shown were Jim Latham and Wilbur Simpson of Hudson Falls; and "Soupy" Campbell, Don Hatin, Gene Pratt, Mort Reynolds, and Phil Smith of Glens Falls.

Let's scan the first issue of forty-eight years ago: September 16, 1949. Three photos dominate the front page, beneath the headline: "POLIO CASES DECLINING IN AREA, BUT DANGER STILL VERY GREAT." The paper stressed the emergency campaign against polio, and the issues were alive with news of the disease's effect upon the community. A photo captioned "Back to School?" shows children crossing in front of "Police Chief Mike Usher...at the corner of Park and Main." The photo had actually been taken back in June, because children had not started back to school yet because of the "polio ban on school" issued by the state Department of Health. School opening had already been delayed two weeks.

Poliomyelitis was so widespread and contagious, and no one knew what caused it. Fear bred sadly ineffective precautions, such as banning kids from swimming if they were overheated, for example. In 1949, a method of growing the polio viruses was discovered. Five years later Dr. Jonas Salk developed a successful vaccine and widespread inoculations began.

But in 1949, Dr. John McCann was urging officials to keep the schools closed, regardless of how long the delay. Mothers at home were not happy. (But did we have sad kids? Please!)

The second cover photo, an aerial shot by photographer Ed Durling, shows the Union Bag and Paper Company when it was right next door to Sandy Hill Iron and Brass Works (now Valmet) in Hudson Falls. The accompanying caption said the paper would periodically "print pictures of the industries that furnish the bread and butter for many residents of our hometown." (A smart editorial move!)

The third cover photo is a dramatic one of Morris "Muff" Nassivera, quarterback of the Greenjackets semi-pro football team. Nassivera, later Village Mayor, is in the air and about to fire the second of two "straight-as-an-arrow touchdown passes" that defeated the Glens Falls Commodores. The Greenjackets played at Derby Park, Hudson Falls. Ironically, they're at East Field in Glens Falls now and their arch rivals, the Commodores, are history.

The headline on Ed Churchill's article inside said it all: "Greenjackets Smear Commodores." (As successful as they are today!) Churchill praised "running backs Faicco, Perotta and Santora," as well as "Sal Canonica, Frank DePalo, Ray O'Brien, Stub Stautner... [and] Ray Greenwood."

Next week, we'll look at some more of the issues and news of *The Graphic*, including the "other" Greenjackets – the semi-pro baseball team. In the meantime, if you have any issues, could you contact me care of *The Post-Star*?

"OVER MY SHOULDER" COLUMN FOR SEPTEMBER 14, 1997
Graphic stories continue

W e've been discussing a weekly newspaper *The Graphic*, first published in Hudson Falls in September 1949. The paper was a ten-page tabloid, about half photos, half text, that focused on local news, with a one-page summary of world and national news. It even had syndicated cartoons, such as Mutt'n'Jeff.

Edward Churchill, the Sports Editor of *The Evening Graphic* (its formal name) told me it was published on Maple Street and lasted about two years. Herbert Moore was Publisher; Robert D. Francis, General Manager; Audrey Thomas, Art Director; and Edward Durling, Chief Photographer.

As I noted last week, Ed Churchill had written about the triumphant season's start of the Greenjackets, the semi-pro football team which originated in Hudson Falls at Derby Park and now plays in Glens Falls at East Field. However, Ed also had written about another Greenjackets, the baseball team, which had not ended its season with the same success.

It had been a rough year and Ed was sympathetic to the players: Carl Polzer, its manager; Don O'Connor, "Buck" Bovee (replacing Bruce Manelle), "Andy" DelSignore, Jack Havens, George Polzer, Ken Fitzgerald, Gerry Gould, and Francis "Franny" Smith. While errors contributed to the problem, Ed noted that "home field," Derby Park, had been closed for refurbishment at the start of the season and the team was forced to play home games in Fort Edward and other spots. "All this hurt the chances of consistent ball needed to win any loop flag," he wrote.

However, at least one member of the team had to have ended the season in good spirits, for in the October 6th edition we find the wedding photo of Francis E. Smith and Laura Dangelico. (And that team has enjoyed 48 winning seasons.)

Obviously, sports were only a part of *The Graphic*. Let's look at the news from various issues spanning from mid-September to December 2nd, 1949. The polio epidemic kept schools closed until October 10, over a month past the opening date. (Since the Salk vaccine's inception in 1954, I think the Asian flu is the only disease to have caused school closings.) Polio's threat also canceled the Washington County Junior Fair at the old Fairgrounds by the County Municipal Center.

Some of the news was "sensational." While the September 22nd issue headlines were about unsubstantiated "Rumors of Oak Street Shootings," the September 29th issue reported "TROOPERS MAKE VICE RAID; WOMAN CHARGES A FRAME-UP." The raid on a "house of ill fame" turned out to be a false alarm, and Judge A. P. Robertson dismissed the charges against the unnamed woman.

Less sensational, but no less interesting, is the premier issue's report of the proposed centralization of the Hudson Falls and Fort Edward School systems. It would have encompassed a territory spreading from southern Fort Ann as far south as the Town of Northumberland. The Fort Edward School system was larger then and embraced parts of Moreau and Northumberland. One can only wonder what the new system would have achieved.

The personal news coverage included photos of local events, such as the one of the CYO dance at St. Mary's hall, showing Joan Bruce, Anne Dewise, Sylvia Sullivan, Carol English, and Wilda Bovee enjoying cider and doughnuts. Or the one of the Donkey Basketball game (remember Donkey Basketball?) at the recently demolished old high school, with the four faculty members, Homer Dearlove, Ray Heil, Tony Luciano, and Elliot Harris all posed by their donkeys.

Radio listings, marriages, births, etc. Everything was there for Hudson Falls and Kingsbury. My thanks to Wilbur Simpson for his gift of the issues of *The Graphic*, plus other copies of *Public Enterprise* and the *Recorder*, which along with the *Hudson Falls Herald*, were published in Hudson Falls from the 1940s through the 1960s. More about those in a future column.

In the meantime, let's get these papers on microfilm. Please contact me if you have copies of these papers, will you? Thanks!

"OVER MY SHOULDER" COLUMN FOR SEPTEMBER 21, 1997
A look at a nation's birth

NOTE: Some of the major Revolutionary War battles were fought in the region spanning from Ticonderoga to Saratoga. The toll taken on those on all sides of the conflict, Patriot, Loyalist, or neutral party, was heavy. As we near our nation's 250th anniversary, the history in these columns is worth revisiting.

The Saratoga National Historical Park in the Town of Stillwater is celebrating the 220th anniversary of the "Battle of Saratoga," actually two battles that took place on September 19 and October 7 of 1777. Both culminated in the surrender of the British General Sir John Burgoyne on October 17, 1777, what I consider the "other Independence Day" of the United States of America.

Today will be the last of a three-day observance of the Battles of Saratoga. From 10:00 a.m. to 4:00 p.m. you will be able to visit the encampments of the many re-enactors representing the American and the British armies and, from 10:00 to 3:00 p.m., there will be a re-enactment of the second battle of Saratoga. (Yesterday there had been a re-enactment of the first battle.)

Before your eyes glaze over and your thoughts turn to canning peaches, please consider this one fact: if the British had won at Saratoga, we probably would have a picture of Queen Elizabeth II on our money and be singing "God Save the Queen" or "Oh Canada" as our national anthem.

In other words, the "United States of America" would not be.

While Burgoyne didn't exactly invent the concept of dividing the colonies along the water routes of Lake Champlain and the Hudson River, he perfected it, and proposed it so much that, ultimately, he was allowed to follow it through. The problem was that no one wanted to work with him.

Understand that though no intellectual, John Burgoyne was far from stupid, and while not brilliant militarily, he was not inept. It's just that he could be quite arrogant and even when he championed good causes – such as fighting Parliament's racism against West Indians – he did it in a way that could offend even his friends or cause him ridicule. For example, it was not his high living but his better than average treatment of his soldiers that earned him the nickname of "Gentleman Johnny." He sacrificed his fortune to marry the woman he loved, was often in debt from gambling, wrote plays that appealed to high society and, in short, was a complex man – but no buffoon. He could have won the Battle of Saratoga.

From the start, Burgoyne was in trouble. He first proposed his divide and conquer plan when he was at Battle of Bunker Hill in 1775, serving under General William Howe. Howe despised and ignored Burgoyne, as did those in London.

However, Burgoyne returned in 1776, only to serve under General Guy Carleton, who despised Burgoyne and kept him in check, in all likelihood preventing Burgoyne's defeating Benedict Arnold on Lake Champlain. It was not until March of 1777 that Burgoyne wheedled permission to set off on his own from England to "divide and conquer," but even then, London did not give him adequate troops or supplies. And when he arrived, who awaited him but the head of all troops in Canada, General [*Guy*] Carleton, who effectively delayed Burgoyne's departure by two months!

Finally, Burgoyne's army of British regulars, Hessian mercenaries, and Iroquois warriors sailed from St. Jean, Quebec, in May of 1777. Mission: rendezvous at Albany with General Barry St. Leger's army coming through the Mohawk Valley and with General William Howe's army, coming up the Hudson. At least, that was the plan.

Around Westport on Lake Champlain, Burgoyne landed and made a speech that insulted Americans, whom he arrogantly considered as naughty children, and which also blithely announced that he would be able to keep his Iroquois allies under tight rein. While his haughtiness caused rebellious Americans to dismiss Burgoyne as an arrogant schmuck, his naive comments about controlling the Iroquois sparked tremendous fear here, and in England, members of Parliament denounced him as a boob for promising the impossible.

It was a very inauspicious beginning, which, as we'll see next week, led Burgoyne to Saratoga and defeat.

"OVER MY SHOULDER" COLUMN FOR SEPTEMBER 28, 1997
General ignored the signs

In last week's column we watched the British General Sir John Burgoyne successfully lobby the Crown to return him to North America in March of 1777 to divide the colonies with a three-pronged attack on New York: Burgoyne down Lake Champlain and the Hudson, Sir William Howe up the Hudson and Barry St. Leger through the Mohawk Valley. All would meet in Albany.

Problems abounded. Burgoyne had started down Lake Champlain with 8,000 troops – far too few! Second, his widely published appeal for the Americans to return to the fold was unbelievably condescending, actually inspiring colonists to revolt. Third, he infuriated both the colonists and Parliament by guaranteeing "control" over his Iroquois allies, a sovereign people hoping only to use the British to stop the advance on their lands. They weren't about to be "controlled" by anyone.

Burgoyne had little to live for but his plan. The previous year, the overly cautious General Guy Carleton prevented Burgoyne from employing his three-pronged attack and even from pursuing Benedict Arnold along Lake Champlain. Arnold eventually checked Carleton's advance. During this same time, Burgoyne's wife died, only a few years after his only child. He was alone.

Burgoyne's troops disembarked at Westport and split up. One part marched south through Vermont while Burgoyne proceeded to Crown Point, then Fort Ticonderoga, both of which he easily took. His troops chased the retreating Americans to Hubbardton, Vermont, but in a fierce (and prophetic) battle, the British suffered incredibly heavy losses.

Instead of sailing south on Lake George, then marching to Fort Edward, Burgoyne went to Skenesborough (Whitehall), where he dallied. He lost weeks chopping his way through the trees that colonists had felled between Skenesborough and Fort Anne[xliv]. By the time he reached Patrick Smyth's house in Fort Edward (now the Old Fort House Museum) it was mid-summer. (Ironically, Smyth had been arrested that year by Benedict Arnold, who would help defeat Burgoyne at Saratoga!)

Burgoyne had lost so much time. Along the way he received a vaguely worded letter from General Howe that Howe would "attempt" to reach Albany. Hindsight allows us to see what Burgoyne would not see: Howe was not coming. But Burgoyne was possessed and would not halt the campaign.

To my mind, Fort Edward was the "Turning Point" of Burgoyne's Campaign. By then he knew something of Howe's intentions. And, while at Fort Edward, four tragedies occurred that should have stopped him. In July, two sets of brutal murders were committed within two days by Burgoyne's Iroquois allies: on July 26, the Allen family of Argyle was massacred by Burgoyne's Iroquois scout LeLoup; on July 27, Jane McCrea was killed.

The Old Fort House Museum's Eileen Hannay says that amidst the welter of misinformation about Jane's death, two things are certain: the young Tory woman was fatally shot while the Iroquois scouts LeLoup and Duluth were arguing over who would escort her to Burgoyne's lines, where her fiancée, David Jones, awaited her. Second, for whatever reason, her scalp was brought first into the camp, where Jones recognized it.

Burgoyne's promise to "control" the Iroquois backfired. His campaign had produced a martyr. Outraged locals flocked to join the patriots.

Burgoyne's next tragedy, which should have stopped him cold, occurred August 6th: Barry St. Leger' entire army was defeated at the Battle of Oriskany. Then, ten days later as Burgoyne's advance troops started out for Saratoga, the Hessian Colonel Baum and his troops were sent to Bennington for munitions. However, they were met by John Stark and a mass of New Englanders at Walloomsac [*the Battle of Bennington*]. Baum died. His troops were decimated.

Burgoyne, having lost time, local support, soldiers at Hubbardton and Walloomsac, and St. Leger's whole army, should have stopped. Nonetheless, (and ignoring Howe's letter), Burgoyne drove on, crossing the Hudson on September 13. He had arrived at Saratoga.

Next week, the final installment: Burgoyne's defeat and a traitor's partial redemption.

"OVER MY SHOULDER" COLUMN FOR OCTOBER 4, 1997
Arnold's role in victory

We have seen now how British General John Burgoyne, because of treachery from his own people, his own ineptitude and pure bad luck, had arrived at Saratoga (now Schuylerville), on September 14th of 1777 in a poor position to be fighting a battle.

Historians believe that Burgoyne deceived himself, because he knew that St. Leger's army had been defeated at Oriskany on August 6 and he knew that Howe had chosen to keep his army at Philadelphia. Burgoyne's three-pronged attack on Albany was reduced to one prong, now arriving at Saratoga. And his own army, initially too small and under-provisioned, was now reduced to 5,000.

Nonetheless, I believe that it could have gone the other way had it not been for Benedict Arnold. On the British side, Burgoyne still had 5,000 crack troops and the continuing loyalty of many more Colonists than many historians care to admit.

And on the American side, three of the four people later held most responsible for American victory at Saratoga – Generals Philip Schuyler, Horatio Gates, and Benedict Arnold – were "killing" each other with political in-fighting. Only Captain Daniel Morgan was not involved.

Congress blamed New Yorker Schuyler for Burgoyne's capture of Fort Ticonderoga in July, and on August 19 replaced him as commander of the Northern Department with the British-born Virginian Gates. Gates had helped to defame Schuyler, whom New Englanders accused of being a closet Loyalist. (It would take 100 years for Schuyler's contributions to the victory at Saratoga to be fully recognized.)

Gates, nicknamed "Granny" because he was overly cautious, was in many ways like Schuyler. (And ironically, Gates rose through the British military with Burgoyne!)

And then, Benedict Arnold. At Schuyler's command, Arnold went to Oriskany in July and played a decisive role in the defeat of the British Barry St. Leger. Upon return, Schuyler was out, and Arnold's old friend Gates now turned on Arnold because of his friendship with Schuyler. Gates fought openly with Arnold, disgracefully provoking Arnold's famous bad temper.

The only person not to be tainted by these politics was Arnold's friend, Virginian Capt. Daniel Morgan.

When Burgoyne launched the first Battle on September 19, he had a chance to win. In my opinion, one of the major forces in turning that battle into an American victory was Benedict Arnold. Unlike Gates, who remained at the breastworks several miles away, Arnold personally led his own troops in battle, including Capt. Morgan and his famed sharpshooters. Arnold later wrote that he constantly, "urged, begged and entreated" Gates for more troops.

Arnold stopped Burgoyne's advance, but was abruptly pulled back by Gates, leaving Burgoyne in command of the field and technically the winner, although he lost almost 700 troops. He was, however, still alive. The British were belatedly sending General Clinton to help. And Burgoyne still had the ability to fight on or safely withdraw. Against his Generals' advice, he stayed.

More Americans poured in. Gates' and Arnold's fighting intensified. Gates stripped Arnold of all command on October 1, seriously demoralizing Arnold's troops. Arnold was not even allowed on the battlefield.

However, he disobeyed on October 7, when the battle opened with Burgoyne's attempt at reconnaissance. The Americans were overwhelming Burgoyne, but Gates remained at camp. Against orders, Arnold jumped his horse and rode into the fray. He directed Morgan's sharpshooters to kill Burgoyne's priceless General Fraser and then led his former troops to victory at Breymann's Redoubt, during which he was shot in the leg.

Despite his later turning traitor, Arnold made a critical difference at Saratoga. When Burgoyne finally surrendered on October 17, 1777, a direct result was that France recognized our new nation and gave it priceless aid, enabling us to go on to ultimate victory.

As we celebrate that "Second Independence Day," let us honor all the parties, Gates, Schuyler, Arnold, Morgan and, yes, even General Burgoyne, whose defeat secured our nation.

"OVER MY SHOULDER" COLUMN FOR DECEMBER 7, 1997
The story behind an epitaph

O n this day of remembrance of the attack on Pearl Harbor, let me share with you a story from the previous World War, a story with both world and local significance.

My thanks go to my friend Joan Aldous, who uncovered the story behind the mysterious tombstone in the Bay Street Cemetery in Glens Falls, bearing this inscription: "Albert Lloyd Hopkins/September 7, 1871/Killed in Lusitania disaster/May 7, 1915."

Her curiosity led her to uncover an unexpected and far more complicated story than was conveyed by the chilling words on the stone. Joan very graciously shared with me the news clippings she uncovered on the story.

Headlines in *The Post-Star* of May 8, 1915 screamed of the sinking of the Lusitania by the Germans on the day before: "SERIOUS SITUATION, VIEW IN WASHINGTON" and "ILL-FATED SHIP HAD BIG CARGO OF WAR SUPPLIES." The war did not yet include the United States, but the sinking of greater numbers of vessels staffed by or carrying Americans seemed destined to pull us in.

Now the Lusitania had been sunk. While the nation wondered if the country would go to war (which it did not until 1917), the story had a particular significance for the Glens Falls region signified by this headline from the same edition: "MRS. HOPKINS CONFIDENT HUSBAND IS AMONG PASSENGERS SAVED." The article beneath it reported that Albert L. Hopkins was "feared dead," although his wife, in Manhattan, as well as his family, in Glens Falls, hoped for the best. Hopkins, the paper reported, was "the son of Mrs. S. DeForest Hopkins of 71 Warren Street and nephew of Mrs. William A. Wait of 79 Warren Street." Stephen DeForest Hopkins was originally from Vermont and had resided in Glens Falls for the last twelve years of his life, presumably because his sister, Mrs. William Wait, lived there. His brother-in-law William Wait was, if I remember correctly, was the Treasurer of the First National Bank of Glens Falls (now Evergreen Bank).

Very significantly, Albert L. Hopkins was more than just a passenger on this ship of ships, which from the time it was launched in 1907 was hailed as a world class marvel of speed among the world's great ships. Although it was not as large as the Titanic, the Olympic, or the other "monster" passenger ships of the time, it was a record-holder for speed. In terms of international law, it was also, technically, "neutral," because it carried 128 U.S. citizens, the day it was torpedoed off the coast of Ireland.

As the Hopkins family learned by May 10, Albert was among the 149 (of the 1200 lost) whose bodies had been recovered and positively identified at a Queenstown Morgue.

Why was he on the ship? The beginning of the answer starts with the fact that he was one of the greatest authorities in the world on the building of large ships, both passenger liners and battleships. Upon his graduation from the Rensselaer Polytechnic Institute in Troy, he went to work for the Newport News Shipbuilding Company and quickly became general superintendent and, by around 1911, the president of the entire company.

It was on April 30, 1915 that Albert L. Hopkins, president of the Newport News Shipbuilding Company, was forced to leave the United States and go to England on business. Hopkins choose the Lusitania, obviously for its speed, as he was trying to make up time. You see, Hopkins had not been in Manhattan, but had been in Glens Falls when he received word from his firm that it was imperative that he go to London.

Ironically, he had been in Glens Falls to be with his dying father. On May 1, only a day after he left his father's bedside, Albert Hopkins was on board the Lusitania, when the cablegram came to him, bringing the news of his father's death.

Six days later, still on board that vessel, Hopkins would join his father.

"OVER MY SHOULDER" COLUMN FOR DECEMBER 14, 1997
A safe place

W hen you visit the Old Fort House Museum in Fort Edward this December for its beautiful Christmas exhibition, make sure you go into the "Baldwin Barn," a combination museum shop and orientation center.

Pause as you enter the door to the Baldwin Barn. Directly ahead of you, amidst all the lovely things, you will see a massive, very antique steel safe. It bears the words "Contryman and Wing," the two owners of the safe when it was first moved into the pharmacy they started 123 years ago.

Standing over four feet tall, painted red with fancy trim, the safe is huge and lovely, with two thick doors, one with a combination lock tumbler, and sets of lockable inner doors and drawers. And it is very comfortable.

"Comfortable" may not seem like a suitable word for a safe. However, trust me it is, for when I was five the safe was one of my favorite hiding spots, as it was located in the prescription room of our family's pharmacy on 151 Broadway. I could crawl into that safe and very nearly close the doors.

With me inside it, the doors could never have been latched, but the thought agitated my parents enough for them to have the tumbler welded so the safe could never be locked.

A little further into the Baldwin Barn, you'll see a huge wooden sign with the words "Contryman and Donnell" laid over the original names "Contryman and Wing." That sign hung on the outer wall of the back, wooden section of our pharmacy – and now you have the broad outline of the three different pharmacies that occupied the current building at 151 Broadway from 1874 to 1961.

In the beginning, Levi H. Wing, a descendant of Abraham Wing[xlv], and Amos B. Contryman operated the pharmacy from 1874 to somewhere around 1906. (Contryman, I was surprised and pleased to learn later, was the great uncle of a long-time friend of mine, Gladys Contryman Lapham of Glens Falls.)

Two clerks in the store, Ora E. Contryman and William G. Donnell, succeeded the first two partners and the store was "Contryman and Donnell" until 1937, when Contryman died. From 1938 to Donnell's death in 1951, it was "Donnell's Pharmacy." In 1952 my father took it over and ran it as "King's Pharmacy" until 1961.

Oddly, I hold the most records from the store, all of which had been stored in the safe, including Contryman and Wing's two original prescription books, hand written in flourishing Victorian script, listing the hundreds of compounds the two pharmacists concocted. Some make me wince to read as they contain compounds of mercury, arsenic, and other tasty goodies. Some prescriptions are historically interesting as they include salicylates, the basis of aspirin, but predating aspirin's invention.

Also, in my collection are interior photos of the store, taken around 1906, most of that interior eradicated by the time we arrived in 1952. By then all the moveable fixtures and such from the original pharmacy had been sold. The remaining built-in Victorian shelves and decorations were torn out and replaced with modern ones. In the early 1950s, Victoriana was distinctly "out."

Some things had remained: the books and photos I mentioned; a 1919 soda fountain that weighed several tons with its chrome fixtures and solid marble front; and, of course, the massive safe.

I mentioned that it was odd to me that I hold most of the store's records. You see, I'd always assumed the museum had more than I did regarding the store. When I learned the opposite was true, I also learned never to assume, but always to ask. Those records will one day go into the museum, their proper place. Only sentiment has kept me from giving them sooner.

Yes, they'll go back and then they'll be joined again with a big, old safe and a huge sign that reads, "Contryman and Donnell."

SECTION 3: PERSONAL AND FAMILY MEMORIES

"OVER MY SHOULDER" COLUMN FOR DECEMBER 21, 1994
A very special Santa

My mother had a little ornament that she placed on the Christmas tree each year, a tiny cotton Santa that she said she had placed on her tree from the time she was a little girl. The little Santa was, truthfully, in sad shape for its years of wear. But it was one of "those things," something given a special meaning when my mother was so little. Why, no one knew. Not even Mom.

As I grew older, with each Christmas I came to look forward to that Santa being placed gently on a high bough, nestled securely to prevent shrieking children, or cats, from knocking it to the floor. Without realizing it, a part of her childhood Christmases gradually became a part of her children's. It was a good feeling.

The tiny Santa moved a lot over the years. From my mother's birthplace in Mechanicville, it went to Saratoga, then to Fort Edward and then Ticonderoga, at each juncture adding children and years to its life. It sagged, and it drooped, and it faded. Yet it survived, tying each new Christmas into the ones that had passed.

The last time my mother put the Santa on her tree was in Ticonderoga in 1982. Shortly thereafter, she was diagnosed with cancer and on her next Christmas, which was to be her last, she decided she and my father would come to our homes instead. I remember her apology for not having a tree, which I later recognized as her way of saying, "I'm angry because I can't put up a tree, like I should."

So that year, 1983, for the first time in decades, the little Santa stayed in a box in my parents' cellar. At Christmas, 1984, my mother was gone and, again, the little cotton Santa stayed packed away. For that Christmas and the next two, my father would not decorate the house nor have a tree. The Christmas person in the King family was Mom and the Christmas person was gone.

About two and a half years after my mother died, Dad told us he was selling our family home in Ticonderoga. It was too big and too full of memories. "Come and take what you want," he told his children. The rest he would sell. For weeks upon weeks we helped him sort through the remains of a lifetime, as much a reward as a burden. For you must understand that Mom saved everything: family pictures and letters, dad's service records, the kids' report cards, canceled checks, even occupant mail. As I had before, I looked through acres of boxes of Christmas decorations. As before, I could not, amidst them all, find the tiny Santa.

Mom always was fond of saying, "What will be will be." I resigned myself to the fact that it was gone. "Things change," my father was always saying. Oddly,

I think that while he knew that was true, in a way he never resigned himself to his own wisdom. Almost three years to the day after my mother's death, he died. Things had, indeed, changed.

For my wife, Sara, and I, that Christmas of 1987 in Glens Falls was, with my daughter being six, filled with expectations of Santa. It was also an oddly empty Christmas. We got out the boxes of decorations and frantically searched for our tree's special angel, fearful it had been misplaced and then found it packed snugly away. My daughter sighed a big sigh! Under our regular boxes were the ones I'd brought from Ticonderoga. I rummaged through them, looking at the bubble lights and other things from my childhood Christmas trees.

And then, I found it. A tiny box inside of which was my mother's faded cotton Santa wrapped up securely. Lost, but never really lost. Tenderly, I placed it on a high bough. And there it will go again this year, as we celebrate our Christmas and the memories that a special decoration carries with it.

From my family to you, a very merry Christmas.

"OVER MY SHOULDER" COLUMN FOR APRIL 10, 1995
The Captain's willing slave: SQ 293591

NOTE: You may laugh when you read the following, but a lot of you will laugh out of self-recognition.

I am SQ 293591.

To the majority of you, that means nothing. To you who were children in the 1940s and `50s and who drank hundreds of gallons of Ovaltine, while faithfully listening to your radios or watching your TV's, it may spark that long buried memory of "Captain Midnight."

For it is true: I was a member of Captain Midnight's "Secret Squadron." And, yes, I still have my official card, purchased with my hard-earned money (begged from my mother) and Ovaltine seals (from jars purchased by my mother). You're laughing. But, gee, I was only ten. And what ten-year-old didn't want to have that great looking card with the Captain's motto, "Justice through Strength and Courage," and the special secret decoder? I've lost the decoder, a plastic miniature of the Captain's own jet, with a secret writing device and the decoding wheel for messages Captain Midnight sent during his shows. I think I had one because my friend Denny Linehan had one. It didn't matter: I had to have it.

I was a product of radio and television commercialism of the forties and fifties. Watching in Fort Edward, I'd want every blessed thing the TV announcer would tell me I wanted. Actually, it started earlier, on the tail end of radio's Golden Age. I remember listening to "Hi-yo Silver, AWAYYYYYY!" just before the local broadcast of the Fort Edward basketball games. ("The Flying Forts are charging down the court! Ryan goes up for a shot...") Listening? Hah! I was there!

Thankfully, only the nationally syndicated radio programs that had the "special stuff." When Hopalong Cassidy came on, or The Lone Ranger or Sergeant Preston – I was ready. My wallet (my parents' wallet) was theirs. When those same shows were televised, when I could actually see, in living black and white, the products they wanted me to have for my own? I was dead meat.

And when they offered a chance to be a "part of the gang," an "insider" – be still my heart! The Rootie Kazootie show had a special plastic film that you put right over the screen to see the missing parts of the secret message. And the Davy Crockett series spawned all the frontier-style equipment (in shoddy plastic with the look of real leather) a child could ever want.

But Captain Midnight? To me, the Captain had the sine qua non of all commercial junk: your own membership card, with your own individualized number and your own secret decoder. It was the best.

Well, I had to believe that, for I was up against a legend. A while before this, in the days before his voice deepened and he wrote letters to girls, my brother Mike had sent away his money (with forty-nine thousand Puffed Rice box tops) to get a pen from Sergeant Preston of the Yukon. (With a faithful canine companion named "King," wasn't it destiny?) That pen did everything but cook breakfast. It had secret compartments and could write in invisible ink and even had a flashlight built into the tip to light up the paper when you were chasing criminals in the dark! Oh, dear lord!

I couldn't have one. The "higher powers" said that Mike "had saved up for it." (Curse him!) He was "older." (And still is now – hah, hah, hah!) His pen made him partners with Sgt. Preston. Was this fair? No! I needed something of my own.

Captain Midnight supplied it. The membership card, the secret decoder, the warmth of being television slave SQ 293591. As instructed, I carried the card with me at all times. Didn't do anything, but it felt good! With my decoder I decoded the Captain's messages, not all strictly about crime fighting. Commercialism did sully some.

Oh! And my Captain Midnight card is still serving me. It's a helpful reminder for whenever I walk into computer stores and salivate over software CD's, hard drives and Mega-RAMs of memory. Just toys.

"And what do I need with toys?" I laugh quietly to myself, as I look at my card. I am SQ 293591.

"OVER MY SHOULDER" COLUMN FOR JULY 17, 1995
Swimming in summer

Hot, languid, lawn-burning summers like this one make me return to the days when I was little and summer meant swimming.

From the time I was five until I turned nine, my family lived over my parents' drugstore, King's Pharmacy, on Broadway in Fort Edward. As a child of seven or eight, before I began to work in the store after school and during the summer, a day at the beach was guaranteed. Until I was old enough to go alone, my older brother, Mike, HAD to accompany me, three years younger than he and definitely a pain in the neck to him. (In a few years, I'd do the same for my sister.) Once at the beach, Mike could ditch me and be with his friends, I with mine.

Waiting to go was hell. Insects were calling out a scorching day and the apartment cooked in the summer heat. Already we kids would have been down to the "kee-wall" – the quay where yachts came to moor on their way through the canal system. (I can hear my parents' warning to be careful, but we were immortal and ignored it.) The smell of the cottonwoods along the Hudson River beckoned, although back then in the mid-fifties, the smell of the Hudson itself did not always beckon.

Oh, to swim! You could smell the heat in the dust of the dirt alley from Broadway to the yacht basin, smell it in the cottonwoods and in the oil slicks and sewage that floated on the river. The roar of the huge dam by Scott Paper made us need to swim.

Using the foolproof strategy of begging until the parents succumbed, we finally were told (not allowed, mind you, but TOLD) to go to the beach. Mom packed us towels and baloney sandwiches – and suntan lotion I never used. We'd race down Broadway, sneaking past the Powers School for fear it would recapture us, then up and over the bridge to the island. I can hear the crunch of sand beneath my shoes that sometimes I'd foolishly remove. The bridge's hot concrete would roast my feet royally.

After the bridge, it's only a few minutes to the end of the island and the beach, but when you're seven or eight it's the entire Sahara. Finally (tah-dah!): The Beach, in all its glory and skin-soaking splendor. Until 1957, when the pool was put in, "the beach" meant swimming in the Hudson. Coming across the parking lot, we'd see that cool, shimmering river and streak down the hill, past the swings, through the burning sands and into the water, totally ignoring the lifeguards' calls of "No running!" As we bobbed in the water, they'd come up to "advise us" of our transgressions. I can see some of the lifeguards from various times in my childhood: Jack Toomey, Bobby Carpenter, the Newells, Nancy, Billy and Bob. Peter Haley, too. Many of you know of Peter's well-deserved reputation in today's music world. Well, it's a wonder he can hear a note, what with the ear-splitting squeals I'd perform at the top of my lungs, as I kiddingly called out (repeatedly, as kids will): "Life guard! Saaave me!"

It's amazing to think of what we swam in. We'd "bomb" the blobs of toilet paper floating by, dive into oil slicks and occasionally illegally swim beyond the ropes to pick up garbage. The new pool they built up in the parking lot was a godsend.

We swam literally all day, breaking only occasionally. Our towels and baloney sandwiches were always full of sand. I can't eat baloney today without expecting a gritty crunch. We'd swing, collect butternuts or walk on the roots of the trees, exposed so much that they looked like gnarled legs. Sometimes Mom would bring a picnic supper, sister Martha and brother Bill in tow. Scott hadn't arrived yet. Calmed by soft breezes, my mother would catch catnaps assisted by watchful neighbors.

The sun, our friend at noontime, now treacherously headed for the hill opposite the beach, its signal that swimming was over for the day at Sandy Beach. But there was always tomorrow and, when you're seven or so, summer's tomorrows last forever.

"OVER MY SHOULDER" COLUMN FOR AUGUST 14, 1995
Remember the PTs, the expendables

Although the official fiftieth anniversary of the end of World War II will be September 2, 1995, the end of hostilities came on August 15, 1945, the day Japan unofficially surrendered.

My father, George A. King, had been the commander of a PT Boat in the Pacific Theater, the "Other War." After the German surrender, he and millions of others accepted the inevitability of taking part in the invasion of the Japanese home islands. However, following the atomic bombing of Hiroshima on August 6th and Nagasaki on August 9th, Japan surrendered. Invasion talk ceased, for there was no more war. My father died believing "the bomb" had saved his life, a notion that I would like to address. But first, a little background.

Recently I came across photographs my father had sent home to my mother throughout the war. By 1945, they portrayed what war had done to a cocky, handsome young Naval officer, handsome enough even to model for photographs in a national magazine in 1943. By 1945, he was far less cocky and, like most PT Boat commanders, constantly in a rumpled uniform, tieless and often without a hat, sleeping in his clothes, never knowing when he'd be called out on solitary reconnaissance missions or to lead the massive offensives of U.S. fleets. In near-suicidal assaults, the PT's sped in below the range of Japanese large guns, firing torpedoes at only a few hundred yards off, then scurried away, often to be sunk by enemy fire or blown up as the Japanese ship exploded. "The Expendables" the PT's were called.

PT Boat people were independent, yet conservative; usually religious, though if not in the beginning of the tour of duty, then definitely by the end. You prayed to survive. While always afraid, conversely my father always believed he would live. In 1945, however, he learned and fatalistically accepted this reality: the invasion of Japan would increase the already high death rate among PT Boat squadrons. So, when surrender immediately followed Nagasaki, my father logically deduced "the bomb" had saved his life. He never would entertain any discussion about its demerits.

I will not debate his logic, although I personally think the radioactive nightmare that followed the bombing of Hiroshima and Nagasaki is tragic and horrible beyond words. However, I will not judge, god-like, the propriety of Truman's use of the bomb, like some now who state Truman knew the bomb was unnecessary since the Japanese were about to surrender. Fifty years of those haunting photos of Hiroshima have given us a perspective not possessed then.

What troubles me is that, amidst the rightful recognition of the civilian tragedy of Hiroshima and Nagasaki, we are forgetting the history that preceded "the bomb": the butcherous conquest of hundreds of millions by the Japanese military, Mongolia in 1931, China in 1937, and southeast Asia and the Pacific by 1941-42. If we know more now of Nazi Germany's evil than of the Japanese Empire's, perhaps it is because of the unprecedented scale of the premeditated, precisely executed horrors the Nazis performed in exterminating Jews, Gypsies, and "enemies of the state" – horrors so grotesque that paradoxically they must never be forgotten.

Just as the atrocities of the Japanese Empire must not be forgotten: nerve gas in Manchuria; the slaughter in China; forced prostitution of Korean women; Pearl Harbor; to name a very few. The Japanese prison camps my father and his crew liberated lacked only the size and the theme of "racial purification" to match exactly the concentration camps of their Nazi allies. The barbarism was equal.

We should remember. Not to foster hatred of today's Japan, the majority of whose citizens, like myself, were born after 1945 and had nothing to do with the war. Nor to excuse any of our government's grievous wartime actions, such as the internment of innocent Japanese Americans. Nor to gloss over the sorrowful legacy of Hiroshima.

Rather, we remember in order to keep a balanced perspective on the history that brought our families, their community, and every community into a war started by power-hungry men who left their humanity behind in the name of God and country.

We remember that history so as never to repeat that history.

"OVER MY SHOULDER" COLUMN FOR DECEMBER 4, 1995
Remember the old Ti coffee club?

A letter from Judy McLaughlin, in Ticonderoga, brought back memories of what I've dubbed the "Coffee Club" at Burleigh's Pharmacy, where my father was pharmacist from 1962 until his death in 1987. While the names differ, I think you'll recognize the faces from your town. Coffee Clubs are the same everywhere.

Now, I'm going back to the sixties and seventies. My parents, Jane and George King, were alive then, both active in the Coffee Club, which wasn't really a club of course, and its morning "coffee hour" was usually more than an hour. Its "members" were the regulars, clustered at the counter, some quietly reading the paper until they fully awoke, some having arrived chattering and happy.

My parents' morning routine was predictable in its unpredictability. George would roar in, frantically groping for the keys, usually late. Often Jane's driving was the source of agitation – and entertainment for the Club. Mom had gotten her license after turning forty and Dad, a PT Boat commander in "the war," unwillingly gave over the helm, keeping up a litany of instructions and gentle cursing that could set a tone for their entry into the store. He would dart to the prescription area, she to the counter, where Judy or one of the other "girls" (all young women, but I am using the language of that period) on duty that morning had hot coffee going, while they prepared the salads for the lunch hour. The sulfurous smell of hard-boiled eggs mimicked what we called the "smell of prosperity," the sulfurous smell of the paper mill.

With each new arrival, the regulars interrupted their conversations about births, deaths or the intimate details about their kids or their spouses, neither who were there to defend themselves. They'd always ask Jane, "What's George done now?" I can see the Club: Paul and Thelma Joubert, Betty Curtis, "Toot" Hurlburt, who had the cab stand by the bank. Paul, a bear of a man, who worked for the phone company, and my mother had both graduated from Albany Business College and so had a mini-alumni association going. There's Virginia "Babe" Smith, a former mayor, and banker Tom Gibson, a Canadian by birth, who always looked to me like a dashing British RAF pilot. There's Jean Brown, Carolyn White, Cy LaPointe. That's only a few. Forgive my faulty memory.

To the rear, in the prescription room, dad would meet his boss, "Bunny" Bevilacqua, the Mayor of Ti, and a wise and wonderful man. The two were like cousins. George would then migrate to the counter to "exercise his humor," which could be piercing. He nicknamed everyone, especially the girls behind the counter: Roxanne, Lolita, etc. And he had eagle eyes. A girl whose boyfriend had bestowed upon her a "hickey" would always get caught. He'd walk back to the prescription room, pretending not to have seen, but then would boom out to her, "An old war wound on your neck?" The Club would go wild! She'd run to the cellar, only to be kidded by Hayden P. Wallace, a WW II veteran whom Dad had nicknamed Sgt. York. Haydie, who cleaned at the store, had heard every word through the metal chute that conveyed the soda fountain's garbage to the cellar. In revenge, the girls would often dump massive quantities of pickle juice down the chute. Sgt. York's profanity, piped up through the chute, would send the Coffee Club into near hysteria.

Sometimes – how can I say this gently? – George would "overindulge," and Jane would offer loud critiques of said behavior, to the delight of the Club. It irked her no end that she rarely drank and had migraines, while he "partook" and had none. Jane's driving offered him revenge. Such as the time when she slid off icy Champlain Avenue, slicing away the D&H switching mechanism, and halting all freight traffic into the village for days! And offering a source for George's sarcasm for months.

While Burleigh's and its soda fountain still exist, there's no pharmacy now. And those old days, like so many of the Coffee Club, are gone. But all will be remembered, especially with friends like Judy to remind us of the good times.

Hey Judy! Pour us another cup, will you?

"OVER MY SHOULDER" COLUMN FOR DECEMBER 18, 1995
Truly a gift from the heart

This is a Christmas tale some of you may have heard before. My friend JoAnn Adams suggested I relate it in this column and so I will. It is a personal story, about a lesson that I learned at a Christmas that was almost thirty years ago, although it still seems like yesterday.

By the time that my mother and father had reached their forties, two of their four children were in college and the other two were of an age that now allowed Mom and Dad to relax a bit...something that they certainly deserved and certainly looked forward to. Which made what they did all the more difficult for their children to understand at that time. For, in their mid-forties, my parents adopted their God-child, who was a little boy, only five years old.

When my brother Scott came to live with us at age five, he was so shy and so withdrawn that we thought he'd never come out of his shell. I should say, we kids didn't think so. My parents felt far more confident about the whole thing. Or at least that's the impression they gave. Parents are like that, you know.

Over the first few years our new little brother gradually carved his niche in the family. By and large he was a quiet boy and around the time he was seven he began to hoard things, keeping them close to himself and hidden, as if he would never get them again if he were to let them go. It had taken him awhile to get used to the fact that he had his own bed and could have his own things, but this year, when he was seven, he really did hoard things away in an almost miserly fashion, especially money that my mother would give him: pennies, nickels, dimes. He hoarded it all. To me he became a little Ebenezer Scrooge, but then I was away at college most of the year and was not as understanding as those still living at home: Mom, Dad, and my sister Martha and brother Bill. My parents had an idea that it was because of our family just having moved to a new house. The move, they said, had made Scott insecure, because he thought that he was going to change homes...and families...again. I thought to myself, "Well... That could be." But, honestly, I just clung to the thought that he seemed very greedy. What a lesson I was to learn.

It came Christmas time, our first Christmas in the brand-new house. With Scott a seven-year-old still believing in Santa Claus, you can imagine that we were all up at the crack of dawn. Presents were being opened, and Scott, uncharacteristically for him, insisted that we open his presents. We did and, as with the youngest child in every family, did so with a great deal of fanfare. It was a fanfare that was truly deserved, and I will never forget those presents. Mine was incredible. A wooden box, originally used to package salted codfish, but now filled with nails. It was his favorite wooden box. And the nails he had collected because he knew I needed them. As everyone opened their present, it was slowly dawning on us all that Scott was giving us his things that he cherished most.

At last, it was time for my mother's present. What a special glow Scott had on his face as he gave it to her. She opened it and took out...his wallet, filled with ALL the money that she had given him over the year. He had given away, as Christmas presents, EVERYTHING he owned, everything that was most precious to him. We all sat, with tears in our eyes, unable to speak, until Scott said, "Did I do something wrong?" And we all rushed him at once to hug him and to tell him, "No, no! You did everything right, just right!" He beamed all over.

I still have that codfish box with the nails. It is a constant and wonderful reminder of what giving really means...a lesson my brother taught to me on a Christmas long ago.

Merry Christmas to you my brother, wherever you may be.

"OVER MY SHOULDER" COLUMN FOR JUNE 30, 1996
A summer through the mill

In 1966 I got a summer job at the old International Paper mill in Ticonderoga. A mill job meant real money, union wages: $2.61 an hour. Back then, IP occupied the center of downtown. It's all gone today, replaced by the present mill, built in 1971 near Lake Champlain.

I started my first workday on the 7 to 3 "tower" (tour). I stood with a group of 18-to-20-year-old "college kids" (not a term of endearment) in the old-time office next to the huge "new mill" that had been built right across Lake Champlain Avenue, cutting the street in two.

Under the skeptical eyes of the regulars, we nervously clocked in (always 20 minutes ahead as a courtesy to the person you were relieving). Thankfully we were interspersed with some full-timers, like Tommy Slattery of Port Henry, and experienced college kids, like Gene Thompson from Moriah. They made sure we didn't hurt the machinery. Or kill ourselves. Even now I see all our faces, but don't remember all the names: Danny Ahern, Bill and the others from Whitehall; Johnnie from above Port Henry, Bob Denn, from Albany; and a kid from Butler College that everybody called Butler.

We walked down a long set of steel stairs into the bowels of the mill, a three-story high basement. The next floor up were the thundering number 7 and number 8 paper making machines, two behemoths we would help feed. In spite of sodium lamps, the basement was dark. Machinery noise was a constant thunder. We shouted to be heard. The temperature was 25 to 30 degrees hotter than outside and rain forest humid. The entire place smelled of rotten eggs from the sulfite process. Our first day. We thought we had arrived in hell. Thirty minutes later, day foreman Jigger Donovan arrived, bellowing a blue streak as he told us how, where, and when to work. Hell was complete.

Bob and I threw imperfect paper ("broke") on a five foot wide, clanking steel conveyor belt, feeding the "Liebeck," a two story steel cone with a whirling drum of blades and superheated hot water that chewed the broke into pulp, feeding it back into Number 7 and 8. The other guys brought broke down in hand-pushed carts from the trimming machines above or in slabs from the splitters cutting imperfect rolls in two. The men above us used it faster that we threw it on. "They're screamin' for broke on 7!" we'd hear. Sweat flowed from us. A red light near the top of the belt would signal when we were to stop feeding in broke. It rarely went on.

We "college kids" tried our best to show we could, and would, work. But I honestly think we probably drove poor Jigger Donovan and the shop stewards nuts in those first days. Dan and I began to ride the battery powered hand trucks around like cars, reciting lines from "Chicken Man, the white-winged, weekend warrior" and singing "Paperback Writer." We all kept filling the Liebeck long after the red light went on. Suddenly a man, soaked head to foot in mushy paper came running, screaming for us to stop. He had been sitting upstairs in the computer room where the tops of holding vats were. The liquid pulp had overflowed the tops of the tanks, gushing down over him and his co-workers, washing them to the floor. He looked like a giant clump of wet toilet paper. We tried not to laugh. I think we tried.

In that first week we worked doubles constantly, from 7 a.m. to 11:00 p.m. After 16 hours of body-building work, we'd shower and run up to the Burleigh House, also known as Willy Roundhead's. Willy had live bands who'd play the Beatles and Motown hits at deafening decibels. With teenage energy, we'd drink too much beer, dance until two, and then go to Burgey's Cave in Hague to do the same until three.

A little over three hours later, at 6:40 a.m., we'd be clocking in, groggily grabbing breakfast from Mr. Good's "Goodie Cart," and doing the same thing all over again. Including the dancing – from that night into the next morning.

And summer had just begun.

"OVER MY SHOULDER" COLUMN FOR SEPTEMBER 22, 1996.
The day a schoolboy ran away

Fall always triggers one particular memory of elementary school that I hope you will allow me to share with you. Let me set the stage by drawing a picture of my grade school, typical of the hundreds of large brick buildings built in the late 19th century. Mine, the Powers School on Broadway in Fort Edward, still stands. Though no longer a school, it will always be my grade school.

When first built in 1893, the three-story brick building held kindergarten through grade 12. [xlvi] By my first year there, first grade with Bessie Green, it held only grades Kindergarten through fourth. I can still see the high ceilings; smell the new paint in the huge hallways; hear the creaking wood floors. Everything smelled of chalk dust, floor polish, and that funny sawdust they put down when kids threw up.

Each room had enormous windows, a separate cloak room for coats, the flag, and a picture of Washington or Lincoln. Many rooms still had the combination cast iron and wood seats, bolted to the floor. The toilets, located in the basement, had bathroom fixtures for high school sized children. To first graders, the urinals looked like shower stalls. For years, the words "basement" and "toilet" meant the same thing in my vocabulary.

My "particular memory" goes back to my first day of fourth grade. A seasoned veteran by this time, I was sauntering up the front stairs of school, amidst the usual screeching and other healthy noises of kids saying goodbye to summer. I was nodding sympathetically to the frightened "little kids," and getting ready for Mrs. Wagner, who would have us all recite Longfellow's "The Children's Hour" every day thereafter. I still know it to this day.

Perhaps I wasn't paying as much attention as I could have to the major ruckus a few stairs in front of me. An adult man was attempting to get his child into the first day of kindergarten. Step by step up the stairs the father literally was wrestling the shrieking boy, whose arms and legs flailed. Soothing words were giving way to those that were, shall we say, more forceful. I was examining how to get around the two, when the boy did something to his father. I'm not certain what, but whatever it was the man gave out with a raging bellow and, never looking around, reached back to give some velocity to the whack he was obviously about to administer to his son's backside.

Unfortunately, my head was in the way. As soon as the back of the man's hand made contact with the side of my head, I let out with a huge yelp, and he dropped what he was doing and reached around, tenderly and apologetically looking after me. But he was no longer clinging to his son.

The word "freedom" never had a better demonstration than at moment. The little boy, free of his father's grip, ran up the remaining stairs, shot over the expanse of the first-floor hallway, bolted down the back stairs and out the rear door. His poor father was torn! With multitudes of apologies, he followed his son, joined by many teachers and the janitor. We kids ran to the east side of the building to watch this posse of adults chase after the boy whose little legs were carrying him toward the partially filled-in feeder canal out back of the school.

Of course, he was caught. And we were wholly satisfied. Why should he go free if we couldn't? Life resumed its proper pattern. But I thought as I was hustled off to class, here it was, my first few minutes in school on the first day of fourth grade and already it was teeming with adventure. "What next?" I wondered!

And shortly thereafter I was introduced to Henry Wadsworth Longfellow.

"OVER MY SHOULDER" COLUMN FOR OCTOBER 9, 1995
The horror of being a newcomer

Our family has just moved and my daughter, Julia, has started a new high school, bringing back memories of my anxiety at starting my junior year at Ticonderoga High School. Also known as "Ti High" – properly pronounced "Toi Hoi."

The accent was notably different between Fort Edward and Ticonderoga. With my flat upper Hudson Valley twang, I'd send kids into laughter as I pronounced words like "laugh" or "cat" in my usual Fort Edward way, which sounded to them like "leeyaff" and "keeyat" said quickly. I thought their twang was funny because they pronounced words like "mountain" as "ma-ountain." Or "my" as "moi."

On my first day, my history teacher, Charlie Royce, asked where I lived. "On the Creek," I replied. With tongue in cheek, but with an eye toward helping me acclimate, Mr. Royce told me that I lived "on the Crick." I said it that way afterwards. It made life easier.

High school was my main consideration. The larger centralized school was in a conference league that included (to me) exotic places like Lake Placid and Plattsburgh. And we had to wear regulation gym outfits which I hated. I later learned the joy of them. You brought them in to school in September, back home once at Christmas and then at year's end, for the safety of all, threw them in a dumpster. Gym outfits were equalizers. No one, not even the team captains, like Rick Bartlett, could really ever look good in those outfits, although I was sure Rick looked better in his than I ever did in mine. I was sure everyone else did but me.

There was also the phenomenon that almost every male except myself and a few other guys left school on the first few days of "Huntin' Season." I remember walking into Mr. Harris' chemistry class on the first day of hunting season. The room was a sea of women. Later in college this would have been a marvelous prospect, but now, 15 and shy beyond words, it was "the chemistry class from hell." I was short, skinny, and positive my face had been borrowed from a gargoyle.

As a teen, the most difficult part of acclimating to a new school is being a teen. Being embarrassed. Even naturally outgoing students will have embarrassing moments entering a new school. It's a rite of passage. It stinks.

One of my worst memories concerns a lovely young woman whom I met shortly after I arrived. I was infatuated. She was "just friendly." The "incident" happened in the cafeteria. Now, just walking across the long cafeteria was an excruciating experience. Then again, in those early days, constantly certain my Clearasil had failed, everything was an excruciating experience.

It was the end of lunch. A Thursday, I remember, because the menu selection was "pennies from heaven," that gastronomic treat of sliced hot dogs in spaghetti sauce over white bread. I had walked the long walk across the large floor to put away my tray and turned. There she was! Signaling me! Asking if she could come over to speak to me!

My heart raced. I smiled and nodded. She walked toward me. I searched for the right words. She spoke first as she arrived: "Can I speak to you?" A goddess asking permission to speak to a mere mortal? Wonders of wonders!

And then she said, with care and obvious concern for me: "Your fly is unzipped. I wanted to tell you so that you would not be embarrassed."

Years later it certainly would not have meant what it did then. As it was, I mumbled a horror-stricken thank you and contemplated climbing through the same window into which I had just put my tray. Instead I walked out, clinging to the wall as if I were part of the paint. No one else noticed thanks to her. I laugh about it now. Although I'm still uncomfortable in cafeterias.

I survived and like all newcomers was adopted by my new hometown, which has a big heart and great people. And I survived high school. And Ti High managed to survive me, my sister, and two younger brothers.

Thanks for the memories, Ti High!

I mean, Toi Hoi.

"OVER MY SHOULDER" COLUMN FOR AUGUST 25, 1996.
School daze

A recent conversation with my seventh-grade homeroom teacher, Mr. Charles Mullen, plus a visit to Fort Edward High School for the first time in many decades were two reality checks I'm not sure I'm handling well. You see, I've carried a memory of the building from the 1960s. But it has expanded so that I barely knew it, although some of the oldest section, the front, looks much as it did then. It amazes me to think that the oldest part was only built in 1924. As a boy, I thought it had been commissioned by the Pilgrims. Reality: the older you get, the younger old things seem.

Ironically, the one thing that remains identical is the auditorium. I stood aghast at the scene of the dreaded "Assembly" – a reprieve from class that turned into horror as Principal C. Archie Hopkins would announce that we'd be listening to the band or a lecture on traffic safety. I gazed with no joy at the hard, wooden, unforgiving seats, unchanged since 1924, seats that caused our bottoms to go numb. That caused us to squirm. That caused Mr. Mullen to threaten a trip worse than an assembly. Yes! To the office.

Frankly, Junior High would have frightened us to death had it not been for the teachers. Mr. Mullen was cool. He taught history. I loved history. He was "okay in my book," as my father's generation always said. Back then he seemed a little stern at times. Much later, as a parent of a seventh grader, I developed an intense sympathy for him, as well as a unique insight into my survival as a human. I don't know how he kept from killing all of us.

Having had mostly female teachers, the experience of nearly all male teachers was weird. Back then for discipline's sake, females did give you a whack. Males were a tad more unorthodox. Take David Ross' math class. Seated at the very back of the room, my friend George leaned back after lunch to take a snooze against the French doors of the storage cabinets. Mr. Ross gently eased an eraser off the chalk board and sent it cruising across the top of George's head and crashing into the doors. George jumped up with a scream and a large chalk stripe across his crewcut. We all howled.

Mr. Jack Toomey taught science. Definitely cool and another one you didn't mess with. His biceps were bigger than our whole bodies. Bob Clarke had a handful in his English class with know-nothings like me. Until I met him, I thought a "classic" was a vintage Batman comic. That miracle worker got me to put down comics and pick up books by Ernie Pyle and Mark Twain.

My discovery of Twain coincided with my expanded interest in drawing, fostered by our art teacher, Miriam Harmon, a lovely lady who passed away recently. Miss Harmon was of the old school, soft spoken so that when the loud word came it was powerful. She taught me a lesson I've always cherished. From the inside of a Huckleberry Finn book, I had copied a drawing of Huck and Jim and proudly presented it to her as my own. Never letting on that she knew differently, she praised my work in a way that told me she knew. From that time on, I never did that again. Her lesson was effective and face-saving. I will always remember her.

Perhaps the oddest sight at the high school was the old gym now serving as a cafeteria. How in the name of heaven they had ever eradicated that gym smell is beyond me.

Oh. And speaking of smells? The school still smells the same: chalk and cleaning fluid and paper supplies. I haven't been in school for how many years, but those odors made me depressed all over again at the thought of fall coming.

Reality doesn't cure everything.

"OVER MY SHOULDER" COLUMN FOR NOVEMBER 17, 1996
Holiday's forgotten course lives on

In my home is my mother's first cookbook, a "Better Homes and Gardens" cookbook from 1943. Mom was a war bride and the well-worn, gravy stained pages of that book still serve me today as I search for recipes. Although the wartime advice on rationing is no longer applicable, and the cholesterol count of the meals would give an elephant a heart attack, I still fondly look at the recipes, phone numbers and "to do" messages scribbled in her hand.

That cookbook is at the root of our family Thanksgivings. To its basic recipes were added others. A voracious reader, Jane – forgive me if I call her by her first name, but as we kids grew older we started affectionately calling her by both "Mom" and "Jane" – culled recipes from *Good Housekeeping*, the *New York Times*, or the latest book she was reading. As she aged, she grew more experimental, adding new recipes, but never replacing old standards. And understand: the larger the feast and the more people to feed, the better her meals were. Special occasions produced a feed so incredibly huge we dubbed it a "Jane Meal."

"The Pumpkin Soup Thanksgiving" is a perfect example of a Thanksgiving "Jane Meal." As we kids had moved away, Jane adjusted her cooking habits for fewer people. Each holiday meal, then, provided her with an eating audience and an outlet for those pent-up recipes. By the 1980s, with all her kids gone from the nest, her Jane Meals had grown to gargantuan proportions. Thanksgiving came to match the three-day feast of the Pilgrims.

"The Pumpkin Soup Thanksgiving" followed the usual ritual, both in food and in actions. Huge platters of cheeses, dips, crackers, fresh veggies, and more were served in the living room, wherein my father sat enthroned in front of the tube, watching one of umpteen football games.

Mom, in a kitchen the size of a big closet, juggled various dishes on and off the stove and in and out of the oven, readying dishes prepared days in advance. We kids had several crucial jobs, including wrenching father from the tube and getting him to the table to carve the turkey, possibly an ostrich, given its size. Another was keeping Dad's mother out of the kitchen. Grandma did not observe the rules of war that preclude meddling in a daughter-in-law's kitchen. The always uneasy truce nearly exploded into battle as Mom's voice rose to a bellow, strained through her teeth: "Please take Grandma to her seat!" Ritualistically, Grandma would stage whisper, "I was only trying to help!" Grumble, grumble. Tension building.

Once in the dining room, festooned with Indian corn and things Thanksgiving, silver and crystal polished, the meal began. Out came – pumpkin soup. A hush fell. My father, never adventurous in his eating habits, eyeballed it. Jane, in full authority, ladled it into his bowl anyway. He paused. Jane gave a murderous look. He ate. It was delicious, he truthfully conceded. It became another standard.

Courses flowed from the kitchen from heaven only knows where. The table was a juggling act of plates, platters, and dishes sailing around, with every flat surface recruited to hold food. Jane was a blur, never sitting for more than a mouthful before popping up and bringing in something else, the traditional oyster casserole or a new vegetable creation from "The Times."

By dessert, we sat gasping our praises to the chef. And, then, suddenly, Jane sprung up, dashed into the kitchen saying, "Oh, no!" and returned with – a forgotten course! Of all the traditions of a Jane Meal that was "the" one for which we waited. To this day, none of us recalls a Jane Meal in which she remembered to serve everything she cooked.

Jane may be gone, but she and her Jane Meals live on. I'm wondering what we'll forget this year.

"OVER MY SHOULDER" COLUMN FOR DECEMBER 22, 1996
Warm memories of our 2nd Christmas

A small, framed painting in my home recalls sweet memories of two people who gave our family a second Christmas celebration on Christmas day.

The painting, of a Native American, was by my Aunt Kinks, actually my great-aunt Cornelia. She was the sister of Nina, my mother's mother. Until I was ten, we would have Christmas at our house and then go to the home of my Aunt Kinks and Uncle Frank in Stillwater.

After we moved to Fort Edward in 1952, our family Christmas became centered around the family pharmacy, open every holiday, Christmas being no exception although the hours were shorter. It made things harder, but we still managed to go to Stillwater.

For the first four years in Fort Edward, we lived in a small apartment over the store. Let me recall a typical Christmas from when I was, say, seven, the year my brother Bill was born. Christmas morning we'd awaken (as if we had ever really been asleep?), absolutely dying to know what we got. Naturally. But, we did have to go to church first. Our parents had the luxury midnight mass. We did not. Grumble, grumble.

Dutifully we'd dress, and somberly peek at the tree on our way to the early mass at St. Joseph's, where we'd thank Father Doyle in our hearts for keeping the mass short. Back home, Dad had already been to the train station to pick up Grandma, his mother, who'd come up from Saratoga for the day. The adults dutifully arranged, we children then proceeded to "unwrap presents": to shred wrapping paper and make a chaotic mess.

Dad would then go down to open the store. Mom would start cooking some things for the next part of our Christmas. Around noon, Dad would close up shop and we would pack the car full and head off to Stillwater. Things were a bit tense, but I would see a change in my mother as we arrived. It wasn't until I was older that I understood the special relationship that existed there.

You see, when Mom was just an infant, her own mother, Nina, died. This left my grandfather to care for Mom and my Uncle Jim, only four. Mom's father asked Aunt Kinks if she and Frank would temporarily care for Mom. They did so – for the next two years – until my grandfather remarried and brought his daughter back home.

So, besides Nina, my mother had two mothers: her stepmother Irene and Aunt Kinks, both of whom she loved as a mother. Thanksgiving we'd spend with my Grandmother Irene and Christmas with Kinks.

Something special happened when we entered that house: my mother became a child again. Kinks and Frank had had no children of their own, but Mom was their child. And we, their grandchildren. The house would be filled with the smell of Christmas dinner. There were presents galore stacked under a small table top tree that Frank cut out of his own back yard. (This using a tree from your own land was incredibly radical to me for some reason.)

The stress and the tensions of a large family, a small apartment and a new business all melted away from Mom, as Kinks hugged her and lifted the weight from her, as if taking off her coat. We opened presents in the front room, where Kinks' painting hung. I can still see that room. And I can still feel the love and warmth that radiated from those two people as they fussed over us. We ate, we played games, we ate some more, and in the tranquility and peace of their home, we as a family found tranquility and peace restored in ourselves.

Kinks and Frank moved away in 1958 and in 1960 Kinks died. And yet she did not. For the love of those special "second Christmases" live on in my heart. And will always.

A Merry First and a Merry Second Christmas to you.

"OVER MY SHOULDER" COLUMN FOR FEBRUARY 9, 1997
Warmth of a Ti welcome

The first time I saw Ticonderoga was right around this time of year in 1962. My father had just taken a job with John "Bunny" Bevilacqua in Burleigh's Pharmacy in December and my parents decided I should see what my new town was like. I was fifteen and adamantly opposed to our moving. But, then, at fifteen, nothing a parent does is right.

And, I was scared to move. "What were these Ticonderogians like?" I wondered as we drove up Route 4 through Fort Ann. By Whitehall, where we stopped at the Silver Diner, the snow had gotten higher and the hills had changed to mountains. Things looked very different, even ominous, to me as we headed up Route 22.

Part of this feeling was intensified by Route 22, which in 1962 was under construction and in shambles. The road's horrible condition was driving local people to distraction. I got my first inkling of what these mountain people were like when I learned that some of them had issued a public invitation to Governor Rockefeller and his pregnant wife to drive up Route 22. The trip, they said, would speed up her delivery date by several months.

"Boy," I thought to myself, "This is one tough crew."

As Dad swore at the make-shift bridge crossing Lake Champlain at South Bay, I enjoyed the breath-taking view. Near Black Mountain, I learned another definition of "breath-taking," as an unlicensed log truck barreled down on top of us, missing us by inches and careening off down the road – never stopping, its logs slopping around the back of the overfilled truck like near-death on four wheels.

"Boy," I thought to myself, "These people are wild."

My introduction to Ti itself came as a scent that lingered around my nostrils as we crossed the flats of Putnam, with the wind whipping off Lake Champlain at about 90 mph and the snow raging around us. But as Dad said nothing, I remained quiet until the Fort View Inn. By that time, it had become an overpowering stench. Still Dad said nothing. I blurted, "Dad! What is that horrible smell?"

He smiled knowingly, and a few minutes later, as we entered the village, he waved his hand toward the paper mill just coming into view, and said, "That's the `smell of prosperity'" – the local phrase for the thick white-blue haze surrounding the mill and every house within a half mile and smelling like rotten cabbage: the by-product of the sulfite process of International Paper Mill that took up easily half of downtown Ticonderoga.

"Boy," I thought to myself, "These people are nuts." What were we doing here? Dad knew. I was soon to find out.

We drove past a threatening wood pile, many stories high, that fed the belching mill, which produced paper 24 hours a day. The mill ran along "the crick" from the village limits for almost a mile into the very core of Ticonderoga. It was overwhelming.

We went directly to Burleigh's Pharmacy, which was practically on top of the mill, as most of Montcalm Street was. Shyly I followed Dad in past the lunch counter, beyond which were the booths in the back where the kids hung out after school. The store's smell was a combination of medicine and soda fountain – oh, and egg salad with olives. Which mixed perfectly with the sulfurous odor of the mill.

Suddenly people came over to greet my father and to welcome me, especially Dad's boss, Bunny Bevilacqua. I was stunned as I realized that in only a few weeks, my father had been welcomed into town and accepted. In my first few minutes walking into that store, I, too, began to learn the intrinsic secret of my new hometown-to-be.

On this cold February day, the intensity of that "secret" – that free and generous welcome – warms me now, as it did thirty-five years ago.

"OVER MY SHOULDER" COLUMN FOR MAY 25, 1997
Sully's precious lessons

With spring and the baseball season upon us, a reminiscence about my little league years, especially about the man who coached me, seemed in order. Sadly, a tragic accident recently claimed the life of that man before I had a chance to tell him I had written about him. So, I hope that what I had intended to say about him in life will, in some small way, serve to eulogize him now that he is gone.

His name was Loren Sullivan. Some called him "Lornie" or "Sully." Hell, in Fort Edward if at some point you don't have a nickname or some variation on your name, you wonder if you're weird. I knew him as Sully. Although I certainly didn't have the advantage of knowing him as well as others, my experience reflects what everyone has told me: that Loren Sullivan was a fine, fair and caring man who was deeply cared for in return.

Sully was my coach for the Knights of Columbus little league team. He was the kind of coach I, as an adult, would consider perfect. As a child I thought otherwise. You see, Sully was fair. With Sully, everybody got to play. Everybody got on the field. And everybody got to bat.

It's probably no surprise, then, that during the first two of my three years with the team, it was in last place. And I was a contributing factor. Oh, I could catch – both hands. Played right, left and center fields.

The problem was I couldn't bat to save my life. And Sully knew I couldn't hit the ball if it were lying still on the ground and my bat were three feet wide. So did the team. It was agony. Yet because of that, I came, belatedly, to appreciate Sully's fairness.

I can see it now. It's a hot, dry, and dusty day at the Harry Hodgman Little League field on Rogers Island. The Knights are behind, as usual. I'm in the field. I catch a ball. "That's the way to go, Joe!" Sully cries. We stave off the opposing team from making any further advances and actually have a chance to catch up. And then Sully says, "Joe. You're up to bat."

I don't know if I begged him not to, but I distinctly remember my teammates begging him not to send me to bat. I must admit it was more than a little humiliating to hear, "Please coach, don't send in Joe!" When I stepped to bat the most we could hope for was that I'd get hit by the ball and walked, always a possibility as several pitchers had been successfully beaning me with a few fast balls, only adding to my aversion to batting. I'd say to Sully, "How about the next time?"

But Sully stood his ground, patiently and firmly, and always with a smile and word of encouragement. "Everybody gets to play" was his rule.

Well, a funny thing happened. In my third year, our team got out of the cellar and went up a notch to third. I decided not to play the next year. I think Sully was disappointed, but he accepted my decision and wished me well. I couldn't explain that it wasn't him or my teammates. I just didn't care that much for baseball. I'll never know for sure if my leaving made a difference, but next year my team went to first place – with everybody playing.

By chance, I ran into Sully recently at Town Hall, only a few weeks before his death. I had wanted, but didn't get the chance, to tell him that I had taken from him a lesson, although I had to grow to adulthood to realize it fully and to put it in these words: life is best when everyone gets to participate, and we thrive as a people when everybody gets to play.

Bye, Sully. And, thanks.

"OVER MY SHOULDER" COLUMN FOR AUGUST 24, 1997
Rockin' memories of the club

Recently, my friend JoAnn Smatko Taylor and I were reminiscing about the old Republican Club in Fort Edward. She arranged for us to get together with the two people most responsible for the club existence from 1954 to `64, Nicholas and Olympia Ruotolo – in Fort Edwardese, "Nicky and Limp." We reminisced, as we looked through their photo album filled with all our memories.

Let me describe the club from a kid's perspective, then give you a bit of "adult history." It was heaven on earth, located on the second floor of the old Merchants Block (now gone), over Murray Rosenberg's Five and Ten Cent Store. I'd run down Broadway, charge up the huge, creaking stairs to the second-floor room with wide floors. Rock music, still new then, was roaring, the lights were appropriately low, the soda cheap. The floor bounced with everybody twisting, doing the mash and other insane dances. (How poor Murray had a ceiling left is anyone's guess.)

Girls were lined up on one side, boys on the other. Many times, girls danced with each other, waiting for boys to "cut in." School dances couldn't hold a candle to the Republican Club. This was where you went to dance – and to be seen. It was cool.

The Ruotolos said the club had started as the local Republican Party's "Republican Club" that, among other things, celebrated the party's victories. In 1954, it was winding down and Nick suggested setting up a youth center with the money left over. He said that Larry Corbett, Bob Bascom, and the other Republicans jumped at the idea and the "Republican Club," as we kids knew it, was born. For the next ten years Limp's and Nick's lives would not be their own.

Guido DelSignore, who, sadly, just passed away, provided the jukebox at cost and Knobby Knoblauch provided the records – always current – at cost. The first time I heard the Isley Brothers "Twist and Shout" was at the Republican Club, not on the radio. Nick still has stacks of the original 45s from 1954 to 1964!

When you arrived, Nick and Limp always greeted you with a smile. (Many of us boys had a "crush" on Limp.) The couple made friends with everyone, even "the tough kids" who then provided "protection" for the place. I never remember a fight there. And nobody with alcohol on their breath was ever allowed in. The soda was always cheap, much of it purchased out of the Ruotolo's own pocket, as so many things were.

There was a point when the Democrats tried to establish a rival youth center in the same building across the hall, but it failed. Nick laughed as he described the party rivalry that inspired it.

I mentioned photo albums. Look over my shoulder for a moment at these photos from 1963. There's 17-year-old JoAnn Smatko and others standing by the window on which is painted GOP Teen Club (the club's other name). See Mary

Murray and Susie Illucci in prom dresses? Oh! Nice shot of Joe Crossett and Louise Quatrocchi. And Mary Quatrocchi, prom queen. Right after the prom, all the decorations were brought from the high school to the Republican Club for an after-prom party. Look, there's Bobby Bowe twisting, along with Davine Moore and Kathleen McCarty. Although no one could twist as well as the Ives twins, Bobbie and Dickie.

And here's a Halloween party with a great shot of Michael Halloran doing the limbo. And another of Limp at the soda counter. So many photos – too many memories to fit in a column.

In the Republican Club, Limp and Nicky established more than a safe haven that kept a lot us out of trouble. They established a family. By my reckoning, they have hundreds of children – for whom the Republican Club will always be alive.

Okay if we all come over next week, Nick and Limp?[xlvii]

"OVER MY SHOULDER" COLUMN FOR DECEMBER 21, 1997
Jane's spirit of giving

It is difficult to say why my mother was such a passionate gift-giver at Christmas.

Not that she stinted on birthdays, weddings and the like (heavens, no!), but Christmas was a time most special. This was shown in ways that began before Christmas, as when she'd finish her Christmas shopping a little earlier each year. I recall one year, just after the 4th of July, she announced her shopping was done, most certainly a definite benchmark. However, to my knowledge she never came close to that again, I'm sure because the need to shop so outweighed the need to break a record.

Normally it was around Halloween that Jane, as we kids called her, would declare her shopping done. This was her regular shopping, not to be confused with the pre-Christmas warm-up in September, nor her sweepstakes-winning efforts in November. By December, she was on autopilot, with the shopping selective, searching for the truly outrageous now that the fundamentals had been taken care of – except for the perfect foodstuff to add to the Christmas menu, which had expanded yearly until large enough to feed China.

Shopping's largest purpose was gift-giving. Some presents were mailed, some hand-delivered and the rest saved for under the tree. However, buying holiday decorations was essential and over the years Jane kept buying, but without disposing. The house in December came to look like a year-round Christmas store, except these were personal things dating from the year she and Dad married, 1942, and from each year thereafter. The sacred (the creche) mixed with the profane ("Frosty" in a one of those snow-filled glass globes). Lovely hand-woven straw items sat cheek to jowl with ugly plastic Santas from the `50s. ("Oh, your brother loved those when he was three," she'd say.) Cards were strung over doors; all flat surfaces were filled with candy bowls; and donated decorations were conspicuously placed, such as a crocheted Santa toilet seat cover.

From my earliest memories, the centerpiece was always the tree, so filled with decorations (bulbs, tinsel, twinkle lights, bubble lights, sentimental ornaments, candy canes, presents!) that green barely showed and so heaped with presents beneath that it appeared the tree floated on a sea of wrapping paper building blocks. Throughout December, perched amidst all of this in his favorite chair sat my father, who neither shopped (except for presents for Jane) nor decorated nor indulged in the spirit of the season. He loved to say that Scrooge was his hero. How the man stayed alive during each season, I'll never know.

On what would be Jane's last Christmas, she was battling cancer and she actually called to apologize for not being able to have her traditional decorations with all her kids and their family gathered round! I protested: "Mom! You don't have..." She interrupted: could she come to visit our house Christmas morning, she wondered? "Sure!" I said, thinking nonetheless how odd it would be for her without her whole production, most especially the tree and the presents.

My daughter Julia was two and a half Jane's last Christmas morning. Jane roared in, pale, obviously sick, but smiling, with Dad at her arm – and both carrying HUGE plastic bags filled with presents. I can still see it now, what seemed like bag after bag coming in, and present after present coming forth, like a gush. It was incredible. As if knowing she would never have this again, Jane had "out-Janed" herself and her little granddaughter sat buried in presents.

Today, in the heaven for shoppers, there's a Brinks truck slowly trailing behind a short, white-haired woman softly humming to herself, stopping to buy at every store on an endless street of stores and pausing only to send the Brinks truck back for more money.

And on earth, at our house, are spread out a creche...a Frosty, a 1950s plastic Santa...well, you know. Merry Christmas.

AFTERWARD

Please pause for a moment, would you? These columns could only have come into existence because they were published in a newspaper, *The Post-Star* of Glens Falls, NY. The columns combined history and commentary, but they had to be grounded in fact. That was my editor's rule. *The Post-Star* always has been and is now about the factual, honest presentation of real news.

In my opinion, but one expressed by so many, newspapers are under siege and threatened with extinction. The onslaught of the internet has caused newspapers, daily newspapers especially, severe revenue losses resulting in shrinking staffs and truncated editions. Even publishing online, newspapers still face economic competition from internet advertising, and, far worse, competition from online opinion sites disguised as factual news sources.

The newspaper, on paper or online, remains unique as the central source for factual, vetted, unbiased news.

You could say that, today, I could easily start a "column" via a blog or some other internet format. You could say news is available everywhere on "The Net." But the reality is that no personal blog, no Facebook page, no Instagram, nor any form of social media devised as yet, can provide the newspaper's centralized, professionally edited, fact-based, open-to-scrutiny information.

In rural regions like that *The Post-Star* serves, the newspaper is the **only** central registry for community news—births, deaths, elections, upcoming cultural events, political infighting, school news, building projects, crime, stories of human interest and compassion, etc. The newspaper is not a perfect source. But as a self-governing gatherer and purveyor of facts, the best newspapers operate under ethical standards universally held by all true journalists. When I need the surest source for the facts, I turn first to a newspaper.

We are drowning in a sea of online opinion. We need to defend and promote factual information in all media, but especially the original bulwark of it, the newspaper. In my opinion, there is no replacement for the newspaper—the Fourth Branch of government, after the Executive, Legislative and Judiciary. It is the guardian of our freedom.

We must support the newspaper—daily, weekly, and monthly—and help publishers find new ways of bringing young readers into the fold.

Whether your newspaper is printed on paper, delivered electronically, or sent by heaven knows what invention yet to come, support it. Agree or disagree with its news; love it or get angry with it; send in your critiques, corrections, commentary. But always cherish, defend, and promote your newspaper.

Your democracy depends upon it.

That is the view from *Over My Shoulder.*

OVER MY SHOULDER: EDITOR JULIA C. CUTSHALL-KING
DISCUSSING PLANS FOR THE BOOK WITH THE AUTHOR – 1981

INDEX

ENDNOTES

---

i Now Finch Paper, LLC.

ii On Ridge Street, to the north of the building at the point of Ridge and Glen Streets.

iii Artist Douglass Crockwell was an ardent proponent of a "by-pass."

iv Today LARAC's headquarters; built in 1872 as Jerome Lapham's carriage barn.

v It is at 333 Glen Street, Glens Falls.

vi Originally the First National Bank of Glens Falls. Evergreen later became a part of TD Bank (Toronto Dominion Bank).

vii John Snyder, a custodian of the old YMCA downtown (*Remember the old "Y"?*), bought skis at Lapham's Sporting Goods in 1925; now at the Chapman Historical Museum.

viii *Bridging the Years, 1763-1978*. Glens Falls Historical Association. Glens Falls, New York, (1978)

ix Correction: it was first named the 10th Light Division in 1943 and renamed the 10th Mountain Division in 1944.

x LeRoy B. Akins, Jr., Mayor of the City of Glens Falls, (1945-2003), native son, head of the "I Love NY" campaign and a passionate champion of Glens Falls.

xi See Pete Tobey's article on area baseball, "At 94, WWII veteran, former area ballplayer still has love for game" (*The Post-Star*, Apr 29, 2012).

xii R. G. Landry's was located on the NW corner of Park and Glen Streets.

xiii M. C. Scoville Jewelers was at the intersection of Glen and Ridge Streets.

xiv Today, the first building south of Cronin Highrise Apartments on Ridge Street.

xv Today, the headquarters of Barton Mines Company LLC.

xvi Holden, Dr. Austin W., *The History of the Town of Queensbury, New York*. Joel Munsell. Albany, NY (1874).

xvii At the northwest corner of Elm St. and Hudson Ave; used for several years by Adirondack Scenic, Inc.; eventually sold and converted to apartments.

xviii Now Opera Saratoga, located in Saratoga Springs.

xix Wolf Trap National Park for the Performing Arts.

xx The Paramount Theater ticket booth was later installed in the Wood Theatre in Glens Falls, thanks to its dynamic Executive Director, the late Bill Woodward.

xxi See Calarco, Tom. *The Underground Railroad and the Adirondack Region*. (McFarland & Co., 2008) for an excellent history.

xxii DeMasi, Michael. "Company to demolish historic Glens Falls home for parking lot." (*The Post-Star*, July 3, 1996).

xxiii Since 2013 Jonathan Newell has led the restoration of The Strand Theatre in Hudson Falls. Live performances and movies once again grace The Strand.

xxiv The Scott Paper plant in Fort Edward is now Irving Tissue Inc.

xxv Hopkintonian refers to a form of Calvinistic doctrine and was named for Samuel Hopkins, D.D., a Congregational minister of Great Barrington, MA, and Newport, RI.

xxvi Haynes wrote his own autobiography, yet new biographies are definitely needed.

xxvii Mistakenly identified in original column as "Julia Judkins." Corrected here.

xxviii The Village's weekly newspaper vigorously reported on the problem xxix Mullen, Joan Hess. *A Little History of Little Canada in Fort Edward, Washington County, NY*. (1995).

xxx Forerunner of the Adirondack Regional Chambers of Commerce.

xxxi Brown, William H. Editor. *History of Warren County, New York*. Published by Board of Supervisors of Warren County, NY (1963).

xxxii Warren County Airport was renamed The Floyd Bennett Memorial Airport in 2011.

xxxiii In 2016-17, I worked with Chapman Historical Museum Executive Director Timothy Weidner on WATER *& LIGHT: S. R. Stoddard's Lake George*. I wrote the essay and other text for this large book, containing 150 fine reproductions of Stoddard photographs, as well as sketches, a painting, and maps. The essay updates some of what I have previously written about Stoddard and adds new information, as well.

xxxiv Cutshall-King with the Italian Heritage Committee of Fort Edward Historical Association, Inc. *Con Amore – The Italian History of Fort Edward*. (Fort Edward Historical Association, Inc.; 2001). The Italian Heritage Committee consisted of Leo Altizio, Anita Amorosi Arcuri, Nicholas "Chuckie" Cantiello, Andrew "Jerry" Cimo, Pauline Massaro Corsall, Sadie Trackeno Dean, Andrew Esperti, Fanny Sarchioto Gaulin, Joseph Giorgianni, Josephine Cardinale Harris, John Mandolare, Joseph Munoff, Anne D'Angelico Murray, Christine Catone Murray, Mary Ann Choppy Nicholas, Mary Casini Smith, and Frank V. Williams (Francesco Vincenzo Guglielmini). The author, the only one of non-Italian descent, was rechristened "Giuseppe."

xxxv My column mistakenly identified the aqueduct as a "viaduct." My 9/22/1996 column carried a correction from historian R. Paul McCarty. The viaduct carried a road over the creek; the aqueduct the canal over the creek. Both still stand.

xxxvi Johnson, Crisfield. *History of Washington Co., New York*. Everts & Ensign, Philadelphia (1878).

xxxvii Heck fled Cambridge in March 1776 as the Continental Congress had restricted Loyalists' rights, especially to possess weapons. She went to the Province of Ontario and founded the first Methodist church in Canada.

xxxviii Smith, H. P. *History of Essex County; with illustrations and biographical sketches of some of its prominent men and pioneers*. Everts & Ensign, Philadelphia (1878).

xxxix Hyde, Louis F. *History of Glens Falls, New York*. Glens Falls, N.Y. (1936)

xl LaRowe, William. *From Circuit Rider to Episcopacy* (1970).

xli Smith, H. P. *History of Warren County*. D. Mason & Co., Syracuse (1885).

xlii In this column, I wrongly stated that the *Lake George Mirror* ended in 1979. Started in 1880, it is still proudly being published.

xliii Sacred Heart Roman Catholic Church in Lake George Village.

xliv My serious omission in these articles was The Battle of Fort Anne, July 7-8, 1777. A major site, Battle Hill in Fort Ann, was preserved for posterity in 2015.

xlv Levi was a descendant of Abraham Wing's brother Edward Wing.

xlvi Corrected here, originally I had written the School was built in 1899. It was 1893, as Union School Building No. 1, also serving as the high school until 1924. It ceased being a school in the late 1960s. My old school still stands as of this writing.

xlvii Olympia "Limp" Aurelia Ruotolo died in 2002; Nicholas F. "Nick" Ruotolo in 2012.

Made in the USA
Columbia, SC
26 October 2018